"When God Shows Up: a Pastor's Journey, provides great insight to pastors and seminary students and others who want to hear and follow the voice of God if they are to lead a missional church. Henry Wildeboer writes out of the crucible of fifty years of ministry experience that describes many of the challenges and opportunities he faced in leading congregations to fulfill the great commission. Willing to be a risk taker for the sake of the kingdom of God, Henry was not willing to settle for a 'care taker' ministry. In some instances this proved to be very costly but at the same time he saw the 'hand of God' working in surprising ways. I have always known Henry as honest, forthright and transparent and these traits are clearly revealed as you read this book. Henry tells it "as it is." Above all you will discover a great love for God and his desire to follow Him...regardless."

Rev. Dr. David Sherbino,
Professor of Pastoral Ministry and Spiritual Formation,
Tyndale University College and Seminary, Toronto, Ontario
Minister, Cornerstone Community Church (Presbyterian Church in Canada)
Kleinburg, Ontario

"With a varied and diverse experience, Henry brings a wonderful sense of the practical and the theological as he looks at ministry and leadership past, present and future. He weaves the themes in a way that makes it accessible to all and relevant for leadership in the 21st century. A great read!"

Dr. Gary Nelson,
President and Vice Chancellor,
Tyndale University College and Seminary, Toronto, Ontario

"Wildeboer shares his journey of faith, joy and pain. Through life and ministry experience and struggles he grew in dedication and obedience to his Lord. He took risks as he responded to God's call, walked by faith and preached prophetically. For that there is a price to pay. This book will comfort and challenge preachers. It will inspire church leaders and members to serve with biblical courage and boldness in spite of one's shortcomings, even with opposition. To those considering ministry, he recommends that you not go into it unless you "have" to."

Rev. Louis Tamminga,
Director of CRC Pastor-Church Relations (emeritus)
Grand Rapids, Michigan

"Henry is a friend and mentor who challenged me to be a better leader. His prophetic edge in preaching and his risk-taking courage made me aware that his life and ministry story needed telling. The many publics a pastor serves can cause one to freeze, staying with the conventional - afraid a prophetic vision will upset. It will. Henry learned that the hard way. Yet it is the only way. It is the way of the Spirit. Breaking through doubt and bucking tradition pastor Henry leads his people into a new dimension of faith. This story of leadership is inspirational and models the merging of the prophetic and pastoral.

His pastoral leadership is such that anyone beginning or on the path of ministry would do well to read. Learn from this veteran of life and ministry, allowing his narrative to inform and encourage, direct and convict, but most of all to help you see what God wants to do with your life and calling. Read this and pass it on."

Dr. Brian C. Stiller,
Global Ambassador, The World Evangelical Alliance;
President Emeritus, Tyndale University College and Seminary
Toronto, Ontario

"When God Shows Up…" is both an historical and a pastoral treasure. Henry Wildeboer has captured a physical and emotional journey that has been experienced by thousands of post-war immigrants, wonderfully recalling those early years in a new country.

But of equal -- perhaps more -- significance, it is a story about a person's spiritual development as a pastor and also of the spiritual development of the early Christian Reformed Church in Canada.

This is a 'must read' for every seminary graduate. There are profound lessons to be learned about those early years in ministry; lessons about the sense of calling and of servant leadership.

While Henry Wildeboer may have intended this book as a legacy to his grandchildren, it is more profoundly a legacy to future generations of pastors."

Keith Knight,
Executive Director,
Canadian Christian Business Federation
Guelph, Ontario

When God Shows up:

a Pastor's Journey

Henry Wildeboer

Chapbook Press

Chapbook Press
Schuler Books
2660 28th Street SE
Grand Rapids, MI 49512
(616) 942-7330
www.schulerbooks.com

Printed at Schuler Books in Grand Rapids, MI on the Espresso Book Machine®

When God Shows Up: A Pastor's Journey

ISBN 13: 9781936243549
ISBN 10: 1936243547

Cover Art by Margaret Dijkhuis

For more information, please contact
Henry Wildeboer
hwildeboer@cogeco.ca

Table of Contents

Foreword

In 1994, I began a one-year internship at First Christian Reformed Church of Calgary, Alberta, Canada. It was a wonderful year of growth and learning, and much of that happened in my new office. As I settled in, I found out that the office had a prior occupant whose voice could still be heard from time to time.

One day in 1994, Henry Wildeboer came into church and sat down in his "old" office that I now occupied. I enjoyed then and I enjoy now the conversations that Henry has engaged me in over the nearly 20 years since that first visit.

It is sometimes said that new pastors need to find "their voice" in ministry. I believe that is true, but I also know that finding that voice is fine-tuned by listening to and interacting with the voices of those who have gone before.

Henry, though officially retired, is still very active in the church, and his voice and his story are important reminders of not only where the church has been, but also where it can be led by the Holy Spirit. In this spiritual memoir of his life and ministry journey, you will hear the voice of an authentic, broken leader and follower. Henry is a leader. Henry is also a follower of Jesus Christ.

Henry's voice will challenge and comfort. His story will cause waves but also move you to see the necessity of a biblical, prophetic ministry. At the end of the story, you will see how God molded and shaped Henry and his journey. Both Henry and I pray that God will use his journey to encourage and challenge pastors and leaders of the present and the future to be freshly empowered by the vision of what God is able and desirous to do in his church today.

As president of Henry's seminary alma mater, I am thankful for Henry and the heart that he shares in this journey that celebrates God and the gospel ministry. May you be encouraged! I was. Faith, confidence and trust form the basis of this testimony! May God be praised!

Rev. Jul Medenblik,
President, Calvin Theological Seminary, Grand Rapids, Michigan

Dedication

This book is dedicated:

- to my father and mother **Hendrik Wildeboer** and **Jentje Wildeboer-Groen.** I thank them for the vision, foresight, and courage to look ahead for us, their six children, letting go of their own dreams and moving to the foreign land of Canada, expecting never to see their own families again. The motivator was greater future opportunities for us their children. I now realize the costs paid and the sacrifice made to fulfill this vision and commitment. Thank you, Mom and Dad.

- to my wife, friend and partner, **Janice Claire Wildeboer-DeKorte** for being a 50 year long source of encouragement, support, love, and sacrifice. For me, our children, and others, you are the model of humble servanthood and godly love. You are the apple of God's eye and his love and blessings for you have amply spilled upon every aspect of my life. If the journey recounted in the book has value, it is because you filled such a steady, major role as wife, friend, mother, grandmother and co-worker in ministry.

-to my children Judy (and Edwin), Barbara (and Andre), Douglas (and Sharon), John (and Grace) and Robert (and Christine) all excelling in love, encouragement and help; who regularly challenge the idiosyncrasies of our aging. You help keep us young and you keep our eyes fresh to see new things in contemporary culture.

-and to, oh yes, those grandchildren, Hannah, Luke, Seth and Mark, and Maxime, Eva, and Zoe, and Jeremiah, Emma and Elizabeth, and Jason, Charis and Michael all of whom sparkle with life, love, and surprises.

-And a very special thanks to God who made life, family, ministry and even this book possible.

In thanksgiving to God, returns beyond expenses will be donated to **World Renew** *to help alleviate* **World Hunger.**

Preface

I began this book to leave something as a legacy for our children and grandchildren. The first four chapters are my journey from birth in The Netherlands to growing up in Alberta and then to seminary in Grand Rapids, Michigan where I met my wife Jan. Jan enriched my life, and then with the children, broadened the story some more. The early years were formative for the rest of my life and were colored by adventure, hard work and deprivation.

But as I wrote about the fifty years since then I knew this book was for more than our immediate family. The years we have been married were filled with ministry. In fact, life and ministry are so interwoven that it is hardly possible for me to think of one without the other. They flow together. Describing the thrills and spills of pastoral ministry has been cathartic. But in the journey I also realized that many pastors today are facing issues and conflicts similar to mine. They may be somewhat different but the struggles are remarkably alike. For the last 25 years I have taught, mentored, and coached younger pastors and leaders. As I shared parts of my journey with them, they were often helped and encouraged to continue in their ministries. I believe this book will benefit members, besides pastors. One doesn't have to be a pastor or church leader to be inspired and challenged by stories where God shows up!

As changes occur in churches some people experience joy, others pain. Those who find change painful often ask the question which each generation tends to ask the next: "What's wrong with the way we've always done things?" My response is that what was done previously was fine for that time. But one generation's response to the Scriptures is not *normative* for the next generation. Because culture is always changing, each generation is called to respond to God's word with a fresh humility, faith, obedience, and creativity. Where God's people serve, new lives and new structures will be built on the foundation of previous generations of believers. While Jesus Christ is the same yesterday, today, and forever, the way we make known "the good news" is unique for each time, place, and generation.

I pray this book will empower those presently in pastoral ministry to have hearts to preach the gospel with compassion, tenderness and love so as to give comfort, but I also pray they will have the courage and an urgency that challenges and warns His church when needed – and it will be needed! Stand on the wall and blow a clear prophetic trumpet sound of warning.

This book is also for those who sense God's claim on them possibly *calling them* to a pastoral ministry. My basic advice has long been, "Don't go into it unless you *have* to and get out when you are no longer impassioned with a sense of His calling." He deserves and looks for servants who are sold-out to Him and who respond with all they are and all they have. The assignment is that big. Read this journey, I hope it helps you discern His plan for you.

Finally, I describe and share my journey for those who serve God everywhere. If you see your work as your ministry to God and others, you are called. Your calling may lead you to a school, a job site, a kitchen, a hospital, an accounting office, a farm or a factory anywhere in North America or in a totally other part of the world. Just be *willing* and *available;* to *be* what He wants and to *go* where He wants; that's all He asks.

Our family's story is not about us, it is our testimony about how God honored His commitment as Father to us. He honoured His commitment to us better than we did ours to Him. He promised to provide for all our needs. We look back and know He did.

We know that God is always present but there are situations and times when we experience the power of God in a special way. He may show up through a burning bush as He did with Moses; He may lead and guide with the fire of the Holy Spirit of Pentecost, as portrayed by artist Margaret Dijkhuis in the cover design. As you read you'll discover Him showing up throughout events, actions, and stories but also in times of utmost helplessness, sin, and failure. You might well be reminded of times in your own life when God showed up. Often the point of humble brokenness and repentance became the place where I met Him. As you read this book, look for times when God shows up!

When times were tough the temptation to quit became strong; but as hard as I tried I couldn't walk away. I had said "yes" to God that I would give Him my life, my time, my all, and I could never find the "strength" to walk away from it. Every time I asked Him "What would you have us do?" He seemed to whisper or shout words like surrender, be still, and wait on the Lord. It was often accompanied with a quiet but overwhelming sense of, "Trust me!"

God has given me a deep love for His Word, His church, and especially for those who see their call as a call from God to His ministry regardless as to where it is fulfilled. I share this journey as the one Jan and I traveled in response to His call. We tried to "Seek first His kingdom" and then discovered that all other things indeed were provided. (Matthew 6:33) I invite you to travel the journey of seeking Him and His kingdom first. It will be tough at times, but you will not regret it. The rewards are amazing!

As Jan and I look back over 70 years of life, 50 years of marriage and ministry, we are surprised at how we see God's guiding hand in both the good and bad times. He has been faithful. We desire this book to be a source of encouragement to you especially when you find yourself going through tough times. We wish you a good journey. Saunter with Him at the leisurely pace of three miles an hour and watch for places where, and times when He shows up, even surprises you.

Henry Wildeboer

Chapter 1

The Netherlands

I came into the world on a warm Thursday afternoon about 4:30 PM on July 6, 1939. My mother, Jennie Wildeboer-Groen, told me I gave her a fairly long, sweaty time before I yelled out to the world that I was here! The doctor was present and so was my dad who was kept busy trying to keep my two year old sister entertained and out of that bedroom. At that time it was deemed unnecessary to go to a hospital for this most natural, common event: the birth of a child. Thousands of other Dutch couples were having babies at home as well. I suspect there were occasional complications, but I never heard about any of them. Upstairs in my parents' bedroom, I got my first swat to which, I am told, I loudly expressed my disapproval.

The house I was born in was located in a small village called denHulst, near Dedemsvaart in the province, Overijsel, the Netherlands. At the age of two my family moved to the city of Zwolle to be closer to my dad's work. By then, World War II was raging. I do not remember much of my first five years; they were war years, only a few events from the later part of the war in 1944 and 1945 stand out.

No Lights after 8:00 PM

I do remember the time that the Germans enforced an 8:00 PM curfew each night by shutting off all electricity into our homes. One could go to bed, find some candles, or sit in the dark. Circumventing the curfew became the challenge of the night. Dutch people tend to be feisty by nature, especially when they are offended or mad. And they were both when the light curfew was imposed! Their anger about the curfew and their hatred for the Germans became passionate fuel that fired their ingenuity to create light in the darkness. A group of neighbours, including my father, decided *they* were going to have light!

Houses in our area were semi-detached. Wires could be run from one house to the next. Someone found (or stole?) an old bicycle which was placed on blocks in the shed attached to our house. For Dutch people, bikes were a prime means of transportation both day and night. Each bike had a small generator on the front wheel from which a thin wire ran up to a headlight

1

attached to the handlebars and to a red taillight attached to the rear fender. At night the generator was flipped onto the tire, and as the bike was pedaled the small wheel on top of the generator spun around, which in turn generated electricity to power the lights.

The men found about eight of the small bike generators and attached them to the frame of the bike on the rear wheel in such a way that when the wheel was pedaled, all the generators spun. The combined electricity from the eight generators flowed into a larger wire which was strung from the bike to five or six living rooms where each family had rigged a flashlight bulb through a hole in the shiny tin lid of a common metal cigar box. The lid reflected the light down into the room. All the shades on the windows were tightly drawn, and I can still see my parents -who loved reading- sitting under the tiny flashlight bulb scanning the latest newspaper for war news or reading a book. The fathers of the families would each take 30-minute turns pedaling the bike and thus extend the curfew by a few hours in each of the homes. Ah, the joy of victory inspired all pedalers! I believe the joy did not come so much from the extended hours of light, but from the satisfaction of defying the curfew. When my dad's turn came, I would sometimes sit on the seat behind him as he pedaled away on this stationary bike. It was a nice time to be alone with him; talking was minimal because he was pedaling hard and had little energy left for conversation. One could always tell that the pedaler was approaching the end of his half-hour cycle; as he tired the reading light dimmed. I learned early in life from this experience to manipulate: If you don't like a certain rule, you can find a way around it.

Where's Dad?

Another war memory stands out. At various times German soldiers came to our house with guns over their shoulders to ask mom where my dad was. He was always "away" when they came, and she never had "any idea" where he was or when he'd be back. I never knew where he was either, even though they asked me many times. Later I learned that he would hide in a stack of firewood in the shed attached to the house that looked like a random pile of wood but had a carefully hollowed-out center. I am sure that at the age of four or five, had I known dad was there, I likely would have told these nice, dignified men with their guns where he was.

Later I learned they had good reasons to look for him. Across from our house was a field along a canal where on many mornings German soldiers would practice target shooting. At lunchtime they usually cleaned up by putting their stuff away, but sometimes they left without picking up anything, assuming they would be back shortly. Long after the war had ended, I learned from mom that dad and a few others would watch the soldiers leave. As soon as they were gone, the men would steal the ammo and whatever else they could find. It was a dangerous thing to do. The Germans were suspicious of dad and a few others but never managed to catch them. Had they done so, we might never have seen them again. It was another act of defiance.

My father would never talk about those war years, even when years later we would ask him about them. It seemed to have been such a painful period that he wanted to bury it deep in an irretrievable part of his soul, never to review again. I heard enough about the Germans to feel no guilt about hating them. My mother called them "rot moffen," (rotten Nazis), my dad despised them to the degree that it seemed to me he felt they were not even worthy of being named. To most Dutch people, however, the Germans were less despicable than their own fellow Hollanders who were NSBers (friends with the Germans and betrayers of Jews and the Dutch who sheltered them). They blended in with all the other Dutch people, including resisters, so that very few knew who they were. They watched and reported those who were hiding Jews, or those who were working underground to oppose the Nazis. Long after the war ended, they were still hated, pursued, marked people who were brought to justice. They had betrayed their very own and to the Dutch there was nothing more despicable.

Cellar Dwellers

In the last year of the war, I also remember waking up in our little root cellar below the kitchen and stair area where mom kept potatoes, carrots, onions and a few cabbages, red and white ones. Food was in very short supply, so whatever we got was carefully protected and preserved. I am not sure where the food came from, but I suspect it came from some of our farming relatives. The cellar was cool, and since we had no refrigerator, it kept the potatoes from sprouting early and then rotting. Night-time bombings would occur often. In my mind I can still hear the whistling

3

sounds followed by explosions. They obviously made a deep impression on this little five year old boy. When my parents heard the planes overhead, usually at night, they would wrap us in blankets and take us down into the root cellar hoping to save our lives in case the house was hit. Fortunately, it never was. I slept in the potato bin. The little cellar was crowded with mom and dad, my sister Helen, my younger brother Bill, born in 1941, and me. At the time mom was expecting my brother Alex who would arrive in March 1945, near the very end of the war. We were under God's protection in this damp potato cellar, but I knew it not.

Chocolates and Oranges

When suddenly the war ended in May 1945, Holland went wild! Canadian tanks and trucks rolled through the streets, with soldiers tossing out cigarettes, chocolates and colorful "orange balls." Later I learned these orange balls could be peeled and eaten. Oranges! They were delicious; I don't recall ever having seen one before. Even today an orange is still a treat! I learned early to view food as a very special gift from God never to be wasted. When one doesn't have much food he realizes just how precious it is. The adults were wild about the chocolates, especially the mothers and women. Men eagerly grabbed cigarettes and, macho-like, puffed away. Ah, how good it was! The party was exuberant; flags appeared on every car, bike and window. We were free! Church organs, long silent, roared again as services celebrated with loud praise and deep gratitude. Holland was free again after five long years of fear, horrendous oppression, suffering, and violent, merciless deaths. Liberation! Hallelujah; uninhibited praise was released. People danced in the streets. Life was good again.

But it was a bittersweet celebration; there was deep pain and many tears as the losses of lives saturated the minds, hearts, and souls of Dutch families. Many of them faced an uncertain future with thousands of fathers, brothers, cousins, friends, and neighbours missing or dead. They had not returned and they were not ever going to come back. The pain of those losses was shared by all. It fed a spirit of revenge, hatred and disdain for Germans for a long time.

4

What Now?

Rebuilding the Netherlands started at a furious pace by the fall of 1945. Holland would not just survive -she would thrive again. Pride and nationalism ran high. The Dutch with help from allies, had defeated the Nazis, and now they were rubbing it in with rapid restoration. Employment opportunities were many, and hopes were high. Churches were filled with people. Marketplaces were filled with cattle, chickens, vegetables, artwork, and everything else necessary to replenish what had been lost.

Something else was also happening, especially in large families. Although World War II was over, a quiet fear set in that another attack might well again come from the east. This common fear prevailed. With Russia growing in power, people wondered whether World War III was just around the corner. And if it struck, would our sons and daughters be called up to go to war again? Would more young deaths be grieved?

Moreover, the Netherlands, being a tightly squeezed, overpopulated little country, would have limited career opportunities for larger families. Would *all* our children find meaningful employment? These fears gnawed at many minds. If another war erupted, would our children survive? Many concluded they did not want to take that risk. By 1948, with the encouragement of the Dutch government, many larger, more adventuresome families, including my mom and dad, were exploring the idea of immigration.

I had no idea until many years later the significance of that decision and the sacrifice and cost these Dutch people took on. Some went to New Zealand and Australia. The great land of America was attractive to others, especially if they already had friends or relatives there. But it seemed that Canada was the biggest draw. It was also our family's country of choice, mainly because we already had some friends there. Between 1948 and 1952 thousands of Hollanders packed their valued, meager belongings in a "kist" (large wooden crate) and via the Holland America Line, particularly the Veendam, Rijndam, and Volendam, set out for the 8-10 day ocean crossing from Rotterdam to Halifax. Pier 21 in Halifax became the port of arrival and the beginning of a journey into a new land, a journey which by no means was complete once foot was set on Nova Scotia soil. From there, immigrants packed into trains which headed west, dropping off passengers along the way. Many disembarked in Ontario. Others with friends or family in Alberta stayed on the train and sat in soot for another two days while traveling to Calgary. There they were either met by friends or transferred to a train heading 150 kilometers north into central Alberta or farther north to Edmonton. Others stayed on the train and still went further west to British Columbia, as far as Vancouver. Central Alberta was to be our destiny.

A Better Future

Dad had a strong yearning to go to Canada primarily for the sake of the children. But mom especially, although usually compliant and submissive, really wanted to go. Once they had announced they were going to immigrate to Canada, there was no turning them back. Both Mom and Dad were committed to it and family could not dissuade them. By now two more boys had entered our family, Harry on Easter Sunday, April 6, 1947, and John, some 12 months later, March 26, 1948. Now there were eight of us: Mom and Dad, one older sister Helen and then five younger boys of which I was the oldest.

Dad had a high school friend, John Mulder, who had gone to Alberta and offered to help us. To expedite immigration, each family needed a "sponsor" who would guarantee a house and job for the first year in Canada. After that, each family was on its own. Since there was ample work in the vast Canadian agricultural expanses and with rapid growth in the construction industries, a job was easy to find for a willing worker. Providing a place to live for a family with six kids was a bigger challenge. However, John Mulder found us a place on a farm 50 km west of Innisfail, Alberta with an older, Danish farmer, Edgar Jensen. Once that was in place, serious preparations could begin for the journey, one part of which was the dreaded "keuring" (the health exam). It must have been tough for it seemed every potential immigrant talked about it and feared it. It consisted of a thorough medical examination by a Canadian-authorized physician. Canada only wanted complete and healthy people. My parents were anxious about the medical especially because my younger brother Bill (Wim then) was born with one hand. His left arm ended with a stub where the hand should have been, with five little balls on the end, where the fingers should have been. Only when the entire family was approved, including clear X-

6

rays of the lungs to indicate the absence of the feared TB, would they be allowed to line up, pay for tickets, and wait for passage space on the boat.

The Keuring

Our family's exam was scheduled for some time in the spring of 1949. Everything moved smoothly until the doctor came to Wim. He examined the hand thoroughly and then told us we had failed the medical and could not go to Canada. My mother, who was really behind this move, asked why and pushed the doctor to tell her what Wim needed to be able to do to pass the exam. One re-exam could occur about a year later. Absolutely determined, she worked hard with him so that when we came back for the re-exam, she had helped him become so agile that he could do most of the things that the rest of us could do. The doctor made him do a variety of maneuvers, including tying shoe laces with the non-hand, all of which he could do, much to the doctor's astonishment. By the end, he shook his head and said he could see no reason to refuse us. We passed!

The tempo now became more hectic. May 16, 1950, Helen's 13th birthday, was the scheduled day for departure on the Holland–American line ship, the Volendam, leaving from Rotterdam. My father's parents were not in favour of our leaving since my father was the oldest son (of four children). His sister was a single mom raising a son, Klaas, who, two months younger than I was a good friend. He was often included in our family's activities. We all liked him and I think he felt at home with us. Leaving him was hard for us but I think also for this 10-year old boy even though I never realized it at the time.

I learned much later that it was also very tough for my grandmother, dad's mom. She was opposed to her oldest son taking his family to Canada. It became more painful and complicated for her by the fact that her husband, my grandfather, was hospitalized in Zwolle with surgery for major stomach problems. As May 16 approached, his condition had improved, but my parents wondered how my grandmother could cope with the immigration of a son and his family at the same time as the recent surgery of her husband? Would this be too much for this feeble -but rather strong-minded mother and grandmother to handle?

7

A Painful Farewell

On the morning of May 16, an uncle -who was also a bus driver- arranged to rent a bus, and with various family members, including all eight of us - plus suitcases- set out for the Rotterdam harbor. We started in the Dedemsvaart area at 6:00 AM, and since we came through the city of Zwolle about 7:00 AM, we stopped at Sophia hospital. Mom and dad wanted to drop in briefly to say goodbye to grandpa (Opa) and grandma (Oma), who was staying near him. They decided it would be best that the six kids stay in the bus and wait. After only a few minutes they returned and on we went to Nijkerk where we picked up another aunt and uncle.

The trip had a subdued almost funereal mood about it, created, I think, by the overwhelming thought that after we said our farewells, boarded the boat, and departed, the families left behind and all of us on board never expected to see each other again. Traveling back to visit family was never considered. Who could possibly afford that since for many the cost of the trip to the new land took all they had? Many immigrants had borrowed funds from family and friend -loans- maybe never to be repaid. The courage of these immigrants to say goodbye forever, (so they thought) still amazes me today.

By noon we were in Rotterdam with people and suitcases gathered on the docks near the boat. Cranes lifted and placed crates into the holds of the boat. Names were painted in big black letters on two sides of the crates, and as kids we were fascinated watching for other crates going to Alberta. There were only a few. Most were destined for Ontario; where that was we had no idea. My sister pointed out when our box was lifted and placed inside the cargo hold. Our name and address, **H. Wildeboer, c/o Edgar Jensen, Raven, Alberta**," was painted in large black letters on the side of the box. It was reassuring that our stuff was with us, but it was also disconcerting. It was another sign that we were rapidly approaching the point of no return!

On the dock some aunts still had a few birthday presents for Helen. After all, it was her special day! Since it was noon, out came the sandwiches, thermoses of tea and coffee, and some fruit. While we were eating, an uncle, Oom Klaas, found a phone to call the hospital in Zwolle to see how grandpa was doing. He came back a few minutes later obviously upset and whispered something to mom and dad. Grandpa had been weak because of his surgery and, because of occasional coughing spells due to asthma, his wound had reopened and bled. So an immediate second surgery had to be done. His rather full stomach combined with the anesthesia caused him to become nauseous and vomit. Some of that had made its way into his lungs and resulted in his death. Earlier that morning when my parents stopped to say goodbye, grandpa had been doing quite well. In fact, they anticipated that he would soon be released from the hospital to go home. Instead, at 9:30 that morning just shortly after we had left Zwolle, he had hemorrhaged and died. This was shockingly unexpected.

Now what? There we stood with all our stuff. Do we get on the boat or stay for the funeral? If we stay, we forfeit the fare for eight people since on such short notice no replacements would be available. As a 10-year-old, I was quite concerned. I think it was the first time I had faced death. I had really anticipated this big boat ride and could see that at the last moment it might be pulled away from us. Tipping the scales for going was the fact that all our stuff was already in the boat and would be going with us. I did not grasp the size of the loss to my parents and to the families who were staying. The death of a father and grandfather, combined with the loss of another family moving to the other side of the world (forever!) must have been a huge shock for a grieving Oma. You lose your husband by death at the same time as your oldest son, wife, and six grandchildren move to another world! How does one endure so many final goodbyes in such a short period?

We boarded the boat about 5:00 PM. With hundreds of others, we found space on an open deck looking for family members on the docks to which to wave goodbye. We waved and waved long after distance put us far beyond the point of recognition. Dutch people make a big deal out of saying and waving goodbye. When we could see our family no more and were certain that they could not see us either, all eight of us gathered on a quiet spot on the deck. There, very soberly, dad explained that grandpa had died, although by now we already surmised that. Our parents were just beginning to digest this. I think that was the first time I saw my mom cry quite hard. Dad held her and looked away to wipe away the tears he did not

9

want us to see. We kids just stood quietly numb, intuitively knowing that this was not the time to say anything. It was a somber time with huge emotional turmoil, one I can still feel. I review that day with profound respect for my parents. I deeply admire their vision, love for us kids, sacrifice, determination, and courage. They saw a big picture future and never wavered from it.

Looking Back

I appreciated my parents even more when much later I learned that my father had held a very good position with the government in the Netherlands as a food and meat inspector. He and mom were set for life, pension and all! He repeatedly told us that he immigrated for the sake of us kids and our future, something that did not make a lot of sense to me at the time. Much later, he proved over and over again what he meant by that.

Crossing the Atlantic

After watching the coast fade away, we found our rooms -Mom, Helen, and the three younger boys in the women's section; Dad, Bill and I were shown three small bunk beds on the men's side. Dad slept on the bottom, Bill in the middle, and I on top. We ate supper late- by now it was after 8:00 PM. Shortly after that, all being tired and emotionally spent, we went to bed. Thus began the eight-day journey across the Atlantic.

While on the boat my dad wrote daily in a journal which I found some time after his death in 1975. Though each day's section was brief, it was fairly revealing. After that very long, tough day of departure, I read that both he and mom went to bed in their separate sections about 9:30 PM and - amazing to me- "slept well," after all that! The journal indicates that though they were moving farther away "from home" by the hour, his heart was still with his family in Holland, especially with his mother who would be making all the preparations for the funeral and burial without him. He wrote a letter that would not be mailed for a week, not until after our arrival in Halifax. It would take about another eight days to reach its destination. He sent several telegrams, also on the day of the funeral, expressing his love and concern for his family.

The journey across was somewhat uneventful, though so stormy that I watched family members spend some days when more food seemed to come out than went in! The meals were very good, and a few of them I ate alone or with only a few family members. Dad would sometimes go to the dining room and bring some dry bread to the bedridden ones. Because the food was good, I did not want to miss a meal, even though I too had some meals that stayed with me only briefly. I do not remember much of the ocean voyage except that I wandered around a lot on the decks by myself as a 10-year old kid.

Relatively early in the evening, we'd all go to bed. Dad would usually go to bed a little later, around 10:00 or 10:30 PM but he would be up by 5:30 AM the next morning. He regularly attended "eventide devotions" led by a pastor on board, and he commented in his journal as to the number of people who showed up and how they all enjoyed the devotions as well as the time afterwards to visit with each other. On one occasion he mentioned that he stayed to sing for a while after the devotions, something surprising to me, since I cannot recall ever hearing my father sing. In his journal he commented on Scripture passages, or shared some thoughts that came to him, all indicative, I think, of the hunger for support and a drawing of life from a solid foundation in a time of grief, change, and pain. I see now that the journey combined with the experience of his father's death had a spiritual impact on him. I suspect the evening devotionals had something to do with that as well. His heart was open and hungry. In Holland I recall that I attended Sunday school and occasional church services, but I do not recall hearing anything personal from my father about things of the heart. My mother was more open and verbal; she was pious in a humble and simple way. She had no difficulty telling us to behave because that was the way God wanted us to honour our parents.

On the fifth day of our journey, Saturday, May 20, my youngest brother John (Jantje) was quite ill, as was mom. John, because of high fever and severe diarrhea, ended up in the ship's hospital. That day we were told we had crossed the halfway mark; we were now closer to the new land than the country we had left behind. My father's journal indicated there was no turning back. In his notes he also remarked that he could not grasp that even in the middle of the ocean seagulls still followed the ship. The next

11

day, Sunday morning, all of us awoke to a clear and quiet sea--finally the storms had ended. When we went outside to the back of the ship, we and many others watched a school of dolphins follow the ship for some time. The thrill of the day came when our section of bedrooms received clean sheets and fresh towels. Though Dutch people appreciate high standards of cleanliness, for many passengers those standards had dropped drastically, especially for those who had battled waves of seasickness. By now many longed for the sight of the Canadian coast.

On the evening of the 7th day, we saw land to the north of us. We were told it was part of Canada, Newfoundland. The next morning we slowly floated into Halifax, Pier 21. The arrival truly was the end of a journey. Holland was now far away, and a new future in a new land lay before us. It was a big change and there was much more to come. However, before we could begin our new life in a new land, another long trip awaited us.

Chapter 2

Beginnings in a New Land

It took till noon before we disembarked, processed through immigration, and received a few small welcome gifts from our new government. Guilders were changed into Canadian dollars, and close to the train station was a grocery store where enough food supplies were purchased for a three-day train trip for a family of eight. By suppertime we were on our way with hundreds of others heading north and west into New Brunswick, then Quebec, and by the next morning we were in Ontario. Groups of travelers left at various stops as we crossed Ontario, especially in the Kingston and Toronto areas. Once out of central Ontario, the stops became fewer, a few in northern Ontario, one or two each in Manitoba and Saskatchewan, and then on into Alberta.

Dad's journaling continued on the train. Comments explained what he saw: "Very rocky area, better soil for farming than yesterday, nice, peaceful town, and train stopped for water." In one place the train stopped for "two hours because we hit a child."

Cold, Dirty, Muddy Water, Friends with Hot, Delicious Soup

It seemed to take forever to get to Calgary where all eight of us and about as many suitcases transferred to a little better train heading north to Edmonton. About 115 kilometers north of Calgary the train stopped in Innisfail, where we disembarked with all we had managed to bring with us. Mom and dad, with a bunch of filthy, crabby, and -by now- tired little kids, were met by their old-time friends, John (Jan) and Jentje Mulder. The Mulders had come to Canada two years earlier and by now were experts in helping us settle. They picked us up in an old one-ton farm truck with four-foot-high racks around the sides of the truck bed. It belonged to the farmer where we were supposed to go, another 50 kilometers west of Innisfail into a rural farming area. Mom with two-year-old Jantje, our youngest, managed to squeeze into the cab with the two Mulders. Dad, Hennie (sister), and the four older boys climbed into the back of the truck. It was not a comfortable ride. Even though it was near the end of May, it was cold and rainy and we had nothing over us to protect us from the rain. We huddled in the middle of the truck; otherwise when the truck hit a pothole in the graveled road we got sloshed with brown muddy water. After about 30-40 minutes on this ride we arrived at the Mulders' house. We were invited to warm up with some nice hot soup and sandwiches. While there, we met a few other recent immigrants who also lived and worked in the area. They made special efforts to welcome us into their new community. We didn't know it then, but these people would become good friends with whom my parents maintained contact for many years.

New Names

The group together decided that we now needed Canadian names, and the sooner we did that, the easier it would be. After getting some Canadian money in Halifax, this was the next step in the Canadianizing process. Names were proposed: Dad, Hendrik, would become Hank; Mom would remain Jentje, but that would probably become Jennie. Hennie, my sister, would be Helen; and I, Henkie ("Henk", when I felt less diminutive) would be Henry. They argued about Wim's name. His full name was Willem, which in Canada would be William, but the shortened version of that would be Bill, which was weird to my parents, since "bill" in Dutch referred to the upper part of the thigh, right below the less appropriate section! Alex remained Alex, as did Harry, but Jantje would become Johnnie, and John when he grew up. I had no idea it would be that simple and that we'd be stuck with those names no matter how much we liked or disliked them. All this took place while we enjoyed a warm bowl of soup, a coffee or hot chocolate, and the sandwiches. The men were treated with a Dutch cigar which dad had brought from Holland in one of the carry-ons. I am not sure the women had anything special. As kids, we were happy with the hot chocolate.

Because we were all tired and dirty, it was soon time to go "home." After a few more instructions on how to adjust, we were reloaded in the back of the wet truck and taken another 25 kilometers west. We passed the little village of Raven –about four houses and a small grocery store and two miles past the store, Edgar Jensen owned a farm where we were to settle for dad's first job in Canada. A quarter of a mile (that's how I remember it) past the farm was an old (dilapidated) farmhouse where we would live, a barn, an old chicken coop, a pump-house and a garden, all fringe benefits besides the pay of $100 per month.

Our New Home

When we finally arrived at our destination, mom and dad were stunned. The Mulders had tried to prepare them by telling them not to expect too much, but this was totally outside the scope of their imagination. The old two-story house sat on bit of a hill, with a few scrawny poplar trees around it. There was not a splotch of paint to be found on the entire outside of the house. In fact, it had never been painted. It was a house with a "path rather than a bath." No electricity, thus no lights, no refrigerator, no forced-air heating. No water except a pump some 150 feet from the house. The doors were thin; the windows all had single pane glass with no storm protection. Insulation anywhere? Unheard of. In the kitchen was a wood-burning cook stove, and the living room had a round, thin metal wood heater to warm the rest of the house. Above the living room stove was an 18 by 18 inch square hole in the ceiling with a grill over it. That was the hot air duct to the upstairs. Though adventuresome to us kids, the house looked appalling to my parents. It was empty, cold, and foreboding and did not even come close to my mother's minimum level of acceptable cleanliness.

But it was ideal really! We had a house in the country along a creek, lots of space, a barn where we kids could play and hide, and hills on which to wander and roam. We did wonder where we might find friends. As former city people, we also speculated as to where we would find other stores, a school, a church, sport fields, and swimming pools. If there were any of those around, were they within walking -or at least biking- distance? We soon discovered there was only a one-room school two miles west and a small store with some basic groceries and a few other supplies some two miles in the opposite direction. And that was it, a huge jolt for city slickers for whom everything had been nearby.

Homegrown Groceries

Behind the house was a good-sized patch of freshly plowed garden, and though it was nearly June we were told if we hustled to get some seed, we could still plant a garden and harvest some vegetables by late summer and fall. If we wanted potatoes during the winter -and which Dutch family doesn't- they had to be planted soon. The veggies would have to be canned to preserve them; the potatoes would have to be stored in a place cool enough to keep them from sprouting but not so cold that they would freeze. By August 20 one could expect the first frost. The short season demanded action *now* if we wanted anything for the winter!

We learned quickly that the garden was more than a hobby; it was a major means towards survival since groceries were distant and expensive. As part of the salary we'd better get the seed in the ground. We soon learned that $100 per month simply was not enough to provide the needed food for a family of eight. The garden produced vegetables and the area provided some wild fruit -lots of wild saskatoons (berries like blueberries but more tart), a few raspberries, and tiny wild strawberries, so small it would take one an hour to pick a cupful. But where would a Dutch meat-loving family get meat? More surprises were on the way.

And Meat!

A few weeks after our arrival, Mr. Jensen showed up with a noisy pig, weighing about 150 pounds. Near the house was a barn (about the same age and condition as the house) where we had created a pen and where we fed the pig whatever leftovers we had; it ate pretty much anything that was greenish or grainy. Later when we had chickens they scavenged in the pig pen turning what the pigs hadn't digested into eggs, especially whole kernels of grain, now soft because they had gone through the "system." This was early recycling at its best, efficiently and inexpensively!

By late fall the pig weighed about 300 pounds. The time had come. With help from another immigrant family who had butchered a pig *once before*, porky had to make the ultimate sacrifice in order to feed both families for some time. After killing it -I hated that part, scraping off the hair with boiling water, and removing smelly -still warm- innards, the whole thing was sawed in half with a handsaw right down the middle of the backbone from the tail down. The two halves were hung up to cool in the pen where only a few hours earlier it had slept and happily slopped its food. The next day it was cut up. To preserve it, the hams and bacon were salted; the trim was ground up into ground pork and sausage—and, after washing out the

16

pig's guts, they were used for sausage casing. The rest of porky was cooked, put into jars, and canned! For a meal a jar would be opened and reheated; that was our meat. The first pig took a long time to butcher. After doing it a few times we became quite adept at it. Usually it was done with another couple who helped us for which they were generously rewarded with meat that they took home and put in their own jars. When they in turn would butcher, the favour was returned. Community was strong and generous. Besides, there was just too much pig for one family to handle and use by themselves efficiently in a short enough period of time since there were no refrigerators or freezers.

Savings

The following spring another "savings" program was started by mom when dad bought about 75 baby chicks. Mom raised them by being very gentle with them. Most dared not die! A few did, however. When one died, we heard, "There goes the profit!" The ones that became ill were kept in the house and nursed to health until they got better. The hens were kept for eggs, most of which we ate; a few were sold to neighbours for 25 cents a dozen. The roosters, usually 20 to 30 of them, were fed till they were about five pounds each when they, like the pigs, were "assisted" to make the ultimate sacrifice. After a meal of chicken, the leftovers made great chicken soup!

The chicks were a good investment in that they cost very little. There were some feed costs, but for the rest they scrounged around the yard and produced organic, natural eggs. Occasionally a coyote would sneak up on one, grab it, and take off with it. This really aggravated mom. She would curse it loud enough to warn every coyote within two miles with potent language that we could only hope no one else could hear. If others did hear, it was usually ok because it was always in Dutch! Her tone was not unlike the tone used to describe the Nazis who invaded Holland a few years earlier. It was the only time she let go with language that we did not think she knew and we certainly weren't allowed to use!

School Days

When we arrived in Raven in May, school still had a month to go, but the teacher decided we should start in the fall. It was a one-room school in the country with about 25 students in grades 1 through 9 with each grade sitting together in its own little section. I was in grade 4 when we left Holland, imagine my humiliation when I had to sit with the grade 1 group to learn basic words and reading in English. In math, once I understood what was wanted, I was always ahead of my age mates. I liked math. It was my best and favorite subject. I could read numbers; they were the same in both languages. Here we were, Helen by now age 13, I was 11, and Bill was 9, all put in with the grade 1 group. By Christmas, each of us had moved up into our own respective age groups.

During that first winter, I remember one day when it was colder than minus 40 degrees Fahrenheit when the three of us walked the two miles to school all bundled up. As we arrived at the school, we noticed no one else was there. We did not know the school's policy that anytime the temperature fell below minus 30 Fahrenheit, school was automatically cancelled, but the school door was left open in case anyone showed up. When we arrived we went in and discovered that earlier that morning someone had fired up the coal-burning stove in the middle of the room. We threw some wood on the smoldering coals quickly roaring it into flames which warmed us up. Since we had lunches with us we decided to eat them early. By the time we finished them we were warm enough to walk home. That was our school for the day.

We stayed in the Raven area for two years. By the spring of 1952, it became obvious that Mr. Jensen was not going to improve any part of the living arrangements, salary, meat, or food bonuses. My parents began to look for another place.

Valuable Memories

I believe the rest of my life was very much shaped by those first few years in Canada. I learned to appreciate my parents and their determination to survive and thrive. I learned to respect the cold western winter and the amazing value of a house with heat, especially a heated bathroom! Though I did not really realize it then, I know now that our first years in Canada were years of hardship. Life was tough. It was very cold in the winter. Imagine having to go outside to "pee" or "sit" in a subzero outhouse with temperatures of minus 10 (F) or colder. I can still feel the cold wind blowing around my bare butt. For toilet paper, we saved old Simpson-Sears catalogs with their slick photo pages. They were horrible to use! We didn't know any better, we didn't dare complain. When we did, mom would quickly and frequently remind us that we should be thankful. We had life, health and food and with that we were blessed. Her motto was, "Be thankful." That stayed with me all my life as one of the blessings of hardship. Surely mom and dad must have had other thoughts at times but if they did, we did not know it.

Humble Worship, Authentic Fellowship

This was the time when we also learned about the value of friendship. We tried hard to meet on Sundays somewhere for a worship service. Immigrants explored joining local Presbyterian churches but for various reasons didn't. Later, I often wondered about the significance of the decisions we made to start our own Reformed churches *and* schools. For our first two to three years in Canada, there were no nearby church buildings, so we gathered every other week in someone's home which was more-or-less centrally located . When the group became too large for a living room, a nearby Legion hall was rented for 5-10 dollars per Sunday where anywhere from 7 to 15 families would meet. Community dances were usually held on Saturday nights in the legion hall. Whoever arrived first on Sunday morning would clear out the empty beer bottles and sweep up the cigarette butts from the night before.

Hunger for God and Others

 After that, we worshiped as we sang our hearts out with Dutch Psalms and English Hymns including some with Genevan tunes. We listened to sermons which were read, we thanked God for the week completed, and prayed for the week to come. It was all simple but very sincere. Because our group was small -maybe 20-30 people- and we were in a more remote area, we rarely had an ordained pastor to preach for us. When we did, I remember it being special; I know I listened better to what was said. The rest of the time we would have a "reading service" led by one of the men, usually the one who was able to read a sermon in the most understandable English from a booklet of sermons written by a CRC pastor. Though it was all quite dignified and serious, I remember that for us kids it was rather boring. But as boring as these reading services were for us as kids, as I look back now, my parents grew spiritually during these times, and started making changes in their relationship with us and even with each other at home. These immigrants came long distances in old cars and put in a lot of effort to meet God and each other and to keep up with what was happening in their various spheres of work, family, schools, and acclimation to a new culture and country. After a 10:30 AM service, coffee and sandwiches –and sometimes soup- came out and were shared with all. The adults visited for a while after lunch while the kids played, and by 2:00 PM we did it all over again: another service, a duplicate of the morning one. Usually, one of the men would read another printed sermon. After that, about 3:30 to 4:00 PM, everyone went home happy, refreshed and fulfilled. We had met with God and we had fellowshipped with others. Life was good.

Those Sundays left good memories even though the 30-mile (50 kilometer) winter ride in a 1941 Ford could be brutally cold. Two adults and six kids in a small car with a heater that left a lot to be desired resulted with thick layers of frost on the inside of the windshield. Five or six of us kids sat in the back with blankets and coats wrapped around us trying to keep warm with not one seatbelt among all eight passengers. The group worship gatherings usually were bi-weekly events. It was too costly to do the drive *and* buy adequate groceries *every* week.

On alternate Sundays when we lived in Raven, anywhere from three to five of us kids were invited with our boss, Mr. and Mrs. Jensen, to come with them–in their new 1950 Mercury, -with a good heater- to Caroline where they attended the Nazarene church and took us to their Sunday school. I remember that more than once the Jensens won the weekly prize for bringing the most visitors to Sunday school and were rewarded with pens, pencils, or stickers some of which they gave to us. We were regularly urged to accept Jesus into our lives; I think some of us did although we did not talk about it.

Spiritual Growth

When we were still in the Netherlands, I remember attending church and Sunday school but only occasionally. We were members of the more liberal state church, the Hervormde Kerk (the Reformed Church). I don't remember how often we went, but it certainly wasn't every Sunday. Spirituality consisted mostly of 15-30 seconds of silence before *and* after meals when we all folded our hands, bowed our heads, and talked to God, I guess. It was a meal routine. Occasionally either mom or dad prayed out loud, especially if we had visitors. Otherwise, I do not remember them doing so. It was all pretty private. The more Orthodox Christians were members of the Gereformeerde Kerk (Christian Reformed Church). They attended two services per Sunday, sent their kids to Christian Schools and were more diligent about Sunday keeping.

When Dutch immigrants came to Canada from *either* of those churches, they were welcomed and received by members of the Christian Reformed Church (CRC). The CRC had established "field men," (they were men who helped find jobs and homes for new immigrants.) Funds for their expenses came from CR churches in the United States. I remember the first winter when a field man came with a whole carload of new coats, pants, shoes, underwear, hats, and gloves for all of us. I have not forgotten that big box of clothes coming in the door. It was amazing. I got a nice, warm winter coat which I proudly wore to school, Sunday school, and everywhere else. When it was too small for me it was passed down the line to the younger brothers, as most clothes were. This all contributed to the creation of a new family of people, all immigrants, into a community which was a church! We were all indebted to the Christian Reformed Church, a church that went out-of-the-way to receive us with open arms. My parents' awareness of God grew as they were blessed by the church and as they associated with other people who wanted to serve the Lord. Because dad had leadership gifts, it wasn't long before he was involved in planning and developing the next steps for the group. If most people become Christians through conversion, I think my parents became more dedicated Christians through assimilation. I don't know when or where they turned the corner.

I do know that later when we moved to Penhold (16 km South of Red Deer) for a short time, we attended the Red Deer CRC, a fledgling church that had started the year before, 1951. We were there at the time they were about ready to build a church. I remember dad (only dad, women did not go!) attended a congregational meeting to decide whether to proceed with the construction.

When he came home, the conversation went like this between him and Mom, (all in Dutch).

Mom: "What did they decide?"

 Dad: "The consistory (Council) decided we are going to build."

Mom: "Hoe kan dat nou?" (How can they do that? But really, "How can they pay for it?") Mom was responsible for groceries and clothes and thus vitally interested in this part of the church's life! By then, I too was all ears.

Dad: "They asked each one of us who is working to donate one day's wages per month for the next year or more besides our regular donations."

Mom: "Henk, can *we* do that?"

Dad: "If the others can, we can too."

End of discussion.

It showed, without one sermonic word, what a Christian commitment and sharing community was about. These people cared for each other and were devoted to their Lord. It was no big deal, they just did it. It happened and they were blessed in the process. The simplicity of it all made a deep impact upon this 13-year-old boy. Their vitality and spirituality may well have been the seeds from which my desire to explore ministry sprouted. These were all immigrants who had only been in Canada for one to five years. They expected to make sacrifices to serve God in their new land and were ready to do so. Their commitment to donate one day's earnings per month to build was *their* simple yes to God. Unfortunately, we lived in Penhold and attended the Red Deer congregation for only a few months. While we were there, we supported that church and the building project. When we moved, we joined the nearest CR church (or group) and supported that group. Participation was never an option. As kids we were never told much, but we tried to listen in on conversations between mom and dad whenever possible. We were very interested to know who and what we were competing with for new clothes, a present, or an occasional new toy.

Small Groups

About one night every three or four weeks, similar efforts were made to meet with other immigrants at someone's house for an evening of socializing. The kids would play and the adults would talk. Everyone brought some food to share -soup and sandwiches usually. All the issues of life were discussed: kids and their schooling, the fathers' jobs, and especially the relationships to their bosses. They compared salaries and benefits (free milk, eggs, meat and a garden). Discussions were accompanied by the aroma of strong coffee and pungent Dutch cigars enjoyed as special treats by the men -only on such occasions. By 9:00 PM the adults would start what always proved to be a boisterous game of cards. When they could get it, the game was accompanied with a "slokje" (a potent bit of libation!) They celebrated their good times with little stuff but lots of laughter. Close to midnight, with most of the younger kids now sleeping all over the place, everything was packed up and all went home happily after setting the date for their next "small group" meeting. Though it was never called that, in actuality it was what they were. Those evenings left an impression on me.

I think these small groups did everything small groups are supposed to do. Great, honest sharing, deep caring and helping one another, lots of fun and laughter. Praying together was not done, except before and after meals or maybe if someone had a serious family issue. Though these Dutch people did not wear their hearts on their sleeves, they had an unshakable dependence on the providence of a gracious God. He was always there even if rarely mentioned. Every prayer included thanksgiving. Without saying it, they practiced that they were not their own but belonged body and soul to their faithful God, who had promised to provide for them. They counted on that. And He showed up, every time. He kept his promises and because no one expected otherwise, they were not even surprised.

Chapter 3

Teenage Years in Canada

After spending two years in Raven, dad found a new place on a large farm to work with a wealthy farmer near Penhold, some 50 kilometers northeast of Raven close to Red Deer. Things improved radically, for our second home had electricity, sewer, and running water. It was a great improvement! Mom was thankful for a warm bathroom with a flusher and she expressed that regularly, "Isn't this a nice bathroom?" I could say "amen" to that.

Though our housing had improved, dad quickly realized that the move was a mistake. Leaving one "tight" farmer, he had accepted a job with one who was more generous but whose record for keeping farm help was terrible. He was a tyrannical slave driver, and it did not take dad long -some 3-4 months- to realize that we needed to get away from there as quickly as possible. The setting was abusive.

Before we were even fully unpacked in Penhold dad found a new farm-help position that offered fair wages, a good house, and a good location. We now moved another 50 kilometers northeast from Red Deer to a farm near the village of Mirror owned by Henry and Barbara Neis and their two boys. It was a good spot; I quickly realized dad was happy working with Henry Neis! After we were there two years, Mr. Neis decided he wanted to quit farming and have dad take over the place. They made arrangements for dad to rent the place, buy some of his dairy cows and machinery, and start on his own. Since that was dad's dream, it was an exciting offer and the deal was quickly and easily done and implemented. Both men had integrity and practiced "your word is your bond" and it made things relatively simple. Dad was an entrepreneur biding his time as a farm worker until the right opportunity arose and he could break out on his own. When it came, he latched onto it. By then I was about 13 and able to provide some help, as did some of my siblings.

Farming in Mirror

Dad did well, the farm expanded rapidly, and he built up a nice herd of milk cows and younger replacements in only a few years. Every time he could spare a few dollars, he'd look for another cow or heifer. In fact, by

Christmas 1955 my mom and dad managed to scrounge enough money together to take what then was a rare plane trip to the "old country." Since they had left Holland under the stress of my grandfather's death on the very day we left, they had longed to go back to repair some of the scars left by their leaving. Sister Helen, now 18, was in charge of feeding and taking care of six kids. And since I was 16, I was in charge of feeding and taking care of some 20 cows and 30 young livestock. The milking, cleaning, calving, and all other related activities were in my lap and that in the heart of the cold winter months. It was the time of year we battled frozen teats on the cows and frozen water lines everywhere else. Any calf born in the heart of the winter risked freezing to death before its mother could lick it dry.

The three weeks went well for us at home as six kids living together. But on the farm it was another story. My parents had helped another Dutch family with three boys who had come as recent Dutch immigrants. The man wanted to farm but had never lived on a farm. Dad, in the generosity of his heart, rather than take the man on as an inexperienced helper, took him as a partner in the farm operation, a big mistake. Dad thought he had made clear that because of my five years of farm experience I should be in charge while they were gone. The partner decided that he was not going to let that happen, and because of his age (40s), he was boss. Though he knew little about dairying he stubbornly insisted on doing things his way rather than listen to a 16-year-old kid, who happened to be more experienced. I wanted the cows to maintain high production levels, look healthy, and birth viable calves. I soon knew we were dropping in milk production, we were battling mastitis (a common cows' udder disease resulting in milk which was not potable), and we had other problems. One day he would feed quality hay to the cows, the next day, if he happened to have straw on the wagon he'd try to feed that to the cows. When I told him that straw was for bedding and had no nutritional value whatsoever, instead of replacing it with hay he'd blow his top. The cows would take one whiff, look at us, pull up their noses and give us that "I-am-not-eating-this-stuff" look which any dairyman quickly recognizes as "we're going on strike -no feed, no eat, no meat, no milk, period."

After mom and dad came back, I learned that dad had had the same problems with the man. It was kindness, not wisdom that had motivated dad to make him a partner. Dad's quick grasp of the numbers told him, not long after that, that the farm's income would not be enough to continue to support two families. He knew the partnership had to end quickly. When he mentioned that to the partner the relationship soured, the partnership failed resulting in a farm auction in the spring of 1956. All the cattle, milk and farm equipment went on the auction block and were sold. That was very painful for all of us, especially for mom and me. We loved those cows like family members, and watching others load them onto trucks and take them away felt like we had betrayed our best friends. Dad as usual was quiet and stoic. When he became quiet, I assumed it meant that he had everything under control. Later I learned that was not so at all. It was the only way he could handle emotional times. He internalized quietly or exploded loudly. He began to look for a smaller farm that could provide financially for his family. He found a place about 150 kilometers southwest of Mirror in the area of Rocky Mountain House, commonly called Rocky. It was a harder move for me because by now I had enjoyed five years of school in the relatively small junior and senior high school in Mirror where I fit in quite well. I was a big fish in a small pond. Because the school was only about two miles from our house, we could walk, bike, or take the school bus. I had also made some good friends and I was now in grade 11. I didn't want to move just before the last year of high school but I was given no choice. We were moving; I was too young not to come along.

And in Rocky Mountain House

For that last year of school, I had to make a new start in the new setting of Rocky Mountain House, a town of about 3000 people and just one larger high school serving the town and the greater farming community around it. I found myself the only male CRC student in grade 12 in a relatively large high school. The CRC that we joined had a group of around 30 young people my age but only a few of them attended the high school; as I recall none in grade 11 or 12.

The others had jobs and were making money! So when I turned 17, I too wanted to quit school like all the other immigrant kids, get a job in construction or the lumber industry, earn money to help my parents, and, hopefully, buy a car! That was the "in" thing for young people. Peer pressure. That's when my dad met my plans head on and in contrast with many of the other immigrants, told me that I was *not* quitting school. He made clear his view on the value of education and reminded me in non-negotiable terms that we had come to Canada primarily for a better future for us children. "You obviously have no idea what is best for you! Like it or not, you are going to get through grade 12 with decent grades!"(said in Dutch: when he was passionate about something he reverted to Dutch). End of discussion, and though I asked one or two more times, there was no negotiating room on that. Deep down I think I was actually relieved that he would not let me quit school. I could legitimately say to my working friends: "I'd quit but dad won't let me." That way I could save face.

I went to school feeling strong peer pressure, and I did not like it. I remember sitting in a classroom where right outside the windows a large new gymnasium was under construction involving many of my friends. They were making money while I was ridiculed for being "het studentje" (little student). But I will forever be grateful for my father's vision, sacrifice, stubbornness, and determination to stick with his decision no matter how disagreeable I became about it.

And there were Groceries

Though I was eager to go to work, make money, and get my own car, I instead did what dad wanted. I went to school. I did find a part-time job at the Killico grocery store where my task was to wait on customers and do carry-outs. About six months later I was taught to clean and stock the produce and fruit shelves. I did well with that as I managed to sell pretty much everything so profit margins went up for fruit and produce. I hated to throw out any food. A year later the boss asked if I would like to manage the fruit and produce section when I was finished high school. It was my first temptation to enter the business world, something that would appeal to me again and again also in later years. I blame it on my dad's genes!

In the meantime, after one year of attempted farming, my father concluded that the soil in the Rocky area was not such as to sustain the style of farming required to provide adequately for a family of eight. He wanted a dairy with enough acres of grain and grassland to grow enough feed for his herd. He planned to send his kids to school and knew that would cost. Where he was, he felt that he could see himself working hard for years to produce just enough grain and alfalfa to meet expenses. I remember him saying, "I don't think I can manage to get my own place here, pay for it, *and* feed *and* educate the kids". He concluded we'd have to move again, a tough decision but one that over the years proved to be a wise one.

Farming in Lacombe

After one year in Rocky, we were on the road again with all our stuff, including machinery, cattle and furniture. I remember driving our 1952 "44" Massey Harris tractor with an open but loaded bale wagon behind it east about 110 km on Highway 11 from Rocky Mountain House to Red Deer and then about 25 km north on Highway 2 to Lacombe where Dad had found a farm to rent. Dr. John McKibbon, a good doctor but also an entrepreneurial farmer, had bought some 360 acres 8 km north of Lacombe. The land had nothing on it, no house, no barns, no sheds, just trees! So everything we needed to run a farm, including a house to live in, had to be built that first summer. We rented the place with the arrangement of one-third of the crop for Doc, two-thirds for us. Dad worked the land; mom and the kids milked the 15 cows (twice a day by hand!) outside for about six months, while Doc and crews of workers from Canadian Union College (a Seventh Day Adventist School) built a house, barn, and corrals. It was one amazing summer as a treed piece of land turned into a full-fledged farmyard with fences, house, garage, barn and cattle sheds. Mom, with the help of us kids, managed to plant, weed, and grow a good-sized vegetable garden with enough potatoes to provide for the family of eight for the entire winter. When mom thought any of us kids were out of line, she punished us by exiling us to the garden to hoe potatoes. The length of time or the number of rows to be hoed was determined by the severity of the crime. Regular practice enabled me to hoe weeds in a row of potatoes faster than most of my siblings. I did not mind this punishment. I actually liked being out there. The love for gardening that I still have today was learned in that early potato patch.

When the rest of the family had moved to Lacombe, I was still in my last year of high school, so I was allowed to stay in Rocky to finish the term. After graduation, I had two choices: I could follow my family to Lacombe, get a job there, save some money and get ready to go to school again, or I could stay in Rocky Mountain House and take the full-time job that

Killico's had offered me. I boarded with the Klaas Kikstra family who had made room for me even though they had six children of their own. When the end of the school year came, the Kikstras let me know that I would need another place to live if I wanted to stay in Rocky and suggested that I could find a better-paying job in Lacombe. I think they had met with my parents and together decided that I was traveling with the party crowd. The Kikstras knew some of my friends and probably noticed that I was getting home later and later at night. They thought it safer that I be under the wings of my parents again; I was too young to handle the freedom. Since it was the easier route to go I did not resist it. It helped that I quickly found a grocery store job in Lacombe, so I packed up and left Rocky.

I graduated from grade 12 in June 1957 with the intention of going back to school for something, sometime, somewhere—it was undefined. My options varied. Through some 4-H activities, I had won a partial scholarship for a year of agricultural courses at a college in Olds, Alberta, which appealed to me. It would mean I'd be on my own for about eight months of the fall and winter in a college-like setting. Or, I could take some more high school courses which would build additional credits towards a general university Bachelor of Science degree. Those courses could be taken without leaving home for another year. With my precarious financial situation, that also looked attractive.

I ended up spending the next two years in both of these educational pursuits. The first year I went to Olds Agricultural College (OAC) for a one-year course in agriculture, graduating in the spring of 1958. The school provided two things: it gave me some basic farming skill and knowledge, and it provided some extra credits towards a four-year university degree in Agriculture. By then I had decided that I wanted to do something to help farmers. I felt that in many instances they were taken advantage of by receiving low prices for their cattle, pigs, chickens, milk, eggs, and grains. And because they were not organized, I felt they were victimized. The second year I had a job at the Lacombe Experimental Farm working in the pig barns while during the winter semester I had time off to take some vocational courses at a composite high school in Red Deer. This gave me more credits towards the first year of a university degree. I continued to be focused upon agriculture.

Inner Turmoil

I realize now that I thought if I could help farmers, including my dad, he would be impressed and I would receive his approval. By then, I felt a growing need for his affirmation. I was struggling with self-worth. I only *felt* accepted and loved by him when I *did* well. Since farming was my dad's life's work, I thought if I could improve overall farming conditions and maybe even their returns, he would *have* to like me.

But by now I was also beginning to think-but not talk- more seriously about the possibility of preparing for the ministry. People at the church, a few of my family's friends, books that I was reading, and a radio sermon by Billy Graham were all things God was using to nudge me in this direction. At a time when I did not really pray that much, I caught myself talking to God about ministry. I thought my mom would like it if I went that way but she never mentioned it. I think she thought this was strictly a personal issue to be settled between God and me; anything she might say she would see as interference. My dad did not say anything either. From that I concluded that I probably did not have his approval, but I never really asked him. Insecurity and the fear of possible rejection led me to assume a lot of things without checking to see if I was assuming correctly. It was hard to ask for help from others when by all appearances I wanted to look like I had "it all together."

I was in turmoil regarding my future. Though I wanted to do God's will, I never said much about that to anybody. I just wasn't verbal about God; I was more verbal about the church. That was less personal. I faithfully attended worship, usually twice a Sunday. I met friends at church, but for the rest I was pretty bland. My future was my greater concern. I had been planning to go to the University of Alberta for a degree in agriculture. By mid-summer 1959 the turmoil was intense.

A couple of pastors and others urged me to pray about the ministry and spoke to my parents that they should encourage me in that direction. But I was reluctant. I liked agriculture and took well to it. I liked the sciences and math courses and I hated languages. Agriculture meant science and math at the University of Alberta. Ministry meant languages at Calvin College, the denominational college, in the United States -not a good tradeoff for me. I liked Alberta and was not eager to move to the United States. Besides, at that time, it was not "cool" to talk about serving God in ministry. In my mind, any kind of public mention of God was a sign of weakness and dependence and won no points with peers.

So I struggled quietly: University of Alberta, dad and agriculture; or Calvin College, God and ministry? Those were the choices and that's how they balanced out.

Solution

In the meantime, I had been encouraged to participate in the annual oratorical contest sponsored by the Christian Reformed denominational youth organization called The Young Calvinist Federation. District contests were held first and the winners (male and female) would move on to the larger regional contest. Finally eight young men and eight young women would make it to the final contest at the annual Young Calvinist Convention held in August. I participated and made it all the way to the final at the 1959 Convention held in the Jubilee Auditorium in Edmonton. This was a big event with about 2,000 youth from Christian Reformed Churches from all of North America. All the while I was trying to make a decision -Calvin or the University of Alberta? By this time it was mid-August, and the September school season was looming. I had registered and been accepted at the university. In fact, I had a small scholarship through 4-H (a farm club for students) and most of the funds needed for the tuition costs. I had made no application to Calvin yet. I would need much more money for Calvin's tuition. I needed to make a decision soon. But how?

Ah, the contest! The winner received a year's tuition to Calvin! If I won, that would be the clear sign that God wanted me at Calvin. If I lost, university here I come! It seemed like a good way to solve this dilemma.

As it turned out, I didn't win and I didn't lose. I came in second with the prize of tuition support at Calvin for one semester. I had won enough so that I couldn't ignore it, but I didn't win enough for a year. The decision was still in my lap. Though God was supposed to clear up this uncertainty, He hadn't helped at all! The turmoil was still there. It was like He was saying, "You want me to decide for you? I called you. You are not a robot.

31

I want your willing yes." I had a decision to make. In this case to not say yes was to say no. Whatever I decided, I was not going to be able to put the blame on Him if things did not work out. By now it was close to the end of August, the convention was over, and I was still on the fence.

Now What?

I remember struggling through the night after getting back to the farm from the convention. I was now more inclined to attend Calvin, but I could still go either way. It was hard to lock the "options" door. I arose the next morning at 5:30 AM to milk cows. Dad and I were alone in the barn, and when I saw him suddenly –totally unexpectedly- I said to him: "I am going to Calvin and I need to get my application in!" I made the decision the moment I announced it. All dad said was, "If that is what you want, that's up to you. I don't have money to pay for it." Neither one of us mentioned "ministry," although we both knew that's what we were talking about. I still wonder whether he was disappointed or relieved that it was decided. My independent streak kicked in and I remember thinking, "I'll do it without your money," although I had little idea as to how. The Classis, (the local regional group of about 20 Christian Reformed churches) made some financial assistance available to students entering studies for the Ministry of the Gospel. The committee handling the funds assured me that I would probably qualify and suggested that I apply. With that touch of affirmation, a few saved dollars, and a lot of self-assurance or confidence in God (I am not sure which), I would go.

I was not in the least bit worried about money then. I had at that moment a dangerous spirit of self-sufficiency: Don't count on others, find and earn your own way! But I also had a simple, trusting faith. Early in my life I had developed an awareness of God. I did not talk much about that, nor did I ask a lot of questions. But I reflected regularly and deeply about God. I expected Him to provide whatever I needed, and He always did. I also had a holy fear of God. I did not want to cross Him up. I was keenly aware that He was not to be taken for granted. I felt accountable and had quiet but strong convictions that I could trust and serve him. I did not pray much about this, I prayed more when I was in trouble.

God and I had this practical, no-nonsense relationship. We enjoyed being together as two good friends without having to do much talking. I had a hard time indicating to God and to others that we had this comfortable bond in that I depended upon Him for everything. But admitting that to tough friends seemed sissy-like and weak; I had a tough exterior. When I needed something, I'd let God know and expect Him to provide it. And most of the times he did. In that I was like my mother who also had a simple, practical faith.

All through my adult life, I have felt that my biblical knowledge was weak, partially because I had never attended a Christian school. The only Bible learning I experienced was at home and at Sunday school. My mother would read the (Dutch) *Children's Story Bible* to us from which I learned most of the Old Testament stories. When I was old enough to read for myself, I read the stories about the life and death of Jesus mostly in the Dutch story Bibles for children. I clearly remember the time I read about His awful, totally undeserved, death. Though I was a teenager I cried like a child but I made sure no one saw me. That was probably the first time I realized what He had done *for me*. It put me on the road to conversion and created a desire to be committed to His way.

Touchy Timing

Once I had decided I was going to Calvin I knew I had to get my application into the college. I had only two weeks before classes started. In addition, I needed a student visa from Calvin indicating that I was accepted as a student or I would not be allowed across the border to enter the U.S. This was required for any Canadian citizen taking further education at a U.S. college. On top of that, I had to carry a letter stating that I had all the money necessary for a year of schooling, including room and board, lest I become a liability for U.S. taxpayers. Time was of the essence.

My pastor, Rev. Bert Den Herder, a wonderful, godly man who had been very helpful all along, had the necessary Calvin application forms, and within a day or so they were off to Grand Rapids, air mailed at that. I began to pack clothes and a few other things, bought a train ticket from Lacombe to Calgary, on to Winnipeg, then Minneapolis and Chicago and finally to Grand Rapids. Once I had announced my decision to prepare for ministry, I was convicted that I was following God's call and doing His will so taking care of the rest of my needs was His responsibility. I was confident that all the details would work out, including the in-time arrival of the needed student visa from Grand Rapids. I was scheduled to leave Lacombe by train the Tuesday afternoon after Labor Day, around 2:30 PM. Our mail came into Box 872 at the Lacombe Post Office. The visa was not in the 10:30 AM mail; I was told that another delivery would arrive at 2:00 PM that afternoon. We took my suitcases to the station about 2:00 PM when, matter-of-factly, I asked dad to go to the post office and get my visa. I *knew* it would be there, and it was. It had just arrived, a wonderful affirmation. God showed up with my visa just at the right time. I have reminded myself many times in later years of the confidence I felt in God that day.

We said our farewells, and I spent two long days on the train which brought me into Grand Rapids about 9:00 PM on Thursday night. I was met by Herman Salomons, who was a Calvin Seminary student also from Lacombe. He had arranged for me to stay that night at the home of another Alberta seminary student and his wife, Sid and Marie Greidanus, originally from Edmonton. Thus began the next phase of my journey and my first involvement with *Christian* Education, Calvin College.

I now know that planning for the future was important to my parents. The decision for them to leave family, friends and country did not come easily or quickly. Neither did mine. Every decision involving change and uncertainty meant delayed gratification. This is tough for an adult, almost impossible for a teenager. The pain of that decision for my dad was offset by his determination (and stubbornness!) to provide a good future for his six children. He was utterly consistent about that. Without his insistence, I would not have finished high school. I am indebted to both mom and dad and would love to be able to express my gratitude to them. When we left Holland I had no idea as to the huge price they paid in giving up the comforts of Holland, their families and financial security. Now starting college I began to grasp the price they paid, I dared not fail at whatever I was going to do. I now surmise that the sense of indebtedness to my parents, especially to my dad contributed significantly to me becoming a restless, driven person.

Chapter 4

The Grand Rapids Journey

1959 – 1965

The next morning the Greidanuses showed me the way to the Franklin Campus of Calvin College where I could register to start classes. I walked to the college, was soon registered, bought a meal plan to eat at the Commons, and applied for some part-time work on campus. I knew my funds would not stretch far without some supplement. Campus was the only place I was allowed to work because I was a Canadian. For anything else, I would need a U.S government work permit.

I found a bulletin board to meet my next two needs: textbooks (preferably used ones!) and a place to live since dormitory rooms were few and already occupied by others. Checking the bulletin board, I found the name of a seminarian at 911 Bates Street, not far from the college, who had an extra bedroom to rent for $8 per week. When I visited Myron (called Paul) and Gail Van Houten and their baby daughter, I quickly learned that renting out the room was not an option but a necessity for them. At times it was the difference between food and no food. More than once Gail asked me for an advance on the room rent so she could buy groceries including milk for baby Rachel. They were poor but they were good people. I was happy to pay whatever they were asking although I was not among the well-to-do either! I did feel I was better off than they were; I had only one mouth to feed, they had three.

Living on Little

Later that fall, the Van Houtens' need for food became even more critical. As a seminarian, Paul was invited to preach in a northern Michigan church for a Sunday. The mileage allotment helped pay for his gas to get him there. However, he stayed two extra days to go deer hunting without the knowledge of the seminary faculty. He came back with deer meat, although word of his hunting got back to the seminary before he did. The day he returned to classes, I was surprised to find him home when I came back from my college classes. He usually came home later since he often studied in the library where it was quiet. When I arrived home that day, I was met by a despondent, discouraged couple. Paul told me that he had been suspended from Seminary for a week because he had gone deer hunting rather than attend classes, obviously indicating wrong priorities. But I knew better. I *knew* why he had gone. The seminary didn't, and Paul was not about to tell them that they had no food. It is hard to ask for help.

The next day I made my first visit to Calvin Seminary just across campus from the college. I waited to see Dr. John Kromminga, the seminary president. I told him I was staying at the Van Houtens and had learned that he had been suspended and asked why. Dr. Kromminga did not want to tell me, so I asked whether it had anything to do with the fact that he had missed three days of classes. He tried to dodge the question but after a bit he admitted it. He then informed me that any seminarian more interested in hunting than attending classes might not be the best candidate for ministry. When I told him it was their *only* means for food presently, he was shocked. The next day Paul got a call that the suspension was lifted and he happily returned to classes. They also received some anonymous gifts of groceries. I never told the Van Houtens about my visit. Three years later when I enrolled as a seminary student and I again met Dr. Kromminga, he reminded me that we had met before at which we both smiled without saying anything more.

I had a meal plan for food at the Calvin Commons. Within two weeks I also found a part-time job in the dish-room scraping food off dishes and washing pots and pans (a real glamorous job)! Along with other Canadian students, we pretty much handled all the food line and dish-room jobs. It was one of the few places we were allowed to work. As a kid who remembered his first egg and orange, I was frequently appalled at students loading up trays of food and then dumping the entire plate's contents into the garbage can after eating only a few bites. Every garbage bin held whole, unpeeled oranges and apples, bananas, untouched boiled eggs, meat and countless slices of bread and buns! How could they?

College Challenges

I had taken two years of French in High School, but I didn't remember much! In college I received credit for my math and science courses but had to take all these dreaded language courses. Since I had no German, Latin, and surely no Greek, I had to do them all! So I plugged through two years of Latin, two years of German, three years of Greek topped off by some courses in English literature, including one in Shakespeare (I don't do him well!) after finishing freshman grammar. In my first year at college I was already warned that Greek, which would start in my sophomore (second) year, would get me. Many pre-seminary students dropped out of the seminary preparation courses after starting Greek. I was determined not to let that happen, although a few times I certainly harbored the thought. When I allowed myself to get behind on vocabulary or syntax, even for only a few days, it would be tough to catch up. The monotony of all that memorization discouraged me and at such times I would wonder what was happening on the Alberta farm. I could do the homework; I just couldn't see enough value in it to warrant all that memory work. Unless I could see something make practical sense I had a hard time with it. Ultimately what kept me going was that I was so absolutely convicted that God wanted me to go into the ministry and I had said yes to Him. Now I was too proud and stubborn to let a temporary time of discouragement win out. At such times I would remember things like the arrival of my visa just in time. It became a memory of God's affirmation and yes to me "I will provide, trust me." I often told myself. "I will not let some Greek vocabulary and syntax stop me from fulfilling God's call on my life!"

It was the first time ever that I had to concentrate and discipline myself systematically to do what I needed to get done. It was important to learn that. I now see that one of the major pitfalls of many ministers is a lack of self-discipline and poor time management. I struggled with it too. Greek, perhaps unwittingly, tested it; it was the course that probably spared some churches the problems and pain of dealing with a pastor who was undisciplined and tended to run late. My guess is that failing Greek redirected a number of people into other careers.

Friends

Several other things stand out from my three college years. Early in my first year, I developed some good friendships, most of them with fellow Canadian students. We were drawn to each other perhaps because we were regarded as "Canucks"-in our better moments, "wetbacks," at less complimentary times. (Like the illegal immigrants from Mexico who swam across the Rio Grande into Texas, we were condescendingly joked about as the "illegals" that swam across the Great Lakes into Michigan.) Though intended to be funny, the word "wetback" had a barb to it. If the term was heard often enough we felt like foreigners and were more comfortable hanging around with fellow Canadians. In my first year at Calvin, Glenn Verbrugge, a preacher's kid from Ontario, and I became good friends. The friendship has been enjoyed during subsequent years and we still maintain regular contact.

A New Friend

The second year brought my best friend into my life although it took me a while to realize it. Many Sunday nights a group of students would meet somewhere at Calvin to sing hymns and meet other students in a setting other than a classroom. Many of us would attend a 6:00 or 7:00 PM evening service and then gather in the Calvin Commons dining hall for a time of enthusiastic singing, some refreshments, and checking the field for possible dates. This was a time when both Canadians and Americans socialized openly and enjoyably. But it was a specific group, students who loved to sing robust gospel songs and hymns. These were the same students who tended to show up on Sunday afternoons to visit patients, shut-ins in nursing homes and hospitals, and at times inmates in prisons. The hymn sings were casual, fun and uplifting; everyone had a good time.

On one October Sunday evening, about six of us Canadian students decided to go to the Calvin Commons to see who was there for the hymn sing. Afterwards we chatted for a while as a group, and I noticed a pretty, fairly self-confident girl with a pony tail wearing a bright red dress and coat. I learned she was a local student, and I assumed likely not the least bit interested in becoming acquainted with a Canadian. I did learn that her name was Jan DeKorte and that she had been born and raised in Grand Rapids.

A few days later I saw her again and decided to make an approach. I had just bought my first car, a 1951 Studebaker for $55, which was a lot of money when you saw the outside of the car, but really cheap if you took a ride in it. I made two round-trips with 5 people in it to Alberta. The Calvin Drama Club (Thespians) was putting on a play, and I thought I would ask her out for that and at the same time give her a ride in my "new" car. She accepted the invitation which began a rather slow-growing courtship, with ups and downs. We were both aware of our totally different backgrounds which we felt might not work in a life-long healthy relationship. I was an immigrant kid from a large family raised with few possessions on a western Canada farm. She was a third generation only child not lacking anything raised in a mid-west American city. About the only thing we had in common was that both of us were members of the Christian Reformed Church attending Calvin College. Both of us were desirous to serve the Lord and we soon discerned that in each other. We were serious about doing God's will. Along with Jan's genuine commitment to Christ, I learned that she was a good organist and pianist and sang in the Back to God Hour Radio Choir. My practical side soon saw these all as wonderful assets to enhance ministry. We soon realized that the synergy of the two of us serving together would accomplish far more than each of us serving alone. Every subsequent year has confirmed that evaluation to be correct. God has blessed us and He has blessed our work.

School, Work, and Money for more School

I learned quickly that I could not handle studying every spare hour as my friend Glenn Verbrugge could. He was on a GM scholarship that covered college costs, and to maintain it he needed a high grade point average. Besides, he was premed, and to get into med school required top grades. (He got them.) I knew that I would be more effective as a student if I did something other than study for about 20-25 hours per week so I might as well have a job and use my energy earning some needed "dough" to get through college. I decided early that the extra work required to turn a B into an A just wasn't warranted for me; it interfered with too many other good things. Glenn was really a good model to me. Every time I saw him studying long and hard, I was reminded that I should too and so did more than I might have had he not been around.

In my second year I acquired a work visa from the U.S government allowing me to work off campus. For my last year at the college and the first year of seminary, I worked a part-time night watchman job at a nursing home that housed about 24 state-supported elderly, incapacitated women. It was located on Pleasant Street -certainly a misnomer since there was nothing pleasant about it-near Division and Wealthy, one of the less desirable areas of Grand Rapids. For the number of patients who lived in that home, state law required two attendants on duty at all times. However, from 11:00 PM till 6:00 AM, all the patients were sleeping and one nurse could easily handle whatever was needed. So, for seven nights a week I was the second staff person who merely had to be on the premises from 11:00 to 6:00 while the women slept and the nurse watched them. It met the letter of the law. That work schedule did little for Jan and my dating relationship except help contribute to good behavior; "I have to be at the Pleasant Street home by 11:00." So, though two staff members were present, one received only minimal pay (trust a Dutchman to figure that one out!) My pay was a free room in the attic (hot as blazes in the summer and cold like a freezer in the winter). Meals with the residents were available at the home and considered as part of the pay. I never had so many mushy, bland meals in my life! Oh, and I got $25 cash per month.

And More Work

I finished my college work and graduated in the spring of 1962. I had received extra credits from the dean of students for my agricultural college year and for the extra grade 12 courses I had taken in Alberta. This allowed me to complete all the college requirements in three years of classes plus a summer session. After graduation I started the summer by getting a job at A&P bakery at $1.75 per hour. That was more money per hour than I had ever earned. Things looked great. I would be able to save a good nest egg for the next school year since I had minimal expenses, no rent and no groceries. And I would likely have opportunity for significant overtime hours at a higher rate per hour. But I also maintained that it was important that I not work on Sundays unless the work was essential. Between studying and work, I was busy and felt I needed a Sabbath. Baking bread and pies did not fit the necessary-work category. Before I started the bakery job, the boss agreed that I would not have to do Sunday shifts. Three weeks later he came to me and told me the union and other workers were challenging my free Sundays. His closing comments were, "I am afraid I've got to put you on the Sunday schedule." When I asked, "What if I don't come in?" his answer was, "Your time card will be pulled, and you're done."

The first Sunday my name was on the schedule happened to be a communion Sunday at Fuller Avenue CRC, the church I usually attended. I woke up early, about 4:30 AM, since I had to start work at 6:00 AM. I tossed and turned. Who will I say yes to? A&P bakery union rules or a biblical conviction that Sunday was a day of rest and worship? Do I or don't I? I needed the money for college; that's honorable and the goal is to serve the Lord, isn't it? Or is this a test from God? Do I trust Him so that I can lose that $1.75 an hour and still make it? Am I just being legalistic, and since many others work on Sundays, why shouldn't I? Back and forth it went through my head, so long, in fact, that by the time I decided I wasn't going to go, it was too late anyway. My starting time had passed. I went to church instead. The next day my card was gone and in my mail slot I found my final paycheck with a few extra dollars of vacation pay. It was hard to lose that job; the pay was good and I enjoyed the work. I did remind God several times that I gave up the job in deference to Him. I now felt He owed me one. I am not sure He shared my feeling! Though on the surface it was not a big deal, it *was* a test of faith. Would God indeed provide?

The only work I then had was an offer from Jan's parents to paint their home at $1.00 an hour. I think they felt sorry for me. I did it, but I don't like painting and am slow and not good at it. Their house had a number of large windows divided by little slats into lots of little window panes. Each one had to be painted carefully without smearing paint on the glass.

When I was nearly finished painting the house, I found a job in a brickyard and spent the rest of that summer working in Grand Rapids for a brick distributor. Rail cars containing eight layers of bricks from wall to wall would arrive in the yard of the supplier on Kalamazoo Avenue. Using tongs to grab 10 bricks at a time, we would put 800 of them on each pallet which was sitting in the open doorway of the rail car. With a lift tractor, we picked up each pallet and stacked them three high in the yard. As orders came in, we would take 4-6 pallets on a truck and, with the lift tractor on a trailer behind the truck, deliver them into various new housing developments in outlying areas of the city. That summer I made many trips to the Grandville - Jenison area. But more loads went to the new Calvin College campus now rapidly developing on Knollcrest farms. I think I have fingerprints on a lot of the bricks of the first dormitories and the seminary. I became quite adept at wheeling that truck and trailer throughout the city and surrounding areas and could back the trailer into the tightest spots. I had lots of practice backing up trailers when on the dairy farm I backed a manure spreader into tight corners so as not to have to fork and carry the stuff any further than absolutely necessary. The trucking improved my city driving skills so that by the end of the summer I could get a bus-driving license. The following school year, Immanuel Lutheran School on Michigan Street offered me a school bus driving job paying three dollars for a two-hour trip. That in turn helped me get a job driving busses for Calvin taking sports teams on some of their road trips and other activities all at a dollar an hour!

Union Membership?

Work at the brick supplier left a bittersweet taste in my mouth. The owner was an outspoken Christian Reformed elder who would boast how wonderful it was to have a free enterprise business run without union interference. I was paid $1.50 an hour and due to the number of orders was often asked to work late at nights, most Saturday mornings, and even some Saturday afternoons. Even though my average week came to 60 hours, I never received one cent of overtime. In fact, when we had a national holiday, like July 4th, and we had the day off, I got nothing. I felt he took advantage of me at every turn, and I mentioned it to him but nothing changed. I was powerless. I learned how unions got their starts, and I experienced the very feelings that have enabled unions to thrive and become powerful. Had a union approached me and invited me to sign up, I probably would have done so out of spite, even though, like many other CRC people, I was generally opposed to the power and spirit of "secular unions" as we often spoke of them.

Since that experience, I have been slow to criticize our church members who belong to secular unions. As pastor of Zion CRC in Oshawa, Ontario I served many workers who were members of the powerful United Auto Workers union, (UAW). I walked in their shoes and it changed my outlook! I especially detest the hypocrisy of Christians who use pious talk to cover up their cheapness or to take advantage of employees. My experience helped me to become a thoroughgoing Calvinist with a world and life view of Christianity that also shapes marketplace work and relationships. I learned from English Anglican Pastor David Watson that a Christianity that doesn't start with the heart doesn't start, but a Christianity that stops with the heart stops. Our faith must permeate everything we think, say and do, individually and corporately.

Seminary Education

In the fall of 1962 I started seminary classes. I enjoyed the fellowship of the students and endured the classes. I had to take another language course, this time it was Hebrew. I could not view Hebrew as a language that would really help me gain a richer insight into the scriptures. It seemed like it was another obstacle course to test my self-discipline. We worked our way through the book of Jonah so that I could read it and explain every verb and textual nuance and I memorized it to pass the exam. I was glad we did the four-chapter book of Jonah rather than the book of Jeremiah. I concluded that my Hebrew scholarship would not likely provide any bright, fresh insights not already covered in good commentaries. My guess is that would be rare indeed. I was right. I did enjoy Old Testament studies and learned more intensely the contents of the Bible. I really was not well acquainted with that part of the bible.

Summer Ministry Experience, Grande Prairie, Alberta

Not much stands out from that first year of seminary. I studied, dated Jan, and had to be at Pleasant Street Convalescent Home for my nightly (elderly) ladies "baby-sitting" job every evening at 11:00 PM. About mid-April I was informed that my 10 weeks of summer pastoral and preaching assignment would be in Grande Prairie, Alberta some 300 miles (500 km) northwest of Edmonton. Part of my task would be to lead a team of 10 young people from the Zeeland, Michigan area who would come to serve for three weeks in a Summer Workshop In Missions (SWIM) program. Together we would help a small church in this northern Alberta oil town do community outreach and evangelism. The city of about 7000 had a small church with only a few people, most of them also involved one way or another in the oil industry. It was the summer that I remember best for the millions of mosquitoes; they were big, bit you wherever you were exposed as well as through shirts and socks. You dared not wear shorts or leave your arms uncovered. It was often impossible to be outside in the evening, especially if

43

thunderstorms were threatening. They were hungry and their bites stung and itched for quite some time.

I spent the other seven weeks serving as assistant to Pastor Dick Bouma, a man who had served with passionate missionary zeal in the Philippines. With that same passion he had come to Grande Prairie. We worked with two small CRCs, one in the city of Grande Prairie; a second one some 30 miles (50 km) northwest in an expansive rural area in the little village of La Glace, a village so small it can't be found on most Alberta maps. In the village was a little church, formerly a one-room school, attended by a small group of Dutch immigrant farmers, most of whom had come in the early nineteen hundreds rather than with the large contingent of post-World War II immigrants. They were old-time homesteaders with huge land holdings, many of whom grew alfalfa seed. They were financially well-off but you would never know it by looking at or listening to them. Once in a while one caught a glimpse of it, like when I visited one on a weekday afternoon and he showed me around on his farm. One stop was in a shed where he showed me a brand new (5 ton) truck loaded with alfalfa seed. As he pointed out the load, I asked, "Where is this going?" I was surprised to hear him say "Edmonton." I said, "That's about 320 miles from here." He replied, "I know, that's why I bought a new truck. When the price is right, I'll get up early and take it." When I asked him when that might be, he responded with, "Anytime now, yesterday this load was worth about $6000, when it hits $7000, I'll be on the road with it." (Note: the price for a new car at that time was around $2500).

As pastors we led two services per Sunday at each location, morning and evening in Grande Prairie, and morning and afternoon in La Glace. I regularly preached three times on a Sunday, especially when Pastor Dick Bouma was on vacation. During the week I worked with the SWIM team, the three weeks they were there, doing training, community calling, and I taught the older group of students in daily Vacation Bible School. In between tasks I was trying to write one or two sermons for the Sundays. It was a very busy summer, but I enjoyed every part of it, so much so that it energized me to return to seminary and tackle two more years of classes. The summer truly confirmed for me that ministry was indeed my calling. I had not misread the Lord nor made the wrong turn the morning I told my dad I was going to Calvin.

Life-Shaping Events

One life-shaping event still stands out in my mind from the 1963 summer field experience. The church provided a small apartment for me which was my office but also the place where I slept and cooked some of my meals but I was also regularly invited to have supper with a couple, Joe and Connie, (not their names). Since they had no children and loved the same activities I did, when we had an open evening we often spent it together. We'd go to a ballgame, an auction sale, or visit another church family. At the end of some of those evenings, I would be invited to their home for coffee and a "snack" (a bacon and eggs breakfast at midnight!). Nearing the end of my summer assignment, we were again enjoying what would be one of our last late-night sessions. Well after midnight, with an artery-clogging plate of food in front of me, I looked at Connie and stated what by then had become perfectly obvious to me: "You two would make marvelous parents." They in fact had been that to me.

Connie looked at Joe who had stopped eating. An awkward silence suddenly surrounded us. I felt, "whoops, I blew it" and instantly wished I could take back what I had said. But it was out, a completely spontaneous comment intended as a compliment, but one which had had the opposite effect. Tears began to roll down Connie's usually jovial face. They shared the pain of their hearts. In their 16 years of marriage, Connie had never been pregnant. Some medical consulting had been done, but for the last five years they had given up all thoughts of children and parenting. Resignedly, they assumed that, "It is God's will that we not have children." I asked, "Have you ever prayed to God about this?" Another rather stupid question! (I do that often when I start messing up!) Of course they had, but during recent years that too had stopped. They had chosen not to talk about this matter anymore with anyone, not even with God. Too painful, I think.

I suggested we pray and, like most church members when a pastor suggests that they pray, they compliantly did. I think we joined hands, prayed together briefly, finished our snack, and I went back to my apartment. A few days later I left that community to return to Grand Rapids, to marriage and to seminary.

The following May, just before leaving seminary for the summer, I received a phone call from Joe telling me that they had been blessed with the birth of a son! I had previously heard that they were expecting a child. However, I was stunned when the news came that the baby was born and was perfectly well! For the skeptic, it was a remarkable coincidence. For Joe, Connie, and me? When Joe called, he stated it well: "God answered our prayer. It is a miracle!"

That event in the beginning of my ministry experience impacted my theological reflection and subsequent ministry. My childhood and my faith journey, combined with my ministry experience, shook some of the foundational assumptions that I thought were biblically valid. I, like many others in the church, accepted the belief that miracles ceased once the Canon of Scripture was adopted and closed. That door was now opened, at least a little crack. Little did I know that the crack would be widened through more experiences.

Wedding Plans

While I spent the summer of 1963 away from Grand Rapids, Jan with the help of her parents was busy making wedding plans. At the end of the summer, I accompanied two car loads of young people back from northern Alberta to Michigan. During the summer Jan again had her job with Consumer's Power and both of us saved hard for the coming school year. After being back about a week, Jan and I were married by Professor John Stek on a warm, humid evening, August 29, at Calvin Seminary Chapel overlooking the Knollcrest pond. It was a very nice wedding, but we did not make it a big deal. A short honeymoon in northern Michigan ushered us into year two of Calvin Seminary. We were both students since Jan still had one semester to complete at Calvin College. It was different to return to school as a married couple but both of us adjusted quickly. We worked hard at our studies. Jan, a diligent student, was a good model to me.

Surely the big event that created a profoundly subdued spirit over the entire campus for a few days that November was the assassination of and the funeral for President John Fitzgerald Kennedy.

Another life-shaping event was happening to us as newlyweds. We were busy since both of us were taking full loads of classes. We had two tuitions although Jan's parents had agreed to cover tuition costs for her to complete Calvin. I was on my own with some aid from Classis trying hard to make ends meet without going into debt. I was raised by debt-hating parents and taught to avoid it if at all possible. To reduce the outflow I again found a part-time job. This time I taught four classes of Church school (Catechism) at Plymouth Heights Church. For each class I was paid $5 for a total of $20 per week or about $80 per month. Our rent was $60 per month plus utilities. Obviously, our cash flow was not impressive. Determined to make do, we found a bakery which sold *day-old* white bread for 10 cents a loaf. But on Tuesdays another bakery sold *fresh* bread for 22 cents a loaf. We would splurge once a week and buy one of those. We were amazingly happy and felt blessed with God's provision for our daily needs. We did not at all feel poor. Praying each day, "Give us this day our daily bread," took on a rich meaning! We were happily married and enjoying life. Both of us were surprised as to how easy and comfortable we were together!

Only one issue arose occasionally that we had not resolved. Of the $80 I earned each month for teaching, Jan deemed we ought to tithe (set aside 10% for the Lord's work). I being the "big picture Christian" deemed that everything we had was being thrown into preparing to serve God. Frankly, I saw no better kingdom cause than putting us through school! We needed books, tuition, travel costs etc, *all* so that we could better serve God. Jan had been taught that when you earned a dollar, "ten cents was for Jesus." It was a basic simple formula, ten cents on the dollar. My approach was not to get legalistic! I believed in being a "generous cheerful giver." Since then I have learned that for many (me included at that time) being a generous cheerful giver is often a lot cheaper than being a tither! Though we discussed this several times in the early months of our marriage, we did not come to an agreement. It was no big deal but big enough that it bothered us.

As the middle of November arrived, Jan began to apply for teaching jobs starting at the end of the first semester, mid-January, when she would finish college. She applied at all the area Christian schools, both of us hoping that perhaps some young woman teacher might be pregnant and require a maternity leave. Not so, nothing. She explored Grand Rapids Catholic Schools for possible openings; nothing. Finally, she applied at the public school offices but again nothing. Instead, she received word that there was currently an oversupply of teachers and they would likely not have any openings in January. By now it was late November. In early December I received another paycheck of $80, and Jan gently again suggested we should tithe. "Get off your legalistic tithing; you keep bringing that up," I responded. (I was getting my first lesson in learning how persistent she can be.) We were now three months behind on the tithe for which my quick mathematical mind needed no calculator (we didn't have those then!) It meant 10% of $240 which would be $24 (not rounded to 25!). I concluded it was less costly to write a $24 check than to argue about it. So I did. On the first Sunday morning of December I put the check in an envelope and dropped (dumped?) it in the offering at Grandville Avenue Christian Reformed Church, where we were attending and where Jan occasionally played the organ for their worship services. Now, there! If giving can be cold and legalistic, this certainly qualified. I met both those qualities in spades!

When I came home from seminary classes about 4:00 PM the next Tuesday afternoon, just two days later, Jan met me at the door with a huge smile (more like a smirk). "I got a job today. Oakdale Christian School called and needs a teacher starting mid-January." That Christian school was her *first* choice; it was only a few blocks from where we were living. She did not say, "I told you so," but then she didn't have to. She said it without saying it. I have not forgotten that experience. In fact, since then similar coincidences have occurred several times. Suddenly, with a teacher's annual salary of about $3,000 we felt flush!

Summer Assignment 2, Tacoma, Washington

The rest of my middler year of seminary moved along rather uneventfully. The following summer (1964), we were invited to lead another Summer Workshop in Missions team, this time in the far western beautiful state of

48

Washington. CRC Home Missions had started an evangelistic, outreaching church in Tacoma, Washington with the Rev. Rits and his wife Pearl Tadema (plus eight kids!) as missionary pastor. Today it would be called a "church plant." About eight young people came from Montana to help with summer mission and Bible School activities. It was a good summer for both Jan and me as we spent a lot of time with the Tadema family and observed how one pastor's family functioned in a church setting. They were models to their kids and to us as they served unstintingly. They were generous, even though the 10 of them lived on one pastor's salary. We learned that generosity begets generosity. I think it's the way the Lord out gives us. We noticed as they were generous with others, others in turn were generous with them. They received a regular stream of food, milk, clothes and various other gifts, mostly practical stuff. They showed compassion and love to all and expected the children as well as Jan and me to do the same. It was their way of life and they were a happy family!

We learned from the Tadema family that to honor the Lord is to give oneself in His service, and as one does so unceasingly and unconditionally, the byproducts of peace, joy, and appreciation will come one's way. We saw the power and importance of modeling godliness as leaders. Our tithing experience and our summer in Tacoma with the Tadema family taught us much about living for others and how God blesses and provides amply when that is done. At the end of the summer, having learned some very important, basic lessons we went back to Grand Rapids ready for our final year at Calvin Seminary.

Back in Grand Rapids

It was a bit of a letdown to become preoccupied with classroom learning again after an exciting summer. I enjoyed ministry with its busy ups and downs, and I soon missed it. I knew I had a year to go and was determined to grit my way through it. I immersed myself into classwork and enjoyed the classmate camaraderie again, and as Jan became invested in her junior high students, we resettled into the routine and the year went well.

The year ended with my graduation from seminary followed by Synod's declaration in June that I was a candidate for ministry in the Christian Reformed Church and available for a call. Calls could not be extended until

July 10 so that "outlying" churches would have an equal opportunity to check out and contact candidates as well as the more local Michigan and Ontario congregations. It felt to me like it was hunting season for churches to bag themselves a new pastor. We received five calls in about two weeks from churches in North Dakota, Wisconsin, Alberta, Washington, and from a startup home mission ministry in Webster, New York (near Rochester). It was a diverse choice of challenges. Without visiting any of them but with written correspondence and a few phone calls, after two to three weeks of reflection, listening and praying to God, and talking with others, we felt perfectly at peace about accepting the call from the CRC in Sunnyside, Washington. From August 1 to the end of October, we had to wait to complete the immigration process so that I as a Canadian citizen could become a U.S. resident. The fact that I was married to Jan, an American citizen, expedited the process but not without Jan's mom's connection to Grand Rapids U.S. Congressman Gerald Ford, later President Ford, who helped move the immigration along.

During that last hot and humid Grand Rapids summer, Jan worked at her previous summer's job doing clerical work for Consumers Power and I was offered a position as a student pastor-chaplain at a Christian hospital for the mentally ill called Pine Rest. It was a good experience and one of the rare times when both of us were working and bringing home two paychecks! By the end of the summer together we had saved enough to buy a new (1965!) beautiful green Chevrolet Impala four-door hardtop for $2,781! It was sleek; we were on top of the world.

On to Sunnyside, Washington

By late September 1965, I received my immigration paper and we packed up our belongings in a moving van and sent them to Sunnyside. We left the next day to drive to Alberta to spend a few days with my family. From there we traveled into British Columbia, south into Idaho, west to Spokane, and southwest towards the Tri-Cities of Pasco, Richland, and Kennewick. It was still warm and dry when we left Spokane and headed toward the dry interior of the state of Washington. When we knew we were only 50 miles (80 kilometers) from Sunnyside and all we saw was desert with sagebrush, we wondered what we had said yes to. The desert continued, 40 miles to go, more desert, 35, still desert, 25, sagebrush, sand, a sparse tree here and there. With 20 miles to go and no change, we were becoming more than a bit anxious! When we were about 15 miles from Sunnyside, we came down a hill and saw below us the Columbia River with lush green farms on each side of it. We learned later that farmers diverted water from the river that snaked like a lifeline through the valley.

We were now entering the Yakima Valley, one of the "fruit bowls" of America. By the time we arrived in Sunnyside, all was lush and green, but only where irrigation provided water. Were it not for irrigation, Sunnyside would have been part of the desert. Where there was no water, there was no vegetation -only sand and sagebrush. We were reminded many times in our years there that "the desert shall bloom like a rose" (Isaiah 35:1).

When we arrived in Sunnyside, we found the church and parsonage and were warmly welcomed. Many in the congregation were genuinely happy to have a pastor on the scene again after what they felt was a long pastoral vacancy. Actually, it was only about a year and a half, but somehow the congregation's members felt that the community simply was not complete without a pastor in the parsonage. They wanted someone there especially for times of tragedy, crises or death. Light and life in the parsonage gave them a sense of contentment, security and completeness. It was much more to them than just having someone on the scene. We were seen as a special gift from God. We had to learn to see that and understand it. When we did they became more precious to us as we did to them. We could then sense and appreciate the tone of endearment and ownership when possessively they spoke of us as "our pastor." Ours was a unique privilege when they handed us all the privileges and rights that allowed us to see more and more of their usually well-hidden wrinkles, pains and fears. It was an honor to lead and help them come closer to Him and stronger in His world. It is much more than a job, it really *is* a calling. We were royally welcomed and received.

Chapter 5

Sunnyside, Washington

1965 - 1971

Before we could really start the ministry part of our journey another hurdle had to be crossed. I had to appear before the pastors and elders of Classis for the dreaded Classical exam. Since a number of pastors and elders were suspicious about the orthodoxy of the seminary, the Classical exam was often used to make sure that new pastors were true blue conservative. Where there were any doubts about the student's stance, some Classes did not hesitate to fail the student and in so doing send a loud message to the seminary faculty. We were warned that the exam was not the place to explore remote theological theories or risky, divisive issues. We were told to take the safe, high road and with open-ended questions travel well to the right of the centre yellow line. The exam was the next step.

For us the Classis was Pacific Northwest which included about 18 Washington CRCs, another five in Oregon, four in Montana, and one in Idaho. Each church delegated its pastor and one elder to attend the 1-2 day Classis meeting held twice yearly. The fall meeting was scheduled to be held the 16th of October (1965) in Lynden, Washington, in the very northwest corner of the state.

The Classical Check for Orthodoxy

The examination began about 9:00 AM. Before the meeting started, we were informed that word had come from Chicago that our well-known and loved Back to God Hour radio preacher, Dr. Peter Eldersveld, had experienced a sudden heart attack and died overnight. He was deeply respected by all who heard his radio messages, those who were members of our Christian Reformed Churches but also by many in our communities. When I knew he would be on the radio I tried hard to find a station that carried the broadcast so that I could listen to him. I did the same with Billy Graham. Each of them had something to say that I wanted to hear. The chairman of Classis informed the two of us who were being examined that if all went well that day, our challenge would be to fill the shoes of Peter Eldersveld. I vowed to give it my best shot. I don't think either of us succeeded, although I have thought about Peter Eldersveld many times and have repeatedly challenged myself to keep my preaching basic and simple, two hallmarks of his preaching. It was commonly stated that his sermons used a 500-word vocabulary; they were geared so as to be understood by ten year old children. He felt if they could understand the sermons, so could most others. "Put the feed where the lambs can readily get at it and older sheep will be well fed."

For this meeting there were two of us candidates to be examined. The other candidate was a student named Harold DeJong who had accepted a call to be the minister of the Conrad, Montana congregation. I did not know him well, since he was a member of the previous year's class. He was nervous, as was I. I just hid it better. Questions were alternately presented to each of us. As the exam progressed -and it was a long one- I capitalized on his nervousness. I simply didn't know as much as he did, especially about people like Karl Barth, Nietsche, and some of the philosophers. I knew more about Calvin and Luther because I had written papers on them. Harold gave extensive responses which often led to follow-up questions. My responses were shorter, and if I stopped, the questioner would go to Harold with the next question. By 5:00 PM in the afternoon we should have been done, instead the non-delegates and I were excused, but Harold was invited to stay for more questions. I thought his responses were good but somehow they aroused further questions from other pastors concerning his orthodoxy. Some seminary professors were suspect because they were thought to support Karl Barth's position that the Bible *contained* the Word of God rather than the more traditional Reformed position that stated the Bible *is* the Word of God. We were carefully checked out as to our positions.

Shortly after supper, the delegates in "closed executive session" discussed and voted on our lots. We both passed, and after about eight hours of examination the final hurdle was crossed. We were ready for ordination. All the obstacles to get from high school to ministry were completed. I know everyone called this the process of education, but for me it seemed more like a marathon obstacle course.

I was ordained in the Sunnyside congregation on Friday evening, October 15, 1965. Sunday, October the 17th, was the first time I preached to the congregation, and I did so as their pastor. I had to lead a morning and an afternoon service since every CRC at that time had two virtually identical services every Sunday. I preached on Psalm 2 in the afternoon, and the next week an elder came to me to question me on my exegesis! These elders were diligent and were not about to allow a young preacher to think that they were not going be listening and watching carefully. They let me know early that they were on the job.

Ministry Starts

As I began ministry with the Sunnyside congregation, I found the toughest routine was preparing and preaching two sermons every Sunday. The morning service began at 10:00 AM, finishing at about 11:30, and then I had to do it all over again with another message at an afternoon service held at 2:30 PM in the winter months and at 7:30 PM during the summer. I received no help planning or setting up any of the liturgies for any of the services. The orders for services were exactly the same with about four hymns (from the blue *Psalter Hymnal*); the Ten Commandments in the AM services, which were replaced in the evening services with the Apostles' Creed, always read by the minister. I changed that on my second Sunday and instead had the congregation recite the creed together, as was done in many other churches but mostly out East, like Grand Rapids, where a lot of other "liberal ideas" originated. For this I was properly reprimanded at my first Council meeting by the senior elder who early in my stay let me know that he viewed himself as the watchdog to keep me on the "straight and narrow." If changes needed to be made, Council would make them. Whether they were major or minor, every issue and discussion had the same intensity and passion. Council members feared the slippery slope. And they had been warned about young preachers. I feared I had only a brief window of opportunity to make changes before the window would be closed and painted shut. I didn't want to lose their support by making changes too early, but I did not want to be put in a strait jacket either out of which it would be hard to extricate myself.

Jan and I decided we should become acquainted as quickly as possible with the 500 members of this congregation. Seminary training had taught that good pastoral care is a high priority for many churches. We did it in two ways. Firstly, we made brief visits to each family of the church in their homes, and secondly, the two of us taught most of the older youth (ages 9-18) in midweek church school classes. Jan taught the two younger classes, and I taught the rest. (Looking back, we were gluttons for work.) We did this for the first year, and though it was a killer for busyness, it, and the pastoral visits, really got us into the church.

This was much appreciated, since the previous pastor had been incapacitated for the last 3-5 years of his ministry due to struggles with cancer. He had managed to preach but had done little pastoral or educational work in the congregation and had had minimal contact with the youth for several years. He did his best to maintain the congregation but the church had learned to function socially with minimal involvement from him. This became apparent in the way the congregation first treated us. For the first six months, we virtually received no invitations to socialize with church members except for about three families. We did not know differently since we had no base of comparison. Because we were starting and had no children, we just poured ourselves into the work of the church which kept us busy and too tired to feel lonely. Once the congregation realized that we liked them -and enjoyed being with them- that all changed. Our diligence in serving helped them to see us as people who could be trusted. We soon felt accepted and loved. I learned then that people were more impressed with how much we cared and loved them than how smart we were. I learned that before a new pastor is trusted to lead he has to spend 2-3 years showing that he cares and is willing to serve. Without that trust, leadership is reluctantly accepted, if at all.

A Seven Pound Girl; a Three Months Pregnancy!

In a special way the congregation showed their love and support six months later. As a couple we felt ready to share our home with a child. We had experienced two early miscarriages, and that, along with the social awareness that there were many children in the world who had neither parents nor homes, opened us to other possibilities. Within three months of our arrival in Sunnyside, we heard a radio commercial that the State of

55

Washington had over 1,000 babies who needed parents and homes: "If you are interested, even in considering possible adoption or foster care, please, please contact Washington Children's Aid." This was before abortions were legal and when only minimal financial help was available for single parents. When we learned that Washington State had a Child Welfare office in Yakima, 30 miles west of Sunnyside, we decided the next time we were in Yakima we would visit it to learn what would be required to adopt a child. We found the office and were welcomed with open arms. Before we left, we were given application forms which we filled out and returned as a bit of a test project to see if we would qualify. We had only been married a little more than two years. If this was God's will for us, fine. If we were turned down, fine also. We were open but not invested. Since it was mid-December I remember Yakima streets cheerfully decorated with Christmas lights. We were about to have our first Christmas in Sunnyside.

Three months later, about the middle of March 1966, we received word that a baby girl had been born in Seattle, and we were invited to drive there (nearly 180 miles) to meet her. Since Jan was an only child who had never had any contact with little ones, no babysitting experience either, she felt she would be more comfortable with a girl. It is a rare occasion in life when one gets to choose! To me it didn't matter. We went to Seattle and met the baby who would become our first child, our daughter Judith Kay. It was that simple and that quick. It was good and it seemed oh so right! This has been confirmed over and over again for more than 45 years. Before long we were on the way home with her. We fed, held, and changed her and she slept contentedly in an unattached car bed (totally unsafe, but common then) in the back seat of the car for most of the three-hour ride home.

We returned from Seattle to Sunnyside on Thursday in time for me to attend a Council meeting that night. Early in the meeting, I announced that we had adopted a baby girl, a total surprise to all 16 members of Council. Their unanimous response was a stunned silence; not a word. Later I learned that they did not know how to react. Should they feel happy because we adopted a child or sad because of the possible struggle and pain that likely accompanied infertility? The mixed emotions led them to say nothing. Was adoption a choice or a lesser but acceptable substitute? But the adoption of a child is no small matter and should be celebrated.

I didn't know what to make of their silence, so I didn't say anything more either. About an hour later an elder asked for the floor and timidly asked, "Mr. Chairman (I was the chairman), wouldn't congratulations be in order for your little girl?" When I answered "They sure are," they mobbed me and completely atoned for their previous awkwardness. I handed out cigars with "It's a girl" and chocolates to those who preferred them.

If the Council members were reserved and caught off guard on Thursday night, they and the rest of the congregation recovered well and quickly. The news went through the church like a prairie blaze. The following Monday evening, the congregation held a baby shower for Jan with some 90 women present in the fellowship hall. It more than made up for their initial reservations. We received everything we could possibly need for the next three years. It was an amazing outpouring of love which we later realized had been pent-up for a long time. Judy was the very first baby in the parsonage for the church's entire 33-year history.

Oh Yes, Two Sermons each Week

Though we acclimated quickly to the church, I felt overwhelmed by those *two* Sunday services! Members would often mention to me that they came to church to hear a good sermon. All that other stuff (liturgy, prayers, and offerings) was regarded as filler. The hard grind for every startup pastor was spending the better part of the work-week preparing those two sermons. And the Sundays came as relentlessly as the sun arose each morning. Many times I felt a 10-day week would be a much better deal for preachers. Many weeks I seemed to just live from Sunday to Sunday. It was not uncommon for me to prepare and preach a minimum of six -and occasionally as many as eight- new sermons a month. I felt like a preaching machine: turn the crank one more time and out comes another sermon. Occasionally, I had a pulpit exchange with a neighboring pastor which allowed me to use the same message twice. Wow, what a break that was!

It was in Sunnyside that I learned the discipline of diligent reading, studying, and planning three weeks ahead with my sermons. I felt I had no choice. I could not handle the pressure of getting up on a Monday morning -after a busy Sunday- and thinking that I'd have to do it all over again in six days without having a clue what I would preach about. I would do my overall planning and basic work three weeks before preaching the message. This accomplished two things: It reduced the pressure of uncertainty, but more importantly, after doing the basic work, it gave the message time to "cook." I have always enjoyed reading and watching documentaries and news stories on TV, and in doing so I would regularly come across something that was just what the message needed as an illustration or to make a point. Those three weeks were cooking and simmering times. Though I found it tough to come up with two sermons each week, I did learn good preparation and discipline, something that proved helpful also in subsequent years. Since I spent most years in larger churches, I had to learn to use my time well. There just was never enough of it. I tried hard not to place the church ahead of Jan and the children.

Another Three Months Pregnancy

When Judy was one year old, we began to talk about another child. About that time someone from an adoption agency stopped by to see how we were doing with Judy. Her adoption could now be legalized via the courts. When the worker asked if we would consider another girl as a possible sister for Judy, we indicated we were fine with that, and in fact mentioned that we had been talking about that very thing. Again, in only a few months and after only a few visits, on June 22 we received Barbara Joy, born in Yakima, Washington on June 1, 1967. The church again celebrated with us and gave us more stuff.

Now we were four people living in a rather cozy, three-bedroom parsonage. It was a small home, less than 1,000 square feet, with one of the bedrooms converted into an office for me and church members began to realize it was crowded. The home had no basement and no storage. To compensate for that, a large room on the third floor of the church, which was right behind the parsonage, was made available to us as a guest bedroom. For some members, it was hard to believe that anything needed to be done about our housing situation. The former pastor had assured the congregation that the house would serve adequately as a parsonage for many years, and it would have for them, an older family of two. However, it wasn't big enough for a growing family, now of four people, with the possibility of more additions. At that time pastors did not buy their own homes. Salaries were complemented with church-provided parsonages. There was now a contingent of people who were willing to do whatever it would take to keep us from thinking about moving elsewhere! They regularly brought up the need to address the parsonage situation. We never pushed it in any way. The discussion about a new parsonage appeared with regularity on Council agendas as different members expressed their concerns. A large, beautiful, new home was built in 1969 after a time of careful planning.

Looking back, I believe the first 3-4 years of ministry in Sunnyside were a learning time for us, especially for me. If it took Jesus 30 years to prepare for a three-year ministry, which was completed by the time he was 33 years old, I also deemed my time before the age of 30 to be mostly preparatory. It was more like finishing the seminary education *preparation* phase than it was actually *doing* ministry. I knew that the learning phase would be a lifelong process but it is especially big in the first ministry charge. Too late I learned that this is a crucial time for a pastor to have a mentor and coach. Even now in retirement, I see the great value in ongoing growing and learning. When Jan and I were married, our wedding text was Matthew 6:33, "Seek first the kingdom of God and everything else will be added unto you." We were learning that seeking is a full-time, lifelong assignment unfinished until He returns.

The Church's Schedule

Every church has her own unique and distinctive features which make up her character. Sunnyside did too. Looking back, a few things stand out. Our worship times and attendance was deeply shaped by the agricultural seasons.

Milking Cows

Though the church was in the city of Sunnyside, the makeup and flavor of the congregation was agricultural; we had a number of large dairy farms. Times for worship services were set by milking times. Now most of them milk three times per day, then it was twice, early morning and twelve hours later, mid-afternoon or early evening. Thus, the evening worship service was held at 7:30 PM most of the year –after the afternoon milking was done, but really much too late for families with younger school aged children and likewise, it was too late for the elderly. Others, especially the people in town hated the late evening times; they just didn't like coming home that late. Dairy farmers adamantly claimed they could not get to church any earlier. Actually, not many of them came to evening services even though the time was set primarily with them in mind. But generally the overall attendance was very good.

Asparagus

From the middle of April through the middle of June, some farmers did not attend the morning service due to asparagus cutting. Tons of asparagus were grown in the Yakima Valley at that time. In May and June with warm weather and plenty of irrigation water, it grew so fast that it needed to be cut daily. To let it go for an entire Sunday -as some farmers did- meant that on Monday much of the tall stuff had to be cut and thrown away. Most workers were Mexican migrant families who were paid by the amount of asparagus in their boxes. The time spent cutting down the tall growth on Monday put no asparagus in their boxes and no money in their pockets! So, they often preferred to work for someone other than a "Sunday keeper." Our practice of not working on Sunday when imposed upon others was experienced as legalistic cheapness. Intended as a Christian witness, it had the exact opposite effect. Most of the migrant workers wanted and needed to work seven days a week in order to make as much money as possible. It took hard work from the entire Mexican families to make a livable income. Generosity in wages for migrant workers was not great; I am not sure it was different within the Christian community. It became almost impossible to get cutters who would *not* cut asparagus on Sundays. It was only a matter of time before cutting asparagus became a seven-day-a-week operation. At church we could readily tell when cutting season started by the reduced attendance in the morning worship services, especially when many older children also helped parents cut asparagus. During the season, junior and senior high schools in Sunnyside started an hour later to accommodate the farm kids who cut asparagus often starting at 5:00 AM.

Hops

Another major crop grown in the Valley was hops used for malt in the beer industry. Huge trellises criss-crossed large fields with strings or wires running from top to bottom. Hops would grow on those, and when the pods were ready, about August, they needed to be harvested, dried in huge ovens, baled, and shipped. Once the harvesting operation started, it would be a 24/7 operation for 4-6 weeks. That harvest also affected our worship attendance.

Orchards and Grapes

The Wenatchee area was known as the "Apple Bowl of America." Sunnyside and Yakima, being just south but with the same climate also had huge orchards. Truckload after load rolled through the countryside taking cherries in June and early July with apricots following when the cherries were done. When they were picked and shipped, pears and peaches appeared and when it was cooler in August and September it would be apple picking time. The beautiful fruit grown in that Valley is an amazing thing to see. During the fall season one often smelled fresh fruit throughout the countryside.

Already when we were there many farmers had small 5-15 acre plots of grapes which were harvested about the same time, if not right after the apples. Many of them went into juice, others were for wine. Over the years many wineries have appeared so that wine is now one of the major economic products of the area.

Pastoral Work

I recall making many visits to church members, sometimes with an elder but most of the time on my own. I made regular rounds to visit those who were limited to their homes or even to their beds. The church had a number of elderly members, and they appreciated whenever I could stop by. Many of these were routine visits, important but not life-changing. No matter how many visits I made or how long I stayed, I could never come too often or stay too long. The visits helped me to get a good read on what was going on in people's lives. Especially with some of the elderly, one stop would inform me as to what winds were blowing with a whole group of them.

One regular visit still stands out rather vividly. Sophie was about a 45-year-old mother of six children. Her husband, Jesse, was totally deaf but had learned to read lips. Each week I would write an outline of the AM message to give it to him on his way into church on Sunday morning. He would come to church, sit in the back -and it was a long building- and with my outline in his hands follow the sermon. I would beg him to come forward since he could read lips so he would "hear" more, but he refused. He had sat in that pew since the church was built and he was staying there (a stubborn Friesian, if there ever was one). Sophie had abdominal cancer and was deteriorating rapidly, so much so that once a week she needed to go into the local hospital where a needle was inserted into her abdominal cavity to drain out about two gallons of fluid that had accumulated. As the fluid increased, her body was gradually reducing to skin and bones. We both knew she would soon die and we talked openly about that. She wanted to live, but she was obviously losing this battle. She asked me a lot of basic questions for which I had few, if any, answers. "Will I be able to see my husband and kids from heaven, or will I simply be asleep until the trumpet sounds? Will I know what is said at the funeral and how my kids handle my being gone? When I see God, what do you think I'll see? And what will He say to me?"

A Simple Request to God

One sunny Saturday afternoon I stopped at her house and she said, "It's getting close and I am ready to go, but I would like to stay for my children's sake. I really would like to help Jesse raise them."

At that time I think only one or two of the children had publicly made a commitment to Christ. The others were all between the ages of 10 and 18. She felt some of the older ones were perhaps not the best examples for the younger ones at that time.

She continued, "They need me and I want to help them, especially spiritually. And since my husband can't hear, it is hard for him to communicate heart to heart with them, even though he tries. My children need *me*!"

I could only agree. Before really thinking, I responded, "How long do you want?"

With no hesitation, she said, "About five years."

Again rather easily I said, "You know, I have no problem with that. We need to go to God and make a strong case for extending your life for five years. We should ask, and believe and expect Him to say yes. "

So we prayed, briefly but fervently, that God -as with Hezekiah- would extend Sophie's life. Like a lawyer pleading for mercy before a judge, I presented the best possible case for this, and in prayer we tried to convince God that He really should answer this prayer for His sake and for the kids' sake. It was not a selfish request; it was a God-glorifying one, one asked solely to bless others. We asked for five years. I felt God would grant our request. I may have even said so to her at that moment.

Sophie's deterioration continued for several weeks, and her visits to the hospital to drain fluids increased with less time in between. She lost more weight, something she could not afford. It was awful to watch her as she became even more skeletal. We were all aware that her time was short. To each other, Sophie and I stated, "It could be any day now." We spoke openly about the fact that apparently God was not going to answer our prayer for more time. We were both puzzled and wondered why God did not grant the request. It seemed to both of us to make perfect sense to give her the five years.

Suddenly and unexpectedly, the fluid buildup slowed down and after a few days stopped. Sophie began to feel better and stronger and she began to gain weight. Over a few weeks the fluid buildup stopped completely and the drain tube was removed. She began attending church services again, much to the surprise of all of us. We were amazed and expressed deep gratitude to God. This continued for three or four years. I don't believe it was quite the five we prayed for, but it was a significant span. During that time several of her children made public commitments to Christ.

But then, just as quickly as she became well, she became ill again. When I visited her, she told me that the doctor had told her the cancer was active and the fluid was building up again. I asked her if we should pray again and request another extension. Without thinking three seconds, her answer was, "No! God has answered my prayer. I now need to get ready and go home." It was a matter-of-fact response which closed the door to any further discussion. From that day on, she spoke openly and cheerfully about "packing my suitcase to get ready to go home." All my visits with her were future-oriented even though she was in much pain and discomfort.

A Funeral Celebration

In one discussion, she wanted to arrange her own funeral. I thought it was a good idea, but as a rookie preacher I found it a bit morbid, but not Sophie. To her it was as basic as planning her next birthday party. She wanted it to be "a celebration, none of this sad stuff!" She had bought and worn a bright red dress for the wedding of one of her children, and that was to be her funeral dress. Styles at that time were moving towards loud colors, also for men, especially in shirts and ties! I had been involved in the wedding of one of my younger brothers shortly before that time, in which all four of us brothers had worn identical darker green suits with salmon-colored shirts and matching ties. Loud and wild! After the wedding I had worn that suit to some church event -a banquet, I think- where Sophie had seen me. I had never worn it for a service, I thought it was too much. You guessed it -I had to promise her that I would wear *that* suit and *that* shirt for her funeral service while she was "planning" to wear her red dress. Her image was more like we were planning for a dance than a funeral. It had to be a celebration of thanksgiving. Not long after that, Sophie died and though it was very sad, especially for her family, her funeral was a celebration of her life and faith. And yes, she was "there" in her red dress, and I was there in the green suit and salmon shirt. There was joy and laughter because of the stories, but there were also many tears; we were painfully aware that we'd miss her smile, testimony, and mischievous character stunts. For her family it was a difficult time. The service was truly God honoring. Many remembered and spoke about it for a long time.

Mission Hearts and Passion

Overall, the members of the Sunnyside Church were faithful, loyal, conservative, and generous in their support of the church and the local Christian school. They had hearts for missions but more for distant strangers than next door neighbors. Members were reluctant to invite their neighbors to church even though I often mentioned the importance of the harvest. I thought that would really connect with farmers. If it did, it did not show up in Sunday's services. About this time, the Zillah CRC, our mother church 12 miles west of us, had become involved with planting a new congregation in the city of Yakima some 20 miles to the west of them. We too had a growing desire to do more for the harvest in our mission outreach! I sensed an eagerness to be more involved locally. Our members were blessed and willing to share these blessings.

Other congregations had met similar challenges by initiating something called a Faith-Promise Program. The members would be challenged to step out in *faith* and make a *promise* that with God's help they would fulfill. They would be accountable only to Him. Only He would know each person's commitment. The funds were separate from the church's annual budget and were strictly voluntary contributions to the mission vision and work of the church. It was a low-key invitation but it received a response of an annual commitment of some $36,000, a huge sum for that time to be used for world and home mission work. It was indicative of their thankful generosity. It indicated that the church was ready for a more direct involvement with a specific mission ministry.

Missions, Hands on

Direct involvement with our own neighbors developed more slowly. If someone in our community had a physical need, we readily provided whatever assistance or financial help was needed. But when it came to socializing most of our members spent their time with their own families and friends from the church.

We had made a few efforts to reach Sunnyside residents with the gospel. With other church communities in the Valley, we shared a Campus Crusade training week. Campus Crusade people were bold and valiant crusaders who confronted as many Americans as possible with "The Four Spiritual Laws." The presentation consisted of leading someone through a small booklet which began with the question: "Do you know that God has a wonderful plan for your life?" The booklet then led one through a concise presentation of the gospel showing how God had bridged the gap between Him and us through the life and death of Jesus Christ. In about 20 short pages, the learner was invited to accept Jesus Christ as Savior. As shy, reserved, and cautious CRCers, about 25 of us along with a number of Christians from other churches took the training and spent part of a

Saturday and some midweek evenings doing a home-to-home blitz in Sunnyside with the gospel. Through this experience a number of our members were helped to verbalize the gospel and assist others to become Christians. And some did. Few however came to the CRC; none became part of the congregation.

Now, 40 years later, much has changed. The CRC in Sunnyside continues its extensive ministry involvement financially, but the church also directly serves the large Mexican immigrant community. An Hispanic congregation with its own pastor utilizes the CRC facilities. During the sixties, cultural and national boundaries were starkly drawn but rarely talked about. We had "our" churches and the Mexicans had theirs with their own language, worship places, and styles. If I mentioned the idea of working with them or ministering to them, the common response -which pretty well shut down further discussion- went something like this: "Most of them are Catholics, and they have their own churches and they wouldn't be interested in our church." I believe that has changed considerably.

Missions, Church Plants

Beyond providing financial support for missions in another part of the world, what could we do in our local region? Our elders began to talk about planting a new congregation that would include hands-on involvement. I was enthusiastic about it and encouraged the vision that Sunnyside could develop a mission outreach in the Tri-Cities area of Pasco, Kennewick, and Richland, 50 miles to the east of us, which in due time would become a full-fledged, new congregation. The Tri-cities had a total population of about 95,000 people (now about 135,000) and all three cities shared access to the large Columbia River, the life stream of Central Washington.

I had no idea that a mission focus commitment would result in me learning things that would change my ministry and impact my future life. I had no idea I was about to go through "a baptism by fire" which would be a foretaste of more severe trials and tests. My faith would be tried and my desire to obey God would be challenged and tested. I would be faced with the question: "Do I really believe the Bible and say yes to it, or do I believe it only when it lines up with what I always thought it said? When it counts,

66

am I first biblical or traditional?" Or, even more challenging, "Am I first typically Christian Reformed or am I Biblical in my thinking? Aren't they the same?" Basic stuff; I did not realize that those issues existed, needed testing, and had to be faced!

We were aware that there were four families with some Christian Reformed background in the Tri-Cities area somewhat interested in the CRC but not enough so as to drive the 50 miles to Sunnyside regularly to worship with us.

A New Church

Four families was not a group strong or big enough to form a nucleus for a church plant. To make it viable it would need significant support from elsewhere. We in Sunnyside were ready to pour our hearts and funds into such a venture, but we also knew we needed the expertise of our denominational Home Missions Board. To keep the ministry locally "owned," we decided that the Sunnyside Council would take primary responsibility for funding the ministry and finding a missionary-pastor. For the facilities, we would need help from the denomination through our Home Mission Board. At that time the common approach in starting a new church called for a nucleus of at least eight CRC families. They, along with the pastor, would be expected to be committed to the new venture. They would work hard, give generously, and nurture this young, tender plant into a mature congregation.

Our Sunnyside church did two things:

First: We placed an advertisement in _The Banner,_ the denominational weekly magazine of the Christian Reformed Church, with information about a new Reformed church starting in the middle of Washington State that needed some adventuresome families who were sensing a calling to help plant a mission church and were willing to relocate their families. It was an unabashed mission call. The Tri-Cities was a good place for a new start. Employment and housing opportunities were excellent in the area. The climate rather hot and dry and desert-like with minimal rainfall, especially from June through September, was mild the rest of the year. Eight highly motivated families responded, all but one from the Grand Rapids, Michigan area. They quit their jobs, sold their homes, packed their belongings into rental trucks, and made the 2,400-mile trek from humid Michigan to hot and dry Washington State, most of them arriving in late June or early July 1968 after their children had completed the school year. We at the Sunnyside church were excited and grateful and deemed the coming of these families as God's blessing and a direct answer to prayer.

Second: As the calling church, we "called" Pastor Henry Bouma and his wife Mary and family from Palo Alto, California, to serve as missionary-pastor. Both Henry and Mary were known and respected for their focus and passion for "lost people" and their skills in evangelism. Eight families were on the way and a missionary pastor had accepted our call and was moving into the area. "God is good" was the common refrain from our church members.

A Location

A few months earlier, about seven acres of well-located open land on Neel Street in a middle class residential district in the city of Kennewick became available for a reasonable price. The committee from Sunnyside providing leadership to the fledgling group decided to buy this land as quickly as possible as a hedge against inflation since land costs were escalating. These people were practical farmers who regularly saw the price of land going up. Their approach was simple. If the start-up church later deemed the land to be in the wrong location for their needs, they could sell it and buy something better located. A few announcements made in the Sunnyside church accompanied with a small drive raised the needed funds of about $37,000 for the land. Sunnyside also was responsible for the housing of the missionary-pastor and family. Again the committee went to work and found a nice home, adequate in size, well-kept, and vacant right next to the land that had been purchased. A second drive raised almost enough to cover the entire cost of $27,000 to buy it. In every step we felt the blessing, leading, and provision of God. The more that was needed the more excited and generous the church became. It was astonishing to me, I never dreamt about that kind of excitement and generosity.

These numbers seem small now, but they were not then. Consider a comparison: a pastor's salary was around $5,000 to $6,000 annually plus a rent-free house. Our church raised a total of $64,000 cash for this mission ministry in a very short time, indicating the church's enthusiasm and generosity. When it was for missions, the church had passion and a big heart.

The Boumas and the additional families made up a nice-sized group. They soon rented a hall where they could meet for worship. We Sunnysiders were jealous because they had air conditioning for the blistering hot summer months and we didn't.

The church very quickly started community calling. The Boumas were good at evangelistic calling and well trained. In fact, they were area trainers for Campus Crusade. They were passionate about confronting as many people as possible with the Gospel message. They went door to door, into malls and other places where they could meet and talk with people. A number of people from the community became Christians and started attending the worship services. Closely supporting and working with them were Paul and Lois Bruizeman. Others soon recognized Lois's personality and skills for meeting people, teaching and helping them. She was soon speaking to and teaching women's bible classes and studies especially with young Christians and would often be asked where she went to church. A number of them started attending as well and the church began to grow.

Help!

The new church and the Sunnyside church soon realized that the new congregation would need some kind of facility. All agreed that the property on Neel Street was well located for a permanent structure. It was visible and accessible. An architect was hired, plans were drawn, and everything moved along at a fast pace, maybe too fast! But as we began to add up the costs for the facility, we realized that the small group, all recently relocated, and the Sunnyside mother church, though generous in its support, did not have the capacity to come up with the funds of several hundred thousand dollars needed to build the church facility. Sunnyside still had a significant debt on her own building which was about five years old. Our leaders were hesitant to borrow more money. Besides, they had just finished raising funds for the land and parsonage. They hated debt and viewed interest as "wasted money"! The motto was: "Pay it off as quickly as possible." We were stuck; in order not to hold back the church we, a bit reluctantly, asked for help from the denomination through our Home Mission Board.

The board's policies were clear. It could not help finance buildings for a new mission unless it controlled and supervised the church. Each step would require board involvement and approval. The board's experience with bargain "land deals" had resulted in some badly located churches, some of which suffered for years only to end up closing their doors. A good location indeed is a very high priority. The board had gained valuable experience which we didn't have. We had unbridled enthusiasm and were swimming in a pool of excitement.

The board readily approved our choice for locating on the Neel St. property and decided to help. The Council's direct responsibility ceased and Sunnyside was now "the calling church responsible for the teaching and the life of the pastor." We also "held the memberships of the families" which meant they had officially joined our congregation. (Note: We hold strongly that every CRC member lives under an umbrella of pastoral and spiritual protection of a congregation by either being a member by baptism or by profession of faith. As long as a church was small and not yet formerly organized as a congregation, the members and also the pastor usually lived under the pastoral care and guidance of a neighboring congregation.) In this case the board did everything else related to the day-to-day ministry, the development of the building, and planning for the future. The financing too was now taken over by Home Missions. Checks were written in the Grand Rapids office.

As supporting church we soon began to lose the close relationship. Our members began to visit the new church less frequently. Even our prayers for our neighboring ministry declined in number and intensity.

What is "Evangelism?"

All seemed to continue rather quietly until about a year later. The new church's building had been completed and its ministry was flourishing, or so we thought in Sunnyside. Occasional rumblings came our way of tensions developing, and in chatting with Pastor Henry Bouma I did sense some concerns but none that alarmed me. Some of our elders, who had more contact with the new church members than I did, reported at a Council meeting that a number of Tri-cities' members were unhappy with the ministry and especially dissatisfied with the pastor's emphasis on person-to-person evangelism. I began to see that the word "evangelism" did not mean the same thing to everyone. To the pastor it meant talking to people to present them with the claims of the gospel and invite them to surrender their lives to Christ.

However, for many of the Tri-Cities members the word "evangelism" meant teaching Sunday school or Vacation Bible School. It entailed framing walls, painting rooms, cutting grass, pounding nails, sweeping floors, and washing windows. They were hesitant to visit people and face them with the Gospel message. I believe at the core they were simply scared to face community people and I think they could not admit their fears. They had left their families in Michigan only a few years earlier to do exactly that and then discovered it was scary. It called for faith, dedication and sacrifice. Their fears were cloaked with theological arguments about the nature of evangelism. And as long as they did not agree, they felt no responsibility to stretch and cooperate. Instead they formed questioning huddles which soon grew into opposition. In the meantime, the Boumas and the Bruizemans continued the weekly community visitations, knocking on doors and talking to people and leading a number of them to Christ. Well aware of the scuttlebutt, they just kept on going as opposition grew, hoping it would go away. Instead of debating what they were doing, they invited (and challenged) the others to join them. The Boumas' effectiveness was such that stories of people making commitments to Christ made their way as far west as Sunnyside! As is often the case, the new Christians started to worship with the people who had introduced them to Christ.

The unhappy members complained to the staff at Home Missions in Grand Rapids via phone calls since they were now responsible for managing the *ministry*. We in Sunnyside became aware of the tension in the new church because the Sunnyside elders were to supervise the *doctrine and life* of the pastor, and the conflicts were mostly in that area. By the time Sunnyside elders became aware of the it, a number of the families were ready to pack and move back to where they had come from. In the meantime, every Sunday they saw new people coming to church. It was a strange paradox.

71

Part Ways

By then we sensed there were a few key people who were marshaling forces to demand that the Boumas be released. Behind our backs, this message had gone to the Home Mission staff in Grand Rapids who had received complaints about a "dictator pastor" who was destroying the church. I also started getting calls from Tri-Cities church members and Grand Rapids staff members informing me as to how bad things were. The staff members were asking whether they should step in and take decisive action with Rev. Bouma. They would, if we didn't. But they knew they would need the cooperation of the Sunnyside elders to take firm action. According to our commonly adopted <u>Church Order</u> only the Sunnyside elders, responsible for the spiritual life of the members and for Pastor Bouma's ministry, could take disciplinary action. However we wanted to be very careful before doing so. By now the Home Missions staff was fully convinced that the pastor was the main problem. Could nine of eleven families be wrong? They had convinced the staff in Grand Rapids that unless the pastor was released, they would all leave. That scared the Grand Rapids staff but also us. Imagine losing all but one or two families. Or, keeping them and losing the pastor. It was a bad, no-win situation. There was much tension and as elders we were under pressure.

In response to the complaints, our elders decided that in teams of two they would visit every one of the families, and do it all in a one-night blitz. Five teams of two elders made appointments for two visits at 7:30 and 8:45. Though they heard a litany of complaints they heard nothing significant regarding the pastor's preaching or pastoral ministry. Almost all the complaints related to Henry and Mary's relentless passion and persistence on *doing* evangelism, rather than talking or meeting about it. How does one find fault with that? The Boumas were somewhat insensitive and impatient with others but that did not warrant release from a ministry calling. For our elders it was a learning experience. They found the complaints to be similar, and several remarked that by the time they arrived at the second home a phone call from the first had already preceded them.

At our next elders' meeting, we discussed what we could do to rectify the situation. I was about to get a major lesson in leadership. Could a 90% majority be wrong? Two of our elders (of about ten present; another minority!) felt strongly that nine families *could* be wrong *if* they were led by a strong leader. They had figured out by then who it was that helped create a stream of phone calls to Grand Rapids by the other eight families.

Until now in everything we had done our elders had been united, I now sensed that we weren't. For me that created a discomfort. Some were siding with the complainers and especially with the Grand Rapids staff. After all, they said, "They are professionals working full-time with new churches and pastors; we as elders are inexperienced with something like this." And though it was not said we all knew our inexperienced church planting elders were led by an even more inexperienced (29-year- old) pastor! This was a difficult time for us; the division among us was most threatening to me.

Conflict, Pain and Grief

Just when I thought the situation had reached its lowest point, things really became worse. Suddenly, the oldest church member, an original Tri-Cities resident, had a heart attack and died. When Rev. Bouma went to minister to the families it became obvious that a number of families were not eager to have him minister in this tragic setting. The now angry members felt that the church's tensions might well have contributed to the man's heart attack. They were not about to ask him to comfort the family or lead the funeral. Instead, Pastor Bouma offered to call me to ask if I would do the funeral. Reluctantly I agreed and took an evening to visit the widow to make the arrangements but also to spend some time with a downhearted pastor and his wife Mary. A couple of the families spoke with me and immediately let me know how bad the situation was. Things had turned out totally different from what they and all of us had anticipated. We had started as a totally committed, united group eager to begin an outreach-oriented church, and now look what had become of it.

Later that night on my 50-mile trip home alone in the car, I cried; in fact I sobbed. I was confused about the situation and angry at God. How could something that started with godly motivation, love, and sacrificial generosity veer so far off the rails in so short a time? Was this a satanic attack or was God testing us? What good could possibly come out of this for this young church and for us, the supporting church in Sunnyside? I was sure all had

73

started with pure motivation. We had poured our hearts and souls and thousands of dollars into the new church, and now it was all falling apart. We had a lot of questions and personally, I was becoming distraught and totally puzzled.

For the first time in my life, I was experiencing the pain of ministry and didn't know why, and worse, I did not know how to fix it. And that was rather unusual for me. Only much later would the answers to some of these questions become clear; God *was* testing the local church and the elders, but I especially felt He was testing me. Would we believe His word, trust Him, and challenge a majority who were convinced they were right but who by biblical standards were wrong? They were sinning against God and their pastor. Simply put, would we walk by faith or the popular vote? By now things had deteriorated, there was wild gossip, malicious slander, judgmental attacks and all the ugly stuff that often accompanies church conflicts. Disagreement about issues progressed to attacks upon persons and personalities. It was my first experience of conflict, one which, although I didn't know it at the time would be followed by others in which I would be awake at night thinking, struggling, praying, and wrestling with God, and wrestling with others during days.

A Difficult Funeral

Two days later on a beautiful Saturday morning, I again drove the 50 miles to the Tri-Cities to conduct the funeral. Since I was early and the parsonage was close to the location where the funeral would be held, I decided to see how the Boumas were doing. As we were chatting, the phone rang and Mary answered it and told me it was for me. It was a key staff member from the Grand Rapids office who said to me, "Henry, the pastor is now killing the members! This must stop, and your Sunnyside elders need to step in and instruct him to cease from ministry. If you don't act now, we will stop paying his salary."

I was floored. I certainly did not need a "heavy" just then. I now know that when pushed into a corner, I tend to think fast and often respond with biting words. It is a response that cuts to the core. It can be right on; but it mostly results in having to go back and apologize. In more instances now I bite my tongue and hold it, but at that time I didn't. I said, "You do what you have to do, and then come to our next Classis meeting and you can explain it there." His response, "If you are not going to cooperate with us, we'll wash our hands of the whole thing." I mumbled, "Where did I hear that before?" The phone went dead on the other end.

The Boumas and I went to the funeral where the tension was palpable. We got through it, but looking back -even now- it was one of the most difficult funerals I have ever conducted.

Church Discipline

By now our elders were upset and ready to discipline most of the families for gossip, dissension and schismatic behavior. I was more cautious and wanted to buy some time. A few of our elders knew CRC church policies and procedure for dealing with disciplinary matters well and were convinced that official church discipline should be initiated. It would mean that we Sunnyside elders would, in fact, say to the members involved that what they were doing was divisive and schismatic to the fellowship of the church, and we would request them to cease these activities and repent. Until they repented, we would ask them to refrain from the sacrament of the Lord's Supper, to protect them from eating and drinking judgment unto themselves, as the apostle Paul warns in I Corinthians 11:27-29. (In later instances we as elders also asked the persons involved *not* to put money in any offering plates, since the Lord really first wants their hearts and then uses their gifts and donations [see Matthew 5:23-24]. I found that when we asked members to refrain from giving, it made a major impact upon them to bring about change. It is totally counter-cultural; the church just doesn't ask people *not* to give.)

It would be a tough decision to proceed with discipline, especially since our denominational Home Mission Board staff fully supported the dissenting families. The staff was demanding that we sever the pastor's relationship with the church and make him available for a call to another ministry or congregation. The Boumas were fully convinced that God was blessing their ministry and calling them to continue their work, even if nine families left. They frankly stated they were called by God to be there and God would provide. As elders we had no biblical reason to ask them to leave. We felt hesitant to oppose them.

75

A Helpful Visit

Before proceeding with official church discipline the Sunnyside elders decided to invite two key members (the President and the Executive Secretary) of the Home Missions Board to visit the Tri-Cities church for a weekend at our expense. We extended the invitation because we were convinced that they would see the complete picture if they could spend some time with the people and leaders and experience the ministries for themselves. The board chairman, Rev. Ed Knott, and the Secretary, Rev. Marvin (Mike) Baarman, accepted our invitation and arrived in the Tri-Cities on a Friday. Over the next two days, they attended meetings; visited the church's ministries; talked with members, neighbours and friends of the congregation; walked around the church neighborhood; drove through the greater area; and spent time with the pastor and his family including accompanying them on some community visits. On Sunday they attended Sunday school and the worship service followed by lunch with the pastor and family, after which they came to Sunnyside in time to attend our evening worship service.

Just before the service, Rev. Baarman asked me if he could have a few moments to speak to the congregation. When I looked puzzled (I was more cautious then about who gets up on the pulpit although I knew Mike well and trusted him) he assured me that the essence of what he wanted to say was to thank us, and he did exactly that. He gave a profound and authentic thank you to the congregation for its ongoing support for this struggling daughter church and he especially thanked the elders for their loving and firm care of this tender church plant with its tough challenges. He stated that he was going back to Grand Rapids to recommend to the board that they continue to help with the finances but that all other decisions be made by the Sunnyside Council until such time that its help was no longer needed and the Tri-Cities church could handle its own matters. The congregation was more touched by his five-minute thank you than my diligently crafted sermon that night. It was a strong affirmation for the diligent work of our elders, some of whom were becoming weary from all this. For some time now we were so involved with the neighboring situation that we hardly had time to do what needed to be done at the home base. My greatest joy was that through all this we continued to work together as a Council and we grew in love for each other. I believe that is the good news of the Gospel.

Shortly after their visit, the Grand Rapids Board informed us that they fully supported the previous decisions of our Sunnyside elders and recommended to the entire board that the supervision of the ministry be turned over to our elders. The board would provide the needed financial assistance.

New Growth

By the fall of 1969, the Tri-Cities church (now less than 12 members) and the Sunnyside elders faced an uncertain future. As leaders in both churches we felt we had followed biblical principles of honesty, openness and integrity. We trusted God, even though it was tempting to go with the strong pressure to release the pastor. It was a huge test for me and also our elders. The Sunnyside CRC, still with a significant debt, was now also supporting a very small fledgling congregation carrying a much larger debt proportionately. To provide a few more bodies in the pews, we appointed three Sunnyside families per Sunday to attend the worship service at the Tri-Cities church. Amazingly and undauntingly, the two couples who were left, the Boumas and the Bruizemans, continued the work of evangelism. God showed up and blessed as new people started visiting, were converted, and joined the little flock. Two community members became part of the steering committee which enhanced the community outreach.

Over a few years the church became a denominational pilot project of a growing church plant supervised by local elders rather than a board and staff 2,000 miles away. When Henry and Mary Bouma accepted a call to a church in Indiana in 1980 regular Sunday attendance had grown to more than 200 people. They had also added to their building. In a relatively short time the group became a church with many new converts. It was a joy to see it flourish after a very testy start.

And on the Home Front

That same fall saw the completion of a new parsonage in Sunnyside and we moved from cramped rooms to ample space. We were expecting our third child, and the congregation deemed the time had come to create more room.

A Wedding

Between Christmas and New Year 1969-1970, our daughter Judy and I went to Bellingham, Washington for a few days for the wedding of my youngest brother John to Sylvia Reehorn. I conducted the wedding, and Judy (three and a half years old) was the flower girl. Jan stayed home since she was in the last month of her pregnancy and the doctor did not feel it wise to travel across the unpredictable, snowy Cascade Mountain pass in her last month. Since John and Sylvia were driving to Grand Rapids where John was a teacher and Sylvia was attending Calvin College, they stopped to stay overnight on their way back on December 31, 1969.

A Birth

On Sunday, January 18, 1970, son Douglas was born in the local Sunnyside hospital. I took Jan to the hospital about 7:00 AM where a nurse promptly led me to a waiting room where I was expected to wait, or if I preferred, I could go home. I was not allowed to be present for the delivery and –for that matter- did not need to be there for the labor either. It would be a long day in the waiting room, so I went home and led the morning worship service (we didn't have anyone around that we could call on to fill in on short notice.) At about 1:00 in the afternoon, I returned to the hospital and was again shown the waiting room where I read *Readers' Digests* until I was told by the nurse "It's getting close… stay right here!" Fifteen minutes later, the nurse was back, "a healthy baby boy! We are cleaning him up, and in about 15 minutes you can see him in the nursery." I got to see Jan as they wheeled her out of the delivery room on the way to her own room, and a few minutes later they brought Doug to us. We were extremely thankful, especially since Jan's parents had had two still-born babies and we had experienced two early-stage miscarriages. We checked 10 fingers and 10 toes; all the parts were there; everything looked great! A few days later we took our new baby into the new parsonage. Life was good and God is good!

And a Funeral

Only three months after John's marriage, in early April 1970, I experienced the hardest blow that I had experienced up to that point in my life when we received word that brother John had been killed in a car crash in Grand Rapids on his way to work. It was a sad and somber time for all of my family as we gathered in Lacombe, Alberta for the funeral. As can be expected, my parents were devastated; I don't believe my mother was ever happy again. It also took a bigger toll on me than I realized at the time. John was always a happy-go-lucky clown and invariably the center of any party. There were no dull moments when he was around; he was a natural with jokes and puns which often produced boisterous laughter. He was intellectually bright and gifted with great relational skills. He was not only the apple of my parents' eye but he was that also for me and my siblings. When he left for Calvin, we couldn't wait for him to visit home again so we could see him.

It was hard for me to learn after John's death that he had struggled with depression. Because of his seemingly happy and humorous exterior, it remained well hidden. I was left with a gnawing guilt for my insensitivity in not recognizing this earlier. I had visited with him for an evening in March while I was in Grand Rapids for a board meeting. We had had a good time, but looking back later I realized that I did not really inquire as to how he was doing and feeling. After his death, I learned from my brother Bill who visited with John a few days after I did that John had said to him that he tried to tell me he was struggling and felt down but I had not picked up on that at all. I guess I was on a wavelength where it simply never dawned on me that John would have "down times." He was a newlywed and I assumed (dangerous thing to do) that all was well. I am still pained over that. I should have been much more sensitive!

Whenever I am now in the Lacombe area, I regularly go to the cemetery and I stop by a small group of three graves, my dad's, my mom's and John's. I grieve at my parents' graves, but I get angry inside when I am at John's. To lose someone so gifted so early in life seems so utterly senseless. I have trouble even today to see this as one of the "all things work together for good" events. I have to preach to myself that I must believe that, even though I cannot feel or see it.

More Ministry, Different Church

In the fall of 1970, we received a call from First Christian Reformed Church of Calgary, Alberta. It was a large urban church with many youth and mostly younger families. Things were going well in the Sunnyside congregation and in the Tri-Cities church, but after five busy years in our first congregation it seemed like a good time for a change, for me as a pastor as well as for us as a family, since none of our children were in school yet. The challenge intrigued me, and after discussing it with the Council and congregation, we felt free and confident to accept the call. We spent three months bringing closure to the Sunnyside ministry and preparing to move some 650 miles north and east.

To this day, we have good memories of our first five years of ministry; and we still have a few close ties to some members of the Sunnyside congregation, even 40 years later. It has always been a pleasure to return there occasionally to visit and preach.

Reflections and Transitions

The Sunnyside journey ended my classroom education and ministry preparation stage. I was ready to transition into the role of the pastor "with all the responsibilities and privileges thereof." I felt I had learned more from the church than they had benefited from me. I long felt the Calgary church was indebted to Sunnyside for the significant shaping and formation of this pastor. We moved when I was 31 years old and, in the good company of Jesus, as mentioned earlier, I now know that the first 30 years of my life was mostly preparation for ministry. I had begun to learn something about the importance of good relationships, the value of self-discipline needed to prepare and preach two sermons per week, plus all kinds of pastoral work in a large congregation had forced me to use my time well.

I transitioned from reading the Bible as a textbook to be studied to pass exams to reading it for its message. Had I just "bought" the seminary package, or was the Bible really what it said it was, "All Scripture is God-breathed and is profitable for teaching, rebuking, correcting and training for righteousness, so that the man of God may be thoroughly equipped for every good work." (II Timothy 3:16)? Was the Bible really making me a man of God? I think it was. My daily work with God's people and their problems, and my time spent each week preparing two messages from the Bible to shape and change their lives had the major side benefit of changing me! My faith grew deeper and stronger as I taught others. The "two-edged sword" was first cutting into my heart and flesh. Though I had witnessed some miracles I struggled with whether they still happen. That question would be faced and tested again in the Calgary congregation.

At Sunnyside, I developed a deeper sense of the mission of the church and the further expansion of God's kingdom into all of culture and all life's challenges. I felt that outreach was no longer optional. I came out of Sunnyside with the conviction that a church without a mission vision by default becomes a maintenance-oriented club.

Finally, I am indebted to Sunnyside for helping me learn to stand on biblical principles. I shifted from majority rule and practical thinking to a more scripturally based perspective. I began to learn about the cost of discipleship. I had seen that faith in Christ and obedience to His way had aroused opposition both from the outside and from within. Standing up against a majority had been a valuable learning experience, although it did not involve me directly. A similar experience but involving me more directly would happen in our next ministry stop, Calgary.

Chapter 6

A Time of Growth!

Calgary, 1971 – 1974

A Cold Welcome

Even though Christmas had passed by the time we arrived in Calgary on January 10, 1971, we might well sing "Though the weather outside is frightful, the people are delightful." Our family was warmly welcomed, but unloading the moving truck with our belongings in windy, minus 40 degree weather was one of our coldest experiences ever. The parsonage was a split-level home with a north-facing front door that remained open the entire afternoon as we carried in item after item, box after box, with the wind blowing every BTU of heat right out the door. The cold air came in and dropped into the basement, making it freezing cold. Our three children stayed with some families from the church while Jan and I worked for two days to get settled. It took the furnace those two days to bring the house back to a comfortable temperature. Fortunately, I had given Jan a heating blanket for Christmas, so at least we had a warm bed. It was a cold start to the ministry at First Christian Reformed Church, or First Church as it was more commonly known.

The following Sunday night I was installed as their pastor, and the very next day I attended my first meeting of Classis Alberta South. I soon found out that this was quite different from Classis Columbia in stable Sunnyside. We travelled to Lethbridge, a two-hour drive south of Calgary. A traditional elder rode with me and spent at least 50 miles (80 km) of the 140-mile (220 km) ride trying to convince me to deliver a sermon soon warning everyone about the evils of movies. In fact, according to him, it would serve the Lord's work best if I would warn our members to avoid *all* movies. When I replied that I thought some movies were acceptable, even educational, his response was similar to the one my pastor had given me when I was a teenager and wanted to see a good movie: "Just because you find a good piece of pie in a garbage can, are you going to eat it?"

At the Classis meeting, tension present in our sister Calgary congregation, Emmanuel CRC, came to full-blown expression when some of its members laid charges against their Council and pastor. These members were supported by a few area pastors, and the skirmish was shockingly loud and long. I noted early that minor issues quickly flared up into major conflicts. Everything was of equal significance and became a win-lose issue. For me, this was an early portrayal of the intense polarization that existed between a number of pastors who were deemed either too conservative or too liberal and their congregations. In reality, none of the ministers was theologically liberal; some church members just labeled anyone who did things other than the traditional way as liberal. My colleague and neighbour pastor was hounded relentlessly by a few pastors but most noticeably by a southern Alberta colleague. To me, this behavior was obviously destructive and I wondered what I had gotten myself into by joining this Classis. I left that first Classis meeting with this caution in mind, "Be careful, there are no minor issues here!"

Events that Shape

As I began the work in Calgary, I prayed that God would not let this to be a mundane ministry for us but an experience of vital spirituality. Along with that, I re-invited God to take my life and do with it as He desired. I gave Him permission to use me for whatever He wanted to get done so I might be most effective for Him. I had little idea what that might be, but I was sincere in my request. I dreaded a mediocre ministry and a predictable life.

At this time an influence that became known as the "charismatic movement" had begun to make significant inroads into many churches. It started primarily in the Roman Catholic Church on October 11, 1962 when Pope John XXIII challenged Roman Catholics to throw open the windows of the church by inaugurating the Second Vatican Council, an extraordinary gathering of some 2,600 theologians, bishops and cardinals. The Pope and the Vatican Council introduced reforms that redefined the role of the church in modern life. The Council declared that Catholic members should read the Bible for themselves in their own language. It also stated that liturgies and homilies (messages) at the mass should be spoken in the language of the people and should be relevant and practical. As people became more personally interested in the teachings of the Scriptures, they became more involved and invested in the church. They learned that God used *all* the members of his body, not just clergy. Many began to ask, seek, and knock and those who did, found! (Matthew 7:7). They discovered that God still has "gifts of grace" (*charisma)* for His children and with these gifts and empowered by the Holy Spirit, they would better worship and praise Him and minister through His church to a broken world. Vatican II was influential in beginning the charismatic movement which swept through many Roman Catholic churches. The movement spread further and is now worldwide and influences every Christian denomination by emphasizing participation in seeking and serving according to one's gifts. Many ministries have started and much growth has occurred since 1962! Roman Catholicism now is a global religion of more than 1 billion members, profoundly affected by the charismatic movement.

I believe when God's people, Roman Catholics *and* Protestants of various denominations, start reading the Bible seriously the Holy Spirit moves and - sooner or later- shapes and pries hearts to bring about life changes, especially in the area of holiness and sanctification. The charismatic movement had also impacted Christian Reformed churches. First Church was one of those deeply affected by charismatic influence and thinking. I recall reading a statement made by Billy Graham at that time, "How the Evangelical church responds to the charismatic movement and the Jesus people may well determine the future of the evangelical church." At the time, I thought it was a strange statement- but it stuck with me. I questioned it then; I now believe he was right.

Growth

Though we had a feisty start at Classis, at the local level our ministry to First church started well. As we began to settle, we were loved and welcomed with open arms. The positive response to my preaching was dangerous to my ego. New people began to show up at Sunday services, both mornings and evenings, mostly through word-of-mouth advertising. A healthy measure of excitement and vibrancy filled the church. Expectations were high. As pastor and congregation, we soon realized we were a good match. I preached with few notes and much passion, some of which was enhanced by a responsive congregation. My sermons were practical and relevant; people spoke about how they were making life changes. The joy and enthusiasm was contagious. People talked about the messages on the way out of church, but also during the week. Some who had dropped out of church heard what was happening and came back to see for themselves. Many enjoyed their visits and would come again, sometimes with their friends. Some didn't like the service, and we would likely not see them again; we also had visitors from neighboring churches, especially at our evening services. Because the church was large, and I was new, I didn't know who was a visitor and who was a member. Many new commitments to Christ were made. On a regular basis I would hear things like: "For the first time in my life I now *know* with certainty that I am forgiven." Or, "I know that I am a child of God. I'd always hoped it, but now I know!"

It was a dangerous and heady time for me. In fact, although I didn't recognize it, these positive responses were nurturing my ego. I was getting affirmation, acceptance, and recognition by my colleagues, something that was far too important to me. I had a big hole in my life for affirmation and it was being filled. It felt good, maybe too good! In the meantime, I continued to work hard and prayed often that First Church would be a church where many would come to know the Lord and grow in gracious tenderness and holiness. Many of our older Dutch immigrants had gone through a war after which they had immigrated to a new land. Extended periods of deprivation had made them tough and harsh. They brought with them the common historic CRC view, "a world and life perspective," meaning that everything we as Christians do, think and say, individually and corporately, is colored by the teaching of the Scriptures. That is still held up as a high principle by many CRC people. The CRC of North America added another emphasis namely the *practice* of graciousness, the *fruit* of the Spirit, and personal and relational love for God and each other. Many long-time members who had willingly worked and volunteered continued to serve but were now joined by others. Newcomers came with new ideas for outreach ministries and initiated them. As needs in the congregation surfaced, ministries were started to address them. Many, with a bit of encouragement joined opportunities to serve. As the church invested love and compassion into the streets of Calgary, the people of Calgary became more involved with the church, bringing with them fresh energy. I saw the ministries as part of God's answer to prayers that we not be a maintenance church.

God, Are You There?

Shortly after we arrived in Calgary in January 1971, representatives from First CRC met with representatives of the two other Calgary CRCs, Emmanuel on the west end of the city near the Christian school, and Maranatha farther away in the northwest area of the city near the University of Calgary and also the High River CRC, 55 km south of us. We wanted to plan a fall conference that would focus on helping us learn how to become more passionately evangelistic. We wanted a speaker, a CRC pastor who was *actually* bringing new people to Christ and into the church. We contacted Rev. Rits and Mrs. Pearl Tadema, the couple Jan and I had spent a summer internship with at their church plant in Tacoma. They were a godly couple sensitive to the Holy Spirit's leading, and indeed they regularly added new Christians to their current church plant in Fountain Valley, California. We knew we could learn a lot from them and their two successful church experiences.

The conference made a large impact on those who attended, and especially on First Church. But an associated event, the healing of a young man, made an even greater impact on us by showing us that God heals usually by utilizing doctors, medicine, surgery, etc., but He also heals in delightful, surprising, and miraculous ways. Why He doesn't always heal this way I do not know. I do know this healing became a formative experience for me. It boosted my faith and it was a sign to me that God really is alive and intimately involved with His people. This event created enough stir so that six months later I was asked to write an article describing it for a magazine now called <u>Christian Courier</u>, a weekly paper read by many immigrants throughout Canada. I include the story as it happened and as it was printed in 1972 with some minor editorial revisions. It is absolutely as I described it. Though the event occurred 40 years ago, it is still vivid for me. I pray it will boost your faith as it did mine. The article was part of a series the magazine was doing, entitled:

In Demonstration of the Spirit and Power

It all began, as far as I can see, in the first week of September 1971. Rather suddenly, a young man by the name of Scott (not his real name) became ill with a fever due to unknown causes. After entering a Lethbridge hospital, he soon slipped into a deep coma. Though tests were completed and various medications were used, he remained in his coma with a dangerously high fever. On September 30, he was brought by ambulance to the large Foothills Hospital in Calgary to see if perhaps something might be done. Upon his arrival in Calgary with a fever of nearly 105, some of the medical staff questioned out loud why it was decided to transfer him. To them, it was obvious that little could be done in Calgary that the Lethbridge hospital couldn't do; Scott would die, if not, he would likely be left with severe brain damage. For some reason he was brought to Calgary at the exact time of our conference.

A Challenge

On Friday, October 1, the Calgary and High River Christian Reformed Churches were to begin a week of fellowship and training sessions to inspire and equip their members to become more effective in the work of sharing the good news. Rev. Rits and Mrs Pearl Tadema, serving the Lord as home missionaries in the Fountain Valley California Christian Reformed Church, were invited as leaders for the conference. Knowing that God was mightily using the Tademas to draw people into the body of Christ, it was not without trepidation, even fear, that we anticipated the conference. What would God lay upon our hearts? Would He lead us to do something new? If so what? Though we were quite convinced about the importance of reaching others in His name, were we really ready to pay the price of direct involvement?

The conference began on Friday evening with a session for Council members followed by a Saturday morning seminar to train leaders. While at the morning meeting, we received a phone call reporting that Scott was in the Calgary Foothills Hospital in very critical condition. We were asked if we could provide support for the family since ministering to Scott in his coma would be minimal if any. Before the Tademas and I left the house, we turned to God's Word. Could there be a relationship between the conference and this illness, or is this mere coincidence? Does God want to confirm His Word with a sign or wonder as He did in the Book of Acts? We shared thoughts, Scripture passages, and prayed for wisdom, openness and courage to do what He wanted done. We wanted to walk and minister in faith and not fear. Whatever we did needed to be in full harmony with

His revealed will. We wrestled with His Word, and prayerfully we decided that in faith, we would ask God to *fully* heal and restore Scott, and do that for His glory. We would ask and believe. We would boldly venture out on a limb and ask others to pray in faith and envision complete healing.

Faith Wavering

In that spirit of submission and expectation, the Tademas and I went to the Intensive Care section on the ninth floor of Foothills Hospital on Saturday afternoon. Our faith, so firm at home, wavered when we met the family and saw the patient's condition. It sank deeper when the family tearfully shared with us the reality that doctors had shared with them. Things looked bleak. The possibility of coming out of the coma existed; however, after an extensive period of high fever, if there were to be a recovery, there would likely be brain damage. Their positive note was, —"as long as there is life, there is hope." However, realistically, "expect the worst." Did we now still dare to believe that God would make him well again? To pray for that is easier than to believe it. To ask believing and expecting and not doubting— I found that hard, really hard, especially when I stood by that bed.

We read some Scripture passages which were clear and appropriate for the situation. As clergymen, Rev. Tadema and I stood by as Mrs. Tadema (Pearl) led the discussion and prayer. She had faith that convinced, (convicted!) her that God would raise Scott up so that His name would be praised. People would know that God really is God. I remember wishing that she wouldn't go so far out on the limb. What would it do to the family's faith and trust in God if Scott died? And what would it do to us? I know that "faith is the assurance of things hoped for, a conviction of things not seen," but…

At the bedside with the family, holding the quivering hand of a patient who was totally unaware of what was happening around him, we prayed for healing and, falteringly, we sang *Amazing Grace*. We went home, and though it appeared that little had been done for Scott, I believed we had at least encouraged the family. But had we lifted them with a Biblical hope? That question would drive me back to His Word again and again in the days to come.

Congregations Involved

The following Sunday morning, October 3, Rev. Tadema was to preach at the Emmanuel CRC, and I looked forward to conducting worship at First CRC. We had decided beforehand to share with the congregations involved the urgent need for prayer. But what would we request the congregations to do? What should they specifically ask of God? In First CRC we heard a beautiful profession of faith testimony in which a young man boldly declared, "I live in Christ because Christ lives in me," after which I shared with the congregation that another young man was preparing for this same step when illness interfered. And now, rather than standing joyfully before his family and congregation, he is lying on —what appeared to be- his deathbed.

I shared the "hopelessness of the situation" humanly speaking and the fact that only the intervention of a miracle by God would spare his life. I asked the church to pray that God would raise him up, nothing less. I was surprised at what I said! At that very moment, I was fully convinced that God would answer our prayers.

As the conference progressed through the next days, faith increased on the part of the participants. Discussion groups shared conversational prayer; fervent prayers were offered for Scott along with other deep personal needs. By now many were praying, from children in several Christian schools, to the aged who for years had walked close with God. There were from many congregations—his home church in Lethbridge, churches in the Vancouver area, the home mission church in Fountain Valley, California, and all four of the Calgary area churches.

Pray and Believe

In the meantime, with the Tademas staying at our home, we were experiencing a rich time of sharing, prayer, and struggles. Scott's condition, however, remained unchanged. We reviewed Scripture passages and heard what Jesus said. To the father of the epileptic boy who said, "Christ, if you can do anything, help us." He replied, "If I can?" That's not really the question. "All things are possible to him who has faith." To the Canaanite woman, He said, "Great is your faith; be it done as you desire." To another woman who believed that if she could touch His garment she would become well, He said, "Your faith has made you whole!" To the blind men who followed him, "According to your faith, be it done to you." To Peter who walked on water and began to sink, "O man of little faith why did you doubt?" And we noted that in his own home town "He did not do many mighty works, because of their unbelief."

It was obvious that there is a direct relationship between faith and the manifestation of the power of God. Do we not see or experience miracles because we do not expect them? "Faith the size of the mustard seed can move a mountain." We often quote it, but do we believe it? And if that is accomplished by faith, are sincere asking and a deep trusting faith *essential* or just helpful for God to heal? We read more. Jesus commanded individuals to respond. To Lazarus, he said, "Come forth." To the lame, he said, "Take up your bed and walk." To dead Dorcas, Peter said, "Tabitha, come!" Peter and John about to go into the temple said, "In the name of Jesus Christ of Nazareth, rise up and walk." To Aeneas, Peter said, "Jesus Christ heals you, arise and make your bed." And Paul speaking to the cripple at Lystra said, "Stand upright on your feet." The spokesman for God expected a response fully within the realm of possibility.

And Act

As Thursday night approached, we discussed whether perhaps we were not only expected to pray but also to *act* in faith. Obedience and submission is *commanded* not just suggested. Pearl asked, "are we to command Scott to rise up and walk?" The idea frightened me. Lots of questions raced through my mind. What if he did? or, What if nothing happened? What would that do to my faith? And what if he did get up? Though I wanted to move into that area, I was certainly not eager to move that far, what seemed to me like a thin limb, way out there! I preferred to have a safer route. Living by faith can be a frightening and tumultuous experience. Yet, desirous to be obedient and reviewing many biblical examples, we became convinced that we must ask *and* act expecting God to respond.

Pearl, though ready to return to Los Angeles early the next morning, wanted to return to the hospital after the final evening conference session. But she would not go alone. She wanted one of us pastors (Rits or me) to go with her. Her husband immediately said he would stay home and pray. That put it on me; do I or don't I? I agreed to go along, but not without first laying out a fleece. Since it was approaching midnight, I suggested that we would share with the nurses in charge of Scott's unit why we had come at that late hour. If they had reservations about having us at the hospital at that time, I would view that as the Lord's "no" to our plans, and we should return home. That was fine with Pearl. Being weary after a long week, I remember saying that whatever happened would be the Lord's doing, not ours; we were both too tired to do much of anything. We explained our purpose to the nurses in charge; both of them urged us to feel free to go in with him and spend as much time as we desired!

Both our faith and courage took a jolt when we saw Scott lying there. With tubes inserted into his nose and arm, somewhat fevered, Scott lay quivering on his back on a water-cooled bed, with his head shaking back and forth. It was not a pretty sight. Together we read some Scripture passages emphasizing the power and promises of God and the importance of acting in faith, hoping this would boost our hope and courage. Pearl stood on the right side of the bed, and I was on the left. For no particular planned reason, I placed my hand on the side of Scott's head. Pearl did the same on the other side, trying to stabilize his shaking. We prayed and asked God to make His name great among His people. Pearl prayed in tongues and suggested we command Scott to "get up!" I told Pearl I could not do it, but I *could* ask Scott to open his eyes. That was fine with her.

Shortly after that, Pearl quietly stated, "Scott, in the name of the Lord, open your eyes." Nothing happened. She stated it three or four times, but nothing happened. Unexpectedly, I felt stirred to say the same thing and I did so firmly, boldly and surprisingly loudly. It was out before I realized it. At that very moment, a powerful but strange "surge" of a kind of electrifying jolt went through me. It was strong and obvious to me, (there was no mistaking it!), neither frightening nor shocking. It was like an electric shock; but actually it wasn't. It was quite beautiful. An electric shock leaves me agitated and aggravated; this didn't. It was something I had never experienced before. Afraid of being viewed as being "weird," I immediately resolved that I would not tell anyone what I had felt.

91

When God Shows up

After that touch from the Holy Spirit, Scott for the first time stopped all shaking and clearly opened his eyes. With a blank look he stared at us, giving no indication that he was seeing us. We stood in silent awe. It was a sacred and unique moment, but it was also a scary moment. I knew we stood in the presence of God, but I also had an overwhelming compulsion to get out of there and run. So we just stood quietly and watched him look quietly and peacefully at the ceiling.

I, the skeptic, immediately thought, this has probably happened before. So I went to the nurses' station and asked if they would check the charts to see if Scott had opened his eyes at all. They paged through some charts and then stated he had not, so I asked, "You want to come and see him with his eyes open?" They did and followed me into his room and saw him quietly laying there with his eyes open. They asked what we had done, so we explained what had happened. They made no comments, so I have no idea what they thought of that. We stayed with him about another 15 minutes. It was time to leave, and when we indicated that, Scott began to shake, was anxious and restless like he was afraid. Pearl suggested we lay hands on him and that I pronounce the benediction. I did, and when I was finished his eyes were closed and he was shaking again. We were ok with that; both of us believing that God would heal him. We praised God and were strongly convinced that God is real. He answers the prayers of His people and honors their faith.

A little later as we walked out of the hospital, Pearl identified the very moment of the jolt when she said, "The Holy Spirit's power really hit you when you spoke those words." Our hands had been touching Scott's head, the jolt had gone from my hands through him and then through her. I knew something had "hit" me, but I could not explain it. When Pearl later pinpointed the very moment, I knew it was real. I also knew my vow for secrecy was busted!

Deterioration

Early the next morning, I dropped the Tademas off at the airport and on the way home decided to stop at the hospital. With eyes closed and shaking,

Scott laid there just like the night before. When I spoke to him and said, "God is healing you," the shaking again stopped and his eyes fluttered but did not fully open. About two weeks later, Scott gradually began to talk. His mind recalled past experiences, and only a few days later his eyes were open and focusing. We carried on a conversation, even though his mouth would quiver at times resulting in stuttering. This would be followed by a shaking and rolling of his head. We hoped and prayed that he would improve.

He didn't and the shaking actually became worse. A week later as I entered the floor and was still some four rooms away from his door, I could hear him loudly hollering, cursing, swearing, and shouting nasty comments to anyone who came near him, including me. It was awful! I checked with a Christian doctor as to what had happened. He said that to the staff it was apparent that there is some brain damage. He told me that X-rays portrayed a brain scar which would likely affect his speech and motor coordination. In fact, it was not impossible that Scott would spend his life in hospital care or institutionalized. After that conversation with him, I went home thoroughly disappointed and depressed. That was my low point. Over and over I asked myself, "What have we done? Oh, no, no"

I remember the doctor saying: "Now if you want to pray for a real miracle, pray that God take the brain scar away. I can't fathom that happening; it would convince all of us here that it is a miracle of God." Very halfheartedly, I said, "Then we are going to pray that God will heal that." I asked the doctor to do so too. His answer: "I would find that hard."

Though I had replied, "We will pray for that," I well remember that my heart was not in it. Instead, questions and doubts bombarded me. Wouldn't a quiet death following a period of coma have been better than a life of retardation? Were all of us in Lethbridge, Calgary, British Columbia, and California wrong by asking God for healing? Had we pushed too hard to have our own way, which was healing? Should we have prayed "not my will but your will be done"? But Jesus *only* prayed that when He asked for the cup to pass away from Him, a prayer that was obviously against the plan of God. He was *born to drink* that cup. To not drink it would thwart God's plan of salvation and reconciliation. What is God's will in regard to sickness? How are sicknesses and other sufferings part of the "abundant life"? Are they?

I remember getting on the pulpit the following Sunday rather dejectedly. I honestly shared what had happened and I again asked the congregation to pray some more. I even shared that at this point I had little if any faith but was now calling upon the faith of the members of the church to fill in for the lack of it on my part. We again turned to the Lord together. Scott's family and church were also again fervently praying that God would continue to heal him. Children in Christian school classrooms, at meals in their homes, in their nightly prayers, were asking, "God, please make Scott well again."

Improvement

About two hard weeks passed and suddenly Scott began to improve. In a period of a few days, his swearing, cursing, slurring of words and the shaking of his head ceased. Between a Wednesday and a Friday visit, I hardly recognized him. Scott was becoming completely well. On one Saturday, he complained that he still could not walk. The next day at church, we prayed for strength to walk. The following week when I visited him he was beaming from ear to ear as all six feet plus of him jumped out of the bed—and walked down the hall some 40 feet and back. Wow!

The following Sunday, for the first time in several months he was in church. Though still somewhat feeble, having lost some 30 pounds of weight, he was sitting in the back in a wheelchair. As I introduced him, he got up out of the wheelchair and falteringly walked down the aisle to the front. I came down from the podium and stood next to him with one arm around his shoulder to steady him. I did a brief interview in which he shared that he really knew little as to what had happened except for what others had told him. I ended by asking him what he would like us to do. He responded, "Can we sing, 'Great is Thy Faithfulness'"? We did! Did we ever! As we came to the lines "…strength for today and bright hope for tomorrow; Blessings all mine, with ten thousand beside!" the organ was playing, but we were hardly singing. Later, many confessed that they could not sing, their eyes were filled with tears and their voices choked with joy and praise. And they were not embarrassed. The following Saturday, Scott went home—in a car—not in an ambulance or a hearse as many had feared.

God performed a miracle in his "family." Even the specialist had no medical answer, only speculations. He was reluctant to say, "It's a miracle." Many hearts were spiritually touched, even revived. For many who struggled and searched for a meaningful faith, it became an experience of conviction by which they knew that God is really alive. I, for one, assumed for years that miracles belonged only to the New Testament era. Now I believe they're not just limited to that time! G.C. Berkouwer expresses it well when he writes:

> *We find nothing in the Scriptures to indicate a line that we can draw through a definite period to mark off a boundary between the time of miracles and the time of the absence of miracles… The many signs that still appear after Pentecost should make us the more careful not to set limits, in our enlightened era, to the miraculous activity of God. There is not a single datum in the New Testament which makes it certain that God, in a period of strengthening and extending of the church in heathendom, will not confirm his message with signs, in holy resistance to the demonic influences of the kingdom of darkness. He who thinks that he can say with certainty that miracles no longer can occur may seriously ask himself whether he thinks in terms of God's power over the world or from a secret capitulation to determinism."*
>
> *--G.C. Berkouwer*
>
> *The Providence of God, pages 224-225*

Biblical theology includes space for the spectacular, fantastic, and miraculous. In general, I do like things orderly, predictable and in manageable sized packages. I like clean, simple explanations. When I expected no miracles to occur, they didn't. I asked not because I expected not. I prayed, even occasionally asked for the impossible, but I did not really expect the impossible to occur. And they didn't. This experience taught me that my prayers need to be accompanied with faith. I am learning to ask boldly, leaving the results to God without feeling I have to be able to explain what He did or did not do. That's liberating.

<u>(Update, spring 2013,)</u>

Scott recovered fully, later married, and I believe he has four children. For a number of years after 1971, we received an annual Christmas card with a brief update. Since moving to Ontario in 1984, we have lost contact.

Impact upon Us

As a church we had together experienced the healing hand of God; we had publicly cried tears in a worship service without feeling embarrassed. It was liberating for many in that it broke through many years of inhibited, formal church behavior. For a congregation of stoic people to lose control of their emotions was a major event. Afterwards, it became easier for us to laugh -even out loud- at our own foibles and follies; we released our need to be in full control at all times. God was real and walked with us. It began to cure what my colleague Frank Breisch used to call a common case of "TOTS" disease (**T**aking **O**urselves **T**oo **S**eriously). Frank, a non-immigrant former Presbyterian, was great at challenging and pricking some of the common bubbles and practices from our rich immigrant culture, especially those to which we were oblivious.

First Church continued to grow. Visitors came regularly, and among them were people seeking meaning in their lives. We realized that we could not have even *one* boring (or uninspiring) worship service; we could not risk turning off someone on their first visit. This pressure stirred us to greater creativity. We enjoyed an amazing amount of freedom. Not everyone liked what we were doing, but they could hardly criticize the results.

Employment

We also grew because of the dynamic economic situation in Alberta in general and in the City of Calgary in particular, which stood in contrast to the relatively high unemployment in Ontario. Many young adults and younger families moved to Calgary because there was work. Some came to check out this "strange" CRC which they had heard about in Ontario. It was common for me to get phone calls from parents or pastors in Ontario to check us out. If their calls confirmed what they had already heard, they would encourage their young adults to go west.

And Encouragement

One Friday afternoon just before leaving for home, I got a phone call at the church office from a young man who had just arrived at the Calgary train station from Toronto. He had some legal problems in Ontario and his marriage was in trouble, so his father had bought him a one-way ticket to Calgary, and told him to call us adding, "Don't come back until you're straightened out." This young man, as did others, came with high expectations. And because they did, they were wide open to a fresh meeting with God. He had a place to stay for the night with some family friends but wanted to see me the very next day, Saturday, my day off, "to get started." He was serious! I had already made plans for the following day, but when I found out he was staying not far from us, I offered to pick him up at eight the next morning. I suggested he wear some older clothes so "we can do some things together and at the same time become acquainted." He was up for that! We had just bought our own home and planned to use the day to clean up the backyard and remove a number of shrubs and trees which had grown wild. He and a few other church members worked with us most of the day cutting, picking up, and bundling branches and hauling them away. By late afternoon he was tired but by now he knew our family and some members of the church By suppertime he was already feeling a whole lot better than he did the day before! I think it was good therapy. He ended up staying in Calgary, later bringing his family. He made significant changes in his life.

I knew and deeply believed that God had *not* abandoned these young adults, even though they appeared to have given up on Him. The godliness with which they were nurtured in their homes and churches can't be shaken off that easily. I believed that and tried to build on that. When I would talk with young adults, they would often tell me they were not interested in the church and say to me, "It is nice of you to invite me, but don't count on me coming." I'd ask permission to ask a question. When that was granted -and it usually was- I'd ask, "Tell me, do you still pray when things go well or when times are tough?" The answer almost always was yes. Then I would say, "That's great," and ask if I could pray with them. A common response was: "I guess that's okay, it couldn't hurt." I'd pray up a storm asking God to pour out His abundant love and blessings, making sure there was not one word of preaching, judgment, or condemnation. And then I'd move along.

Now, more than 40 years later, living in Ontario, I still meet older folks who approach me and ask, "Are you Rev. Wildeboer?" I often answer with something like, "Depends why you ask." They'll mention some relative who lived in Calgary during their wild days and express appreciation and gratitude for what somebody there did for them. It is gratifying that many good changes lasted. I have also met a number of those wild youth who are now older, wise elders and leaders who shake their heads at the craziness of youth today! I remind them that I felt the same way about them some 35 years ago!

Another Impact for Change

Another reason for First Church's change and growth was a strong influence from outside our own congregation. About 15 months after our arrival in Calgary, we heard about revival services being held nightly at a nearby large Pentecostal Church called First Assembly for the 40 nights between Easter and Pentecost. Each evening started with 30-60 minutes of praise followed by a rather long (repetitive) message. This was followed by a time of prayer, altar calls, and the laying on of hands for the filling of the Holy Spirit, or healing. The services drew large crowds including a number of people from First Church who responded to altar calls and were prayed for and had hands laid on them for empowerment. Many of these people experienced changes in their lives.

The fire spread as more members learned about the revival meetings and larger groups began to attend the crusade. I soon received phone calls like: "Rev. Wildeboer (the common title then), you must go soon. I went last night and responded to the altar call, came to the front, was prayed over, and God gave me this wonderful new prayer language." Or another, "I said yes to God last night and for the first time in my life I have this amazing peace in my heart and now without a shadow of doubt I know that my sins have been forgiven!"

But not All

But there were others who described with vehement language what they saw: "Have you gone yet? I think you need to go as soon as possible!" When I asked why, one described the evening as: "After a period of mushy singing and swaying, our minds became like soft putty, they then gave an altar call and told us to come to the front where they prayed over us and confused our people by telling them, 'Now you are a Christian' or, 'Now you are filled with the Holy Spirit!'" One mother strongly urged me to get on the pulpit on Sunday morning and warn our members *not* to go there. "It is phony! It is hypnotism. It is straight from the devil."

No one who attended those services came home unaffected. Feelings were either strongly in favor or against. Discussions in the fellowship hall after our own Sunday services were heated. Many spoke with evangelistic fervor of having *experienced* the reality of the Holy Spirit in one way or another. Though they had been deeply devoted and sincere Christians for years, now something had changed them. As pastor and elders, it was hard to take a stand for or against. We tried to be discerning and make wise decisions, but I know we made some mistakes. In uncharted waters, we were too tolerant and indecisive while buying time to discern how we could be *most* helpful without putting a damper on the fragile flickering fire of new life.

Many of the changes brought about in church members' lives were in harmony with the very basic teaching of the Scriptures. Some members, for the very first time in their lives, sought out others -even their own family members- and apologized for long-standing conflicts or resentments. They confessed and owned their anger, pride, and stubbornness. Some parents confessed to their children that they had been harsh and impatient with them. When a teenager heard this, it made a major impact on him. A 20-year old young man said to me, "Whatever happened to dad, it's real! I like it!" Others who had stopped attending worship services started coming to church again. They said things like, "Something real is drawing me to come."

Unchangeable people Change

Along with the obvious changes, deeper changes were also occurring in our church members. I noticed an increased interest in prayer and Scripture reading, both personally and corporately. Many longed for more and longer times of prayer. An increased hunger for a relevant, authentic, and more participatory style of worship began to challenge us to be creative and moved us away from the traditional pastor-led service to a more participatory one. A hunger for a "Word" from the Lord was frequently expressed as members began to read the Bible increasingly for themselves, in their families, or in small groups. Families who had never before had family devotions now started. Financial giving increased. Some church members became instant "tithers." (For a Dutchman to do that, it *has* to be the Holy Spirit!) Others became inwardly convicted that they could no longer entrust their children to a secular public school system. It was no longer enough to acknowledge that God merely existed. Rather, he was seen as Lord of all creation, and therefore their children had to be enrolled in the Christian School. Calgary was the only community that I know of where Christian School enrollment increased through involvement with the charismatic movement. In other places, the reverse more often occurred. First Church had been known in the Calgary area as a church with poor Christian School attendance among its members, even though I had preached quite passionately about the importance of Christian education. My impact in changing people's minds was minimal. Imagine revival services in a Pentecostal church causing the local Christian school to grow.

Other changes occurred as well. Marriages were restored. Relationships between parents and children became more tender and gracious. Patience grew. We saw change and growth in the fruit of the Spirit. As Jesus said, "By their fruit you may know them." We were seeing good fruit! Sicknesses were prayed for and amazing healings occurred. Some alcoholics quit cold turkey. A few members who had struggled with depression and had been on antidepressants were gradually able to reduce them. Oh, we also saw some extremes, especially in the area of prophecies which we had to address but without condemning the gift of prophecy.

We realized that the new vitality was fragile and early criticism often killed tender growth. When someone came to us pastors with new joy bubbling out of them, released because some other pastor had ministered to them, our tendency was to feel threatened rather than thankful. We had to be in touch with ourselves on that. But our first response was always positive. We genuinely celebrated what God was doing, including the gifts of prophecy, tongues, and interpretations. We were quick to praise God and encourage the work of the Spirit. We knew something good was happening that more than offset the risks of misuse or even "bad theology." We believed our people when they were convinced that they had experienced a fresh touch from God. We had asked for the fire of the Holy Spirit. Do we now run for fire extinguishers when God answers? Controlling a fire often results in putting it out. We repeatedly reminded each other that patience, love, and time would nurture the good and hone the excesses. We were determined to continue to faithfully teach the Scriptures so as to "let the Word of God dwell in you richly." (Colossians 3:16)

And there were Changes in Worship

Until that time the order of worship was the standard one used in many CRCs, as described in the chapter on Sunnyside. In summary, 4-5 hymns, some prayer times, a 25-30 minute sermon, and in the morning the Ten Commandments were read. The PM service was about the same with minor variations. It was easy, predictable, repetitious, and utterly boring for some. For others, it was completely comfortable. It was hard for me to do that same routine week after week with fresh enthusiasm.

More Praise and Involvement

More church members now wanted involvement in planning and leading worship services. This was a big change for us pastors who had previously led the entire service. Others now led times of praise, they led prayer times; they eagerly and powerfully read Scripture passages. And they did well! We also had some willing to give testimonies –ok, some of them did go too long! Some asked if they could put together a service that allowed some musical flexibility. Instruments like guitars, drums, brass instruments - including jazzy sounding saxophones- began to appear more regularly on our platform, next to the pulpit and communion table. For some services we parked the organ! This was shocking to some. I liked the changes but I had to learn to relinquish control, and that was not always easy. At times I cringed at some of the things that were done.

It's hard to believe now (remember this is the seventies!), but we received repeated requests to incorporate the use of drama and "movements" (liturgical dances!) to express physically the message of the hymns, Psalms, and newer songs. Our Confessions state that God is to be worshiped and praised with our whole being, and to us this meant including the use of all the creative arts. Since we knew that dancing before the Lord was already practiced in Old Testament times, it was hard for us to refuse to include this seemingly new expression. Personally, I found it beautiful and appropriate. In fact I was often moved deeply by the beauty and simplicity of the dances. But we also received loud complaints from some who found it "highly offensive and undignified." As elders we moved cautiously. One woman asked me to call her in advance and let her know when a service would include a liturgical dance, so she and her husband could stay home or go to a neighboring church. Bending over backwards not to offend, I did call them a few times until someone told me that this was ridiculous! I called one last time and informed them I would not be calling again. They kept coming anyway.

In the meantime, our dance group which started small expanded with more young people and children and continued to develop and practice movements for more hymns. Some formerly uninvolved members became excited by the opportunity to express their love for the Lord in this way. They would develop their own movements and motions to a particular hymn, demonstrate to some of us, and ask permission to do so in a worship service. We had various emotional reasons for saying no but no biblical reasons. So we didn't. My partner Frank Breisch's comment would stop the debate, "I can't sing, but now when it comes to dancing…"

We also began to use drama, usually as an introduction to a message. Personally, I found drama very effective—it would pull people together on an emotional level, and I could directly and effectively connect with that. An appropriate drama put me as the preacher "on the five-yard line." I could often take the people from where the drama had left them and move directly into the application or challenge coming from the Scripture passage.

And Mistakes

Though we generally did new things well, we never did them perfectly, especially the first few times! Most mistakes were minor, but we also had the occasional blunder. That's just the way it is when one tries new things. In tense settings, a little mistake creates a big discussion. For some, mistakes were inexcusable. The answer for many was the obvious one: If it offends anybody, especially our older members, put a moratorium on it. It did happen occasionally that someone with a microphone in his hands became oblivious to time and didn't know when to quit! Some services went far too long. Occasionally I too could feel the amplified base guitar or the drums through my feet and we'd notice some people with their hands clamped over their ears! We made mistakes and we apologized for them, but I'd rather do that a dozen times than kill the creativity of God's people. We erred on the side of generosity and permission-giving.

Love Tests

It takes love and flexibility to experiment with new forms and ways of expression. Mistakes are the tests that give a read-out on the love, patience, and spiritual maturity thermometer. Many of us had become emotionally invested in a safe, traditional form of worship which was threatened by change. The *form* for some was as significant as the *recipient* of worship. Some people were resistant to change because they dreaded losing control over their emotions. We received comments like, "Why do we need every Peter, Joe, and Susie up there? Aren't you paid for that?" A backlash was developing.

Due to criticism, we toned down some of the jubilation of our Sunday services; we tried not to "offend," a word readily thrown around! The solution became more apparent as time went on. In order to make room for the expression of all these gifts, why not have a time of praise and worship on Saturday nights for those who want and enjoy this freedom. We can then keep our Sunday services closer to the way they have always been? It seemed like a wise compromise. Saturday night praise services began with some 50-100 attendees. They were led by church members without any pastoral involvement or interference! I showed my support by regularly attending, but I was not involved in the planning, leading, or teaching.

We were trying hard to be wise leaders who made room for flexibility even with such gifts as tongues, interpretations, and prophecies with which some of us -including me- were not fully comfortable. I too made room for these spiritual gifts, questioned them at times, but did not actively participate myself. I played it "safe." Sometimes I felt like a chameleon. When I was with charismatic members, I was one of them. When I was with traditionalists, I could authentically and happily sing the old hymns that I've always liked. In one Saturday night worship we sang, "When peace, like a river," and when we sang the third verse, "My sin, not in part but the whole. Is nailed to the cross and I bear it no more," my arms, along with everybody else's were as high as they could be; I was as joyful as I had ever been. It was wonderful!

However, the next morning as I led the Sunday AM worship service, we sang the same hymn. At first I held my arms next to me and felt uncomfortable and phony. The same "spring" that pulled them up the night before was still tugging. Inwardly I am asking all the basic nasty, introspective questions. Am I a hypocrite, a chameleon, or a religious schizophrenic? These thoughts bothered me, and by the third verse, I inwardly said, "no more, here goes" and I raised my arms, just as high as I had done the night before. "Oh, consistency, thou are a jewel." It was liberating, it felt like God showed up and said something like, "Hang loose." I felt honest in my response. It was an issue of *my* obedience to the Scriptures which clearly speak about clapping one's hands, raising one's arms in praise to God, and dancing in praise and exultation. (Remember, this became common practice in the eighties and nineties, *not so* in the seventies!) I longed to express my love for the Lord both motionally and emotionally. Will I do what God wants, or will I continue to be controlled by the lowest common denominator of safe expression? In short, will tradition or Scripture dictate my response? It was as simple as that. Once I realized that, it *was* simple. I claimed to be "Reformed," and if so, "Sola Scriptura" (only the Scriptures) dictates our response. I now believe it is sinful to be controlled by tradition when the Scriptures clearly teach otherwise.

Sure enough, the word was out. I had gone off the deep end! I was publicly marked. It felt a bit like "Do we have need for any further witnesses? We have heard it from his own lips" (Luke 22:71). The obvious evidence was my upraised arms. Some who had long been suspicious of my "leanings" were relieved that I had finally shown my true colors. I was a "charismatic," not a good label at that time for any CRC pastor. It was thrown at me many times, almost always pejoratively. The journey at First Church was changing from one of joy into one of struggles, opposition, and increasing pain. I was about to enter a tough, life-changing phase.

Another Sunday Baby

Exactly two years after our arrival in Calgary, we made another 7:00 AM Sunday morning trip to a hospital, this time in Calgary. Labor pains, as with the birth of Doug three years earlier, again threatened to interfere with worship, this time the two duplicate services at 9:00 and 11:00 AM. When we arrived at the hospital, Jan's labor had slowed and she suggested I go back to church and lead the first service. I did, and right after I finished the message I broke for the kitchen phone, dialed the number of the labor room which I had in my pocket, and soon heard, "We just took her into the delivery room. If you want to be here for the birth of the baby, come now!" A commute usually taking 20 minutes took me only 10, and I was just in time to gown up and welcome little Johnnie, a dark-haired, beautiful boy. We celebrated again with deep gratitude, counted another 10 fingers and 10 toes. Wow, God is good. After thanking God with Jan, Johnnie was sound asleep—a rough morning for that boy! Jan was also exhausted and wanted to sleep, so she said, "Go away, go back to church and preach the message for the second service." I walked into church just after an elder had started the service and he was delighted to see me! As I took over, I shared greetings from Jan and newborn son John from the General Hospital. The entire congregation stood up, clapped, hooted, and whistled, just the way a covenant child is intended to be welcomed by his church family.

The first few years in Calgary were exciting and busy. I worked hard, but I also played hard. Diligently, I would finish the Sunday messages by 4:00 PM on Friday afternoon and go home and not touch any work again until later Saturday night or early Sunday morning. It was time off for the family, and not negotiable, except for too many Saturday weddings. When that happened, I would block off a good part of Monday, but that was not the same, especially during the school years when I was home but the kids were not.

Chapter 7

Joy in Ministry

Calgary, 1974 - 1977

In ministry we often talk about a pastor's honeymoon with a new congregation. Like newlyweds, in the early months of the marriage of congregation and pastor neither can do anything wrong. That changes, however. For some, the honeymoon is short -a year or less- for others, it is much longer.

In Calgary, my honeymoon was quite long. Things took off with a bang. My ministry as pastor and preacher was appreciated, especially when our fresh way of doing things started to bring back many who had left the church. However, more people meant more pastoral challenges which called for more help which in turn required more space. The increased attendance "problem" on Sunday mornings was resolved rather quickly by initiating double morning services, but that did not meet the need for additional staff. The more people became involved with First, the busier I became. Something had to give.

Staff Growth

During this rapid growth period, we began to build a staff team. In the seventies, the common practice was one church one pastor. If one pastor could not care for all the people, the solution was simple -start a second church in another place. Already in seminary, I had a growing conviction that the CRC needed to put more effort and money into building staff teams to work together synergistically. We had too many facilities being unused for too many hours each week. Our current system spent far too much money on maintaining and building more church buildings. In 1972, a year after our arrival, Council decided to apply for a Calvin Seminary intern to work with our church for a year. It was an easy and relatively inexpensive way of having a second pastor, even though that person was temporary – for only one year- and was a seminary student instead of an ordained pastor.

Seminarian Ralph Fluit came and was responsible for youth ministry and assisted with some of the preaching. I supervised and coached him which was our contribution to the seminary. Ralph was followed the next year by Jake Weeda. Others leading our youth ministry in those early years were Hans Altena and Barend Biesheuvel. The youth pastors served for about a year with us before moving on to other ministries. They worked hard to follow up with CRC youth and young adults, especially those who had come to Calgary to get lost. Some with no desire to be found were found by youth pastors or youth elders and became devoted followers of Christ. Others came once or twice only to disappear again. We were by no means 100% successful.

Using interns as temporary youth workers was a good way to help us grow into a team ministry; we were ready to think longer term. We decided to look for someone who could be co-pastor with whom I could split all the areas of ministry into primary and secondary responsibilities. Both of us would contribute in *all* areas but with clear delineation according to our gifts and responsibilities.

The congregation quickly decided that we needed *two* more pastors, one to co-pastor with me in the areas of preaching, education, discipling, and pastoral care. The second would work with the youth and young adults. Salaries and moving and program costs would add about $100,000 to our annual budget which already was $300,000. It was a hefty increase, and it came in the middle of a budget year!

The elders prepared some printed material explaining to church members what we believed needed to be done. We called a congregational meeting to explain our plans at which we faced a variety of questions and concerns. We boldly asked the congregation to approve the budget increase and add two pastors. The motion was adopted by the congregation by a significant majority, indicating, among other things, that most of the congregation was strongly supportive of the direction the leadership was proposing.

Because I had been at First for close to five years already, Council asked me to commit to staying at least another five years. Team ministries were still rare in the CRC, and many of them failed after one or two years often due to the team leader leaving too soon for another ministry. This usually left disillusionment in the congregations about the viability of more than one pastor in a church. Our elders too were skeptical since ministry teams were often racked with tension and conflict instead of stability and growth. I could see no reason why I should not make that commitment, so I did, clearly adding "Deo Volente" (D.V, God willing), and meaning that God was free to intervene and call for a change or a move. As leaders we wanted to be convinced that it was God's call for me to stay. This was new territory for us. I loved the church and the community, and I could not imagine being more effective or feeling more fulfilled. So I said I was ready to commit to staying.

Growth and Conflict

After the Sunday morning worship service when the material was handed out to members of the congregation, a man, who in the past had exerted a lot of power but now seemed to be losing influence, came to me pointing to the place on the page where I had *humanly speaking* committed myself to staying at least another five years. He looked at me and asked, "How can you possibly do that? The Lord may want you elsewhere and by saying this you make yourself unavailable to Him."

His words sounded pious, but everything inside me said, "That is not the real issue." I was not convinced that this man's concern was motivated by my possible unavailability to God. When I smell phony piety, I tend to react quickly -far too quickly- at times. I shoot from the hip before thinking. Before realizing it, I said, "The Lord knows my phone number and address." (Today, I probably would have said, "He has my email address!")

The man looked at me with a disgusted expression and then said it all: "If that happens, we will never get things back to normal." That was it! "Normal" was when he was in charge. In the past, he, and a few other church members had influenced which pastor was called (including me!), how long each stayed, and when it was time for them to move on. In his mind I think I was close to his moving-on point, maybe even past it! He had been one of the people who "courted" me to Calgary, welcomed me "at the train station," and he and others let me know quickly that since they knew the church I would be wise to lean on them; without their wisdom and counsel I would not thrive. Later I learned they had encouraged two previous pastors to accept calls from other churches before things deteriorated and the pastor lost his reputation.

From that day on, this man and about five others began to challenge and oppose every plan that Council presented. They became unhappy -in fact, at times, plainly miserable- with church activities. They complained about our outreach ministries because they felt the community work interfered with the pastoral needs of the church members. They also accused us as Council of giving too much responsibility and power too soon to new members.

As they became more strident in opposing church leaders, they pulled back from congregational ministries. Some even boasted that they were no longer supporting the church financially. As they alienated others, they became more isolated which led to more anger, and for some, even bitterness. Ironically, their complaints actually accelerated their loss of control as other church members became tired of them.

I now realize that the heart of the conflict was really the cost of discipleship. Without knowing it we were becoming a "mission-focused church." We constantly asked ourselves, "How can we better fulfill our calling to be the people of God in the world?" We emphasized that Christian integrity meant *ongoing* sanctification and growth of *all* Christian Reformed members; it was not just for outstanding saints. Lifelong CRC members were not exempt from the calling to grow and change. Some became frustrated with the persistent call and incessant challenge. I think some maybe felt guilty for not being involved with bringing in the harvest, as Jesus speaks of it (see Luke 10:2).

Over time, the contrast between many older and newer members became more obvious. Many newer members quickly invested themselves in church ministries and made changes in their lives, relationships and priorities. The issue of our "charismatic worship" or "Neo-Pentecostalism," wasn't the issue at all for them. The big question was, "Were we willing to deny ourselves, take up our crosses, and follow Him?" As James Elliott said, "Are we ready to lose what we cannot keep in order to gain what we cannot lose?" The call was loud and clear. Many of us were saying, "Yes, but I don't know what that means." Some understandably were more cautious;

some were fearful, even if they never said so. If only we had focused more on the basic question of fear; we addressed everything else but this key issue!

A Unique Ministry Team

In 1974, Pastor Frank Breisch joined us at First Church, coming from a Home Mission church plant in Corvallis, Oregon. He was a solid Bible scholar and a clear thinker. In fact, in his early ministry years he had served as a Bible teacher in Christian schools and had written several books for Bible curricula. He was 10 years older than I was which made up for the fact that I had five years of seniority with the church. We became co-pastors, dividing the work responsibilities, including the preaching. I really appreciated working with him, and we enjoyed a good relationship. Maybe because of his non-Dutch background, I later wondered whether he really ever felt fully accepted by some members of this predominantly Dutch immigrant congregation. Frank disliked the feistiness with which everything was tackled. I didn't like it either but was more used to it.

Frank and I formed a good team. I learned from him how to handle criticism about another person. Church members would come to him and give him a tale of woe as to what someone else had done or about how unhappy they were with aspects of my ministry. He would listen and let them talk until they were done and say, "I am glad you told me this. When I see Henry, I'll let him know we talked and tell him that he can very soon expect to hear from you, right?" Often the person would respond by saying, "But I can't talk to him like I can to you." Frank would then offer to go with him to talk to me or anyone else they had mentioned. "Not to do that would be to gossip, right"? He did not let anyone play us out against each other; this enabled us to work together well in a challenging situation for seven years. He held members accountable for what they said, better than I did most of the time. For that I still respect him.

We complemented each other in other ways as well. I would intuitively do and say things that were mostly right but not always fully worked out. I knew it would work but I couldn't always explain why. Often a Sunday or two later, Frank would explain what we were doing and why. And he would do it in such a biblical and beautiful way that even I was impressed by what

111

I had done, even though at the time when it seemed completely natural and logical, I had not provided any explanation. I acted more intuitively. We were both thoroughly committed to the Scriptures, to a contemporary world and life view, and we were respectful and supportive of one another. The congregation knew it and soon stopped trying to play us against each other.

By 1976, we were ready for a third staff member, a youth pastor. Dean Dyk, a Montana farm boy and recent Calvin Seminary graduate, was called and accepted. He had an unusual mixture of gifts and proved to be the ideal person for the job. He had had some policing experience and could smell a boozer or a druggie a mile away. With a look into a person's eyes, he had a good idea whether he was high and on what. Dean was a ideal pastor for dealing with an urban church's growing flock of youth and young adults. But he also had very credible classical music training. He was a good organist, and as one Calvin professor told me when I was checking references, "He sings like an angel!" During the Christmas season, Dean would often sing solos from Handel's *Messiah* in our special services.

Church 'Police' Work

Dean approached youth work like a policeman who smelled deception and bad behavior and was not afraid to address them. He simply used the youths' struggles as the starting point to address their spiritual hunger. He regularly became exasperated with the intensity of their hormones and their enjoyment of booze. He neither condemned nor condoned their lifestyle but confronted them and minced no words. He challenged them with the will of God. They knew he loved them.

Several memories with Dean stand out for me and still make me chuckle. A number of young adults stayed in various homes and duplexes around the city. Some cheaper rental units in the northeast end of the city were occupied with 12-15 young adults, mostly from Ontario. A group of men would rent one side, and a group of women would rent the other. To be sure, they shared a lot in common. As far as we knew, most of it was wholesome, but we weren't always sure about that. It seemed like a lot of energetic juice flowed in a rather confined area.

The King's House

We also had a duplex owned by a friend of the church, not far from the church called "the King's House." It was occupied by about 8-12 younger people, (ages 18 – 23), men on one side and women on the other. Quite regularly one side of the duplex would cook the main meal and invite the other side to join them. In order to have one larger room for sharing meals together, both sides came to Dean with a request to remove the dividing wall between the two apartments. It was OK with the owner. The removal of the wall would facilitate social activities and joint meals. Dean decided to check with the elders for their advice. It became a controversial issue for them, once they started discussing it. A rather heated discussion ensued. Some felt they must firmly veto the request to remove the wall. One elder wanted to "break up these common-law relationships" and, looking at me, sarcastically asked whether I was "ready to baptize the babies!"

In the end, the wall was removed, and as far as I recall, only one baby from there *was* baptized. One of our youth workers and his wife stayed in the duplex for a long weekend when most of the regular residents were away on a camp-out. Their baby was conceived there! (They had a cute baby; they're wonderful parents and they shall remain unnamed!) To be sure, we chuckled over this many times.

The Beginnings of Sonshine

While this was happening, Jan and I had become friends with a couple named Don and Merviana Cheveldayoff. They were relatively new Christians, joined First Church as members, and quickly took a deep interest in our community ministries. Since he was a realtor and knew the apartment market, I asked him to keep his eyes open for an apartment complex near the church. Repeatedly, members had spoken to our deacons, and one of them, Dan VanderWekken, regularly talked to me about the fact that although we had some duplexes available around the city for groups of young adults (ages 22-27), and we had the King's House for young people (ages 18-23) who often needed help finding work, housing, and food, we had *nothing* to help young families and single parents who were in crises experiencing emotional stress or relational pain with *any* kind of housing. Should we not care for them as we did for our youth and young adults?

These people also regularly appeared in our circles; they showed up at church looking for friends, guidance, counseling, worship, or sometimes just for a place to be with others. Many were broke. How could we help them?

Not long after I shared this with Don, he called and said he had to see me "today!" That was unusual for him, so I made time and he came into my office all excited. "I found 12 apartments for the church, *two six-unit* complexes with mostly two-bedroom apartments *directly across the street from the church* and the parsonage where we were living. The location couldn't be better, the challenge couldn't be bigger. Some of us drooled at the ministries we could provide in these buildings, help for troubled couples, support for abuse victims, rehabilitation into society for recently released prisoners, housing for temporarily separated couples, and places for single parents with children. To some of us, it was an answer to prayer. We were a large church with vast resources to help many people. To us, it was a "no brainer." Still, we had never talked about more than 3-4 units at most, and we were now looking at *12 units*. The total cost was $360,000, -a lot of money– but a fair price that Don indicated would likely result in a quick sale for the sellers.

Dan shared this with the deacons who were ready for something like this. But it would be too major a ministry for the deacons of one church to handle; it needed its own organizational structure and board so as to develop a wider supporting community. The deacons loved the potential but felt the project was too big and came too early for them to make a decision. They decided instead that since a Council meeting was coming up a week later, they would seek Council's wisdom on the matter. Council also was cautious with this big a project, they saw the need and voted in favor of exploring it further. They also thought it should be a ministry endorsed and supported by the church –maybe more than one- but with a separate managing board. Because there was lack of clarity as to who should do this, they were reluctant to make a decision recommending that we as a congregation tie up the buildings. But they are available *now!*

At the Council meeting, Don informed us that two offers were in the making. Time was of the essence. If we first took the time to formally organize and incorporate a board, we would probably lose the properties. So, Don suggested that we tie up the properties with a $15,000 deposit, with the condition that we have 30 days to reconsider the offer. No small task for only 30 days and the more so because there is a large organization to bring along in the process. Some of us stuck our necks out and followed Don's suggestion, and put up the deposit to tie up the property by signing an offer to purchase. It bought us 30 days. After that, we had to say yes or no to remove the conditions from the offer. If yes, we would have another 30 days to raise the down payment of $80,000 leaving a mortgage for the balance of $280,000.

The Ticking Clock

Where do we get 80 grand in four weeks? If we could not come up with the 80 grand, we lose out, but our deposit was not lost. So far, we were safe. These older units were large and good value for the money. They were ideal for families with two, even three, children. The location was perfect for what we planned to do. But it was also a large amount of money to raise at a time when interest rates were really high (about 14% +) and going up, rather than down. The risks made us nervous.

Everybody thought purchasing the buildings was a great idea, but getting (five-year) loans out of their pockets for the down payment was an entirely other story. I learned it is not hard to encourage something if your funds are not involved. With three days to go before the conditions had to be removed we had commitments for $40,000 which was 50% of what we needed. I knew God was in it and it showed when a young couple with minimal income and three young children came with a $10,000 cheque. They had gone to their bank and put a second mortgage on their home. When I asked them why they did it, their response was, "We'd do it for our children, why not for our neighbours?" Through the entire time we were not anxious. We knew without a shadow of doubt that *if* it came about, it would be God's doing. We simply saw the opportunity, presented the challenge, shared the need and only asked for help from those who *wanted* to help, no begging, cajoling, or manipulating. That approach was liberating and did not keep any of us awake at night.

On the Thursday evening before the next day's noon deadline when we had to say yes or no to removing the condition, we had an elders' meeting. Since it was summer, a number of families were away. About 12 were present plus two deacons who came. We shared where we were and that we were $40,000 short of the $80,000 that we would need a month later for the down payment. We asked for informal advice. Most Council members were in favor of the project moving ahead but wondered about us getting involved in buildings *as a church*. We agreed, but what other choice was there for housing help? There was not a rental to be had. We held a straw vote in which most Council members said yes to the concept. All agreed it was needed. Some voted no because they had no money to help it along but all indicated they *would not resist* it if a way could be found to proceed. I suggested that those interested in discussing the decision should come to my office right after the elders' meeting had concluded.

Crunch Time

About 9:30 PM, six of us met in my office, including the two deacons. At that point, there was nothing more to say. I suggested that we each take a slip of paper and write on it "yes" or "no" to withdrawing the condition the next day. If we wrote "yes" we were going to have to come up with the full down payment of 80 grand four weeks later. I thought: "We only have 40 now." While thinking that someone else said: "That should be possible; we *already* have 40!" But we all knew that if we said "yes" that night and we didn't come up with 80 grand in four weeks, we would forfeit the deposit of $15,000. Everyone clearly understood.

We had one pen and one of us handed out the slips of paper and I led in prayer. We sat quietly around the table as one by one we picked up a piece of paper and the pen and wrote one all-significant word. We counted then one by one; three yes, two no, one abstention. The decision was made. That night stands out in my mind as one of the more memorable, beautiful and courageous evenings while in Calgary. We removed the condition the next day, and four weeks later we had all the commitments for the needed down payment. It was done! It was like God's Spirit came and said yes and invited us to say yes with Him. He gave the church an opportunity to partner with Him. And the church said, "We're in." And when we did we became co-partners with Him in this new ministry venture. And He has blessed and more than held up His end through all these years as did a large number of people in the congregation.

116

It was the shot in the arm needed to move forward on a new counseling ministry. Soon, a board was organized and took responsibility for the ministry and the buildings. We now had a building, fully rented with the present tenants, but little else. We began to look for the necessary staff, we knew if the apartments were going to be filled with people with various needs, we would need house parents, counselors, and managers. Salaries for them would require money. We decided to do a faith-promise pledge commitment drive to raise funds to support the staff. We asked the entire congregation to make a monthly commitment to support this new venture, although we still did not know exactly how or what it would be. We received pledges for about $4,000 per month. The church held a special (second) offering on the first Sunday morning of every month when adequate funds were received as regularly as clockwork for a number of years. We were sometimes low but never fell short. First Church took strong ownership of this ministry of justice and mercy for a number of years. Later resources came from other community churches, groups and businesses. Simply put, the Lord blessed it.

Now Staff

The board hired Herman and Betty VanderBurg as the first staff people. They, along with their six children, moved from Toronto to Calgary to take on the challenge. No one who was in First at that time will forget when we heard that the moving van with *all* their belongings had crashed and completely burned up near Swift Current, Saskatchewan as it was traveling across Canada. Everything was lost! This resulted in an amazing outpouring of love from First Church of clothes, furniture, household goods, and appliances, including a new stereo set because someone knew that Herman loved good music. Immediately, Herman, Betty and family were endeared to our church family.

As Herman and Betty loved, reached out, and counseled many Calgary people, the Lord blessed the ministry which by then was called Sonshine. It provided quality counseling and care for married couples and single parents. It quickly became a place of blessing and hope. It provided help and support for abuse victims. As Sonshine grew, additional support flowed in from other congregations, individuals, and businesses. Beginning small in 1978 by reaching out to a few homeless families, those in the pain of a divorce, or in the trauma of abuse, it now has counseling support, help, and housing available for youth, young adults, and families.

The ministry has grown and has won a variety of awards for providing excellent social services. In 1989, the services were adjusted to focus on family violence. Today, Sonshine Centre operates a 24-unit second stage shelter that offers a one-year residential counseling program for women and their children who have experienced violence and abuse. Close to 60% of funding for operating costs now comes from donations from individuals and corporations. The balance is received from rental income, grants and counseling fees. The start and continuation of Sonshine is God's doing. Much credit also goes to some diligent, patient, and persevering board members. And without Herman and Betty, as they are known to all, it would not have become what it is.

Youth Challenges

For First Church, though, the biggest challenge was ministering effectively to our youth and young adults ages 16-25. With them we realized the truth of the dictum, "Communicate the gospel constantly and use words if you have to." We had to model godliness and practice *doing* the gospel consistently, which was the way we earned credibility. Modeling authenticity consistently was our big challenge; if we got that somewhat right, we might be able to help, teach, and counsel our youth and young adults who were constantly tested facing moral challenges every day. They were bombarded with temptations and seductions. In a heated, hedonistic and materialistic culture where everything revolved around achievements, accomplishments, and acquisitions, a lukewarm Christianity would not stem the tide.

Dean especially dealt with these issues on a daily basis. For some of our young adults, alcohol use was a problem. Drugs were less common. Dean and all of us staff addressed these issues in sermons, especially the abusive use of alcohol. We knew drinking parties were regularly happening. At the end of one such celebration, one of our young adults was killed on the way home in a single-car crash. It was a wakeup call.

As pastors we struggled together as we prepared for the funeral. Though we asked Frank to preach the message for the funeral, we discussed as to how we could handle this with biblical, pastoral, sensitivity and integrity. We knew the church would be filled with young people and young adults, all coming with one basic question: "How are you preachers going to handle this one?" They, like most people at funerals, were anticipating a message that would make everything well. It was the proverbial elephant in the room. Someone who seemed to be living a lifestyle like many of them were, was suddenly killed. What would we make of that and what words of comfort would we give? Can we "fix it" somehow? Do we communicate that no matter how one lived, what values he practiced, or what priorities he adhered to, as long as he had correct theological thinking, pastors will comfort with heavenly peace? That seemed to be a prevalent, unspoken attitude present especially at funerals.

Balancing Truth and Love

When the ending is wrong and tragic, we want God to be portrayed as gracious and loving, forgiving and merciful. That's not the time we want to hear about His justice. As a pastor, I have at such times felt the tension between being nice and honest. I have been less than truthful because it was less painful. I have yielded to the temptation to give comfort that glossed over the reality of the two ways -one broad, the other narrow. We are also *not* to be judgmental which creates a tough dilemma at times.

Frank first gave comfort but he also spoke truth. He did not polarize comfort, mercy and justice. Any death, tragic or otherwise, casts one into the arms of the Lord who knows all things perfectly and who is able to combine His perfect justice and mercy, keeping in perfect balance what we can't. The word "perfect" is absolutely essential. God is the only one who is privileged to be fully present in *every* human experience, including sudden fatal car crashes. He was there and knows precisely every thought and word that transpired in those vital last moments. Therefore, with confidence we leave tragic, unexplainable deaths in the hands of the one who dispenses perfect justice, mercy, and grace, because of the work of Jesus Christ. There is absolutely no better place to leave a loved one.

That is the *good news* of the Gospel and provides a measure of comfort for *every* funeral. With every death we have to release our loved ones to someone when the end comes. Doesn't it make sense to release them to the

119

best one possible; the hands of the perfect one? The worst sinner finds perfect justice in the very hands of God who though angry at sin comes to us with mercy and grace. No matter how many challenging questions we have, ultimately we stand before Him empty handed holding them out to receive from Him what only He can give, comfort. No matter who one is, or how he happens to die, at the end he meets his God who knows all and does perfectly right *every time*. Though hard to grasp, this is our comfort. It is the good news for any difficult, tragic death, including a suicide. As a pastor I find it very comforting to leave every deceased person in the hands of the God who "full of grace and truth" holds those two things in perfect balance. Perfect justice, perfect love, every time.

After explaining that Frank secondly gave a stern warning in that God will not be mocked. Because He knows all things perfectly He is knowledgeable about our response to His gift of grace and aware as to how we responded to his knock on the door of our hearts. (Rev. 3:20) God is unmistakably clear about the importance of believing in our hearts and confessing with our lips (Romans 10). The Word is a two-edged sword cutting both ways. It comforts us and pleads with us that we live in a relationship of truth and love with Him. It is also a word of warning by which God pleads with us to be reconciled with Him.

The funeral service challenged everyone present to evaluate their priorities and lifestyles, for "you know neither the day nor the hour." I believe it made a big impact on all who were there but -like most sermons- I wonder about the shelf life of the impact. The funeral was authentic and touched many but not all. As life continues the effectiveness of any event and sermon wears off. It's one of the reasons why we get up on pulpits *every* Sunday and do it again… and again.

Life Goes on

Later that summer on the Tuesday morning after the August long weekend, Dean came into my office. He was deeply troubled. The young adults from a north-end duplex had gone to Kelowna, British Columbia for a campout weekend, returning on Monday afternoon. In Dean's words, it had been a "drunken mess." He was utterly disheartened since it had happened before and he had discussed it with them –more than once. They had promised him it would not happen again, and he thought they had amended their ways. Dean felt he needed to visit them again but he dreaded it. I remember him saying, "What more can I say? I have sung all the stanzas there are of that hymn." On the spur of the moment I asked him, "Want to visit them together? Would you like me to go with you?" He liked the idea and said, "It would really be good for them to know that you too care." He would call each side of the duplex and tell them to be home at 10:00 PM the following night: "Be there," policeman style!

On the following night, a beautiful evening with late Calgary daylight, Dean and I drove to the duplex just before 10:00 PM. We arrived with the car windows open, as were the windows of the duplex. As we were getting out of the car, we clearly heard a female voice say, "Oh s--t, it's both of them!"

That was our introduction to an honest discussion. Did our visit with them make a difference? We'd like to think so. I know that years later when I would meet some of these young adults again, they would remind me of some of those visits and even remember some of the things I had said. When meeting later with them many had become as traditional as their middle-aged parents whom they had earlier criticized. They were now trying to raise their own youth! Makes a big difference as to what end they are on! I have been proudly introduced to their parents, spouses, and even children!

By all Means Win Some, Challenges

New commitments and a flow of new people energized our creativity. We sought all kinds of ways to attract others. We were biblical but not traditional. Many of our newcomers had only traditional services in their arsenal of experience. Our worship services were regularly led with instruments like guitars and drums, even banjos. Some CRC members were incensed when other member - especially those sitting near them- raised their hands or clapped. In the seventies, CRC people just didn't do that! Others challenged the "off-the-wall" singing aided by overhead projectors, popular at that time, now replaced by PowerPoint and projectors. They disliked the repetitious newer songs (later called 7/11 songs, 7 lines sung 11 times- and some were). Some long-time members saw positive changes in these young people and cautiously forfeited their preferences for a more traditional approach. Many genuinely rejoiced when someone's life was changed and the person testified to the fact.

About that time, Dean Dyk received a note from a pastor in Ontario asking him to visit two sisters who had moved to Calgary some six months earlier. They lived with three other young women, and Dean wondered if I would visit this group of five young ladies, all aged from 23-28. I said I would. When I called ahead to arrange the visit, they immediately informed me: "We're kind of done with church and we're not really interested in church stuff." I told them I wasn't interested in a "church conversation" either but would like to stop by and briefly meet them. Permission to visit was reluctantly granted. We mutually set a time.

Costly Furniture

When I arrived around 9:30 PM in the evening, they were waiting for me with coffee and cookies. They told me their parents had trained them that way to prepare for the visit of the "Dominee" (common term for a minister in Dutch). The coffee was served on a unique coffee table in the middle of the room that was about 75 cm wide and one meter long (2' X 3') and consisted entirely of empty cases of beer bottles, neatly stacked in the form of a coffee table with a nice piece of cardboard as the table top. With many new people moving into the city used furniture was hard to find in Calgary; I was sitting on a lawn chair.

As we began to chat, I remarked about the unique coffee table. Rather proudly, one of them told me that they had not bought *any* of the beer! It was all given to them, to which I replied, "Ohhh, this could be an expensive table. What *did* it cost?"

It became very quiet until one young woman repeated my "ohhh," and then asked me what I thought they might have paid for it. I said I didn't know - that's why I asked. "You tell me." This led into a very interesting conversation. As I usually do before leaving I asked if I could pray with them. How does a CRC kid say no to that? I prayed for God to bless them so abundantly that they simply could not fail to see His goodness and love. I ended the visit with our standard invitation: "Come just once and if you don't like it, tell me and I promise we won't bother you again." With some,

122

that promise was more attractive than the invitation to come. I think two of the young women came back. I do not know what happened to the rest of the group. They, like many of them, came to Calgary, stayed a while and then moved on, maybe to Edmonton, Vancouver or back home, and often without anyone of us knowing they were leaving or where they were going.

The Power of Example

Some young adults, after one or two visits at the church, wanted to get involved. They would offer to teach a class of Sunday school kids; sometimes we let them before we knew much about them. (Today that probably would not happen due to abuse issues and protection policies relating to boundaries.) But there is nothing more challenging to one's own morals than standing in front of a bunch of 10-year-old kids teaching a Sunday school class on godly living. If you want to see wild lives changed, that will do it. The teaching experience required them to be genuine. In front of a bunch of curious honest kids they could not get away with hypocrisy.

One afternoon just before I was going to go home I remember a young man with a black, scruffy beard from eastern Ontario strutted into my office. He proudly informed me that he had not gone to church for over five years even though he had been raised in the CRC. He added that he was a singer and loved to play his guitar. It was the perfect time for me to play the come-once invite, "come *once*, and we'll leave you alone." His response to me was, "Only if I can bring my guitar and play."

Stay and Play

A bulb flashed in my brain, and I responded with, "That's fine, but come to an evening service." That was the more relaxed, informal service in which other instruments besides organ and piano were used. What we did at night was not as carefully scrutinized nor as severely criticized.

A few weeks later the young man showed up early on a Sunday morning along with the all-practiced-up-and-prepared Praise Team. He went up front with his guitar and joined the group. No one knew who he was, but they quickly realized that he was a good player. When I came into church a little later for the AM service, one of the leaders cornered me and asked,

"What do we do with this guy? He just showed up, didn't say anything except that you had invited him to come and play."

I asked if he was bothersome, and they said, "No, not really, although our guidelines state that if anyone missed the practice before the service they are scheduled to lead, they were not allowed to play for that service. He also wants to sing a solo!" We decided to let him play, and he sang his solo. Risky, yes, but by the end of the service he was hooked and began to worship regularly with us. But we also heard about this "unkempt guy." Some were offended by his appearance and his church apparel: bushy, dark, far-from-clean hair; a pair of torn blue jeans and a colorful Western shirt, both of which fit far too tight for appropriate worship attire! I know I could have avoided some unpleasant chatter had I stopped him. If I had, he probably would have left and my guess is that we might never have seen him again. His relationship to God was more important than a confrontation with our comfort zone.

Joy in Worship, Life Changes

We did more things like that that seemed unwise to some but quite acceptable to a young person searching for reality. We as staff believed that every person who came our way was entitled to unconditional acceptance, love, and forgiveness as we had read in a book by that title written by Pastor Jerry Cook. Visitors returned if they experienced acceptance on their first visit. We took risks by getting some new people involved early in their journey with us. Most people understood that they needed to present the best of their gifts but they did not have to wait to serve and lead publicly until they could do it flawlessly. Their involvement led to their sense of belonging, which often resulted in their making new commitments and changes.

In Sunnyside, I had diligently practiced what I believed to be the right order: You *first believe*, make profession of faith, and then you *belong*. Believing and profession then opened the doors to roles in ministry and leadership. In Calgary, I learned that young adults were usually indifferent about membership issues. If they felt they belonged (they experienced acceptance), they viewed themselves as members, whether they had made profession of faith or not. Some would come and request "budget envelopes" (CRC jargon) or "tithing envelopes" (for those with Evangelical or Pentecostal background) for their financial support. As staff we celebrated that as joyfully as if they had just made profession of faith. "Believing" often came later as did public profession of faith. Once someone became financially involved, they became a ministry supporter and it wasn't hard to then ask, "Wouldn't it make good sense for you to profess what you believe?" Many did and accompanied their professions with testimonies. We included these in our evening services and the celebrations were often followed with coffee and cake. It *always* added to the vibrancy and the attendance of those services. Visitors, even on a first visit, were often hooked. I think it's the kind of "fishing" Jesus talks about when he is looking for "fishers of men" rather than fishermen.

Fresh Power

All these things empowered us! It was exciting to see lives change. That kept us going even through criticism - carping, was how it often felt to me. But the more lives we saw changed, the less attention we paid to the criticism. As more people responded to the Lord, we took more risks. We began to add altar calls, inviting worshipers to come forward for specific prayer, often accompanied by the laying on of hands. As leaders we encouraged others to clap their hands or raise their arms simply by doing it ourselves. What we modeled, the church would do too, sooner or later.

One evening after a time of vibrant praise and heartfelt prayer, I preached that Christians needed the "whole armor of God" to stand against the schemes of Satan in this "present world, and against the spiritual forces of evil" (Ephesians 6). I introduced each part of the armor and explained its function and then stated, "Now some of you know the reality of this better than I do. So we will sing the hymn "Christian Do you Struggle?" (Psalter Hymnal, 1987 edition, number 575). This is a hymn with simple, specific lyrics about the battle Christians wage against the powers of darkness, and the absolute need for prayer and Holy Spirit empowerment. I then added, "At the end of the hymn, I will sit down, and then if any of you want to share some thoughts on how you handle this struggle, please come forward."

I wasn't sure if anyone would take me up on this request since I had never made it before. I sat down and realized the risk I had taken when I saw another dark-bearded, bushy-haired young man get up in the back of the balcony, make his way to the stairs, and head down the main aisle. I panicked briefly. What might he say? Will I lose control? Oh no, he *is* coming! I had no idea who he was. By now, he was strutting down the aisle wearing blue jeans, a Western shirt, boots -the only thing missing was a wide-brimmed, Calgary cowboy hat! He marched to the pulpit on the stage, began to speak, and proceeded to give a 5-7 minute testimony that "rang like a bell!" Everyone was perfectly quiet and attentive, and I believe he touched more hearts and lives than I did in that service. It was anointed. God obviously spoke through his words and no one ever dared to criticize them. The young man, Ron Dees, became a deeply committed Christian, married a wonderful young woman from the congregation, and has served effectively as a leader and elder for several terms. They have a great family and are still actively involved in the church! Afterwards I was glad I took the risk; the Lord blessed it. Hindsight is so perfect.

Prayer and Prayer Requests

The charismatic influence nurtured many members to become urgent about prayer, both private and public. We began to have extensive prayer times in our evening services, taking time to share prayer needs. At first, prayer requests were quite generic: "for sick people in the hospitals, for the students who are anxious about exams, and for our missionaries for whatever they stand in need of." Over time, more specific needs became requests: "for my mother who is going in for a hysterectomy, for my friend who is failing in school, for a cousin whose parents are separated." Today those kinds of requests are common, but in the seventies they were not.

One night we had two prayer requests that stirred up questions. The first would have been all right in itself. It was from a young boy who asked us to pray for his puppy who had been sick with bad case of diarrhea for nearly two weeks. "It's making a mess all over the house." And then in childlike, non-church terminology, he explained how bad a mess it was creating and how his mother was reacting. After he finished his request, I wondered, "How do I handle this?" We prayed for God to heal the puppy. A second request came from a young man, about age 20, who emotionally asked for prayer for his sister and her husband in one of the Brampton, Ontario churches who were experiencing marriage problems. This was fine, but then he went on to explain how critical the problems were and how the minister who was counseling them didn't have a clue as to how to help them. We had a number of people from Brampton who knew exactly whom he was talking about. It became embarrassingly uncomfortable. I stopped him from providing more details by saying, "I am sure he is offering the best that he has and we will pray for healing." We did. During prayer request time, I learned to think on my feet.

At our next elders meeting, we had a written motion "to have no more verbal prayer requests." The goal was to avoid embarrassing situations. Only written requests would be received *before* the service, and two elders would review them. I admit sometimes for the sake of flexibility and creativity, we stretched boundaries. But this was overkill -in order to make *no* mistakes we would ban *all* verbal requests. If the motion passed, an important part of our worship would become fully controlled, safe and predictable.

The motion did not pass. We instead constantly challenged each other to stay fresh. We vowed to be careful, and over time requests became more specific. The more specific they became, the more often we saw specific answers. Members regularly asked for help to stop smoking or drinking, for peace as they faced major surgery, for help with children or teenagers, for God to move in the hearts of sons and daughters to create a hunger for worship. When God answered our prayers we celebrated and rejoiced. We regularly offered clap offerings of praise to the Lord.

God Shows up and Affirms

About that time, a major tornado ripped through the Woodstock, Ontario area. Homes, farms, schools, and churches were damaged, if not destroyed. Since we had a number of young adults from the area, we immediately heard about how some of their families had been affected. In our evening service it was a major prayer concern. We prayed for the Woodstock community.

Two days later I was at the office ready to go home when I heard a timid knock on my door. It was an elderly man I did not know but I had seen in church several times. After introducing himself as a member of a Lutheran church, he told me he viewed First as his church because he and his wife came for evening services after attending their own church in the morning. They were present Sunday night, heard the prayer request for Woodstock where he had family, and were moved by it. As he spoke, he pulled an envelope out of his pocket and laid it on my desk with the comment, "When the church has an offering for those needs, would you see to it that this is included?" A few more comments and with that he left as quietly as he had come. I took the open envelope, looked inside and saw four new, crisp one-hundred dollar bills. All out of a simple prayer request made a week before!

Often we found that if we tried something new and it had not gone well, a few weeks later the opposite would happen. Something beautiful would occur unexpectedly and virtually outside the realm of possibility. It was as if God smiled and said, "Don't take yourselves so seriously."

To me these were the affirmations we needed to know that God still had His eye on us even though increasing tensions created an air of distrust and hostility. I began to dread Council meetings because I never knew when the next curve ball would appear no matter how carefully we had prepared the agenda. These curves appeared when someone would say something like, "Pastor, can I ask a question that I was asked this week to which I didn't know how to respond but promised I'd check with you?" My response often was a cautious one: "If it's just a question for me, catch me after the meeting." When that was declined with, "But some of the other elders have the same questions," I knew that another agenda was about to take over the order of the day.

Blessed Again!

In the meantime, as a family we were enjoying wonderful blessings of life, health, and energetic little children. Two girls and two boys made us a busy but happy family. On July 10, 1976, child number five, our youngest, announced the time for arrival on a beautiful, warm Saturday morning. Most considerably it was my day off, instead of Sunday morning, the other times! This time we went to Holy Cross Hospital close to where we lived and where our obstetrician-gynecologist practiced his specialty, delivering babies. About 9:00 AM we made our way to the hospital. This time, though, I was allowed to share the entire journey of labor and delivery with Jan, a major change between 1970 when Doug was born and now, 1976. I groaned along with Jan, I wiped up sweat, I held her hands; wiped her forehead, and I cut the umbilical cord! I thought I was extremely helpful!

About noon Robert Scott made his appearance, another healthy boy. We again counted 10 toes, 10 fingers -everything was there! And again we thanked God. Later it dawned on me that counting and thanking God for those fingers with each birth was important. Maybe because my brother Bill's lack of five could have stopped the family from immigration. Fingers and hands have a special meaning for us; they are important! We now had two girls, 15 months apart, and three boys, the first one arriving three years after Barbara and the other two each coming three years after the one before. We felt we had the perfect family, each birth perfectly timed by God. What a joy they were to raise, and what a blessing they are to us. The lines have fallen to us in pleasant places. We look back on a wonderful journey.

Don't Upset Me

Back home in the meantime there is a church. This was the time when we saw more energized young people in church in their street attire, -blue jeans – faded and torn preferably were in. We saw people who were searching and open. Others saw dirt, long hair, beards, or offensively short skirts. I would often hear reports that were so exaggerated I could not even figure out what they were talking about. Some of the critical neighboring pastors and elders heard these stories also. Puzzled, they would ask me or one of our elders, "Why do you encourage things like that when you know how upsetting it is to good people?"

We were not intentionally aggravating anybody. Colleagues would chat with me, and in the course of the visit I felt like I was being examined. Maybe I was becoming paranoid. I was often asked –rarely directly- what I thought it was to be Reformed. I was not asked for a biblical explanation for our practices.

Our view of church as *mission* conflicted with the prevailing view that saw the church's primary responsibility to be taking care of her members, *maintenance* as it is often called. We wanted to be effective in reaching others. As older Christians, we needed to be *most* flexible to stretch as much as was needed to nurture new spiritual babies. In a family the baby sets the schedule, at least for a while. Parents cannot raise healthy children if their predominant attitude is saturated with "it's all about me." When I heard, "But I am just not comfortable with that," I could hardly resist the retort of, "So what? What makes you think that your level of comfort is the standard by which God is honored?" Christ told us clearly that to win and nurture people into discipleship required huge costs and calls for self-denial. That *is* uncomfortable. The underlying self-centeredness --even arrogance-- that evaluates everything on the basis of *"my* comfort level" is unbiblical if not downright selfish. For them it was the standard by which all else was evaluated.

Complaints continued and dissension grew. As staff, we spent an inordinate amount of time teaching, and explaining our actions and how they biblically fit into a Reformed church. Pastor Breisch especially worked hard at teaching contemporary, solid Reformed theology. In due time, the critics would not accept this from him either. In Council meetings, some elders tried to pass motions that would revert us back to earlier days, but they could never muster enough votes. They became more and more frustrated. Their constant request to Council and Classis was, "We just want to be a normal Christian Reformed Church!" whatever that was.

I understood that this was both annoying and disheartening for these church members. Some elders, mostly older ones, resigned in frustration. Their friends who held similar views had so often heard their complaints that when they were nominated for Council they too declined to serve. As a result, the balance of Council became more lopsided as more progressive young men became elders. No women served at that time. The makeup of our leadership team was changing. Sooner or later, a clash was bound to happen.

Chapter 8

The Storm Builds

Calgary, 1977 – 1980

Once talk about the conflict at First Church became public, it quickly spread. Many heard I was in trouble. I received phone calls from colleagues in different parts of Canada; seminary classmates expressed concern. Those who knew us well were generally supportive and concerned with the well-being of our family, including Jan and the kids.

When there is conflict in a CR church, the local Classis (a group of churches in a regional area) can decide to appoint a team of "church visitors," two or more experienced representatives, to evaluate, assist, advise, or admonish a local church Council if needed. Appointed by Classis these teams help hold a congregation accountable to the Classis and through Classis to biblical standards and denominational principles as established by Synod, the largest, top governing body of the denomination. Different teams of church visitors were appointed to First Church, but it seemed to us that the church visitors who were appointed had a common bias against anything charismatic as was also still predominant with the entire denomination.. They started with sympathy for those who were opposed to Council. They met more often with those who disagreed with the direction of the church than they did with Council even though our Church Order makes clear that, to retain responsible accountability, church visitors are *not* to meet with members or groups of members without informing Council, or without having Council members present. That was ignored.

Repeatedly, we had to explain and defend that we could include the charismatic gifts of our members, make changes in worship and ministries and still be thoroughly Reformed. We kept hearing from the church visitors, "Wonderful things are happening and lives are changed for the better but…" and the "but" was always followed by a litany of dissenting comments, out of concern that we retain "good order" and uphold the "ways of the past." The famous black and white question that we heard

131

many times was: "Were we all wrong before when we did not do things this way?"

The church visitors recommended to Classis that the concerns and dissent in First Church warranted investigation. There was no protest or appeal of any kind. The investigation was initiated merely on the basis of complaints, rumors, and gossip. The October 16, 1978 Classis meeting appointed and mandated a committee of six people, two pastors and four elders:

> *To investigate the various movements in the church and the lead personalities involved in order to find out if these suspicions have any grounds.*

We objected to what seemed to us like a wide-open mandate to go on a witch hunt. Classis overruled our objections. The committee and mandate were initiated.

About a year later, that committee issued a report that was predominantly critical of what was happening in First Church, especially in the area of pastoral leadership. Note some of the statements:

We are concerned about the matter of congregational leadership. Have the pastors presented leadership that is becoming to ministers in the reformed tradition? Your committee has a number of serious objections.

1. We cannot escape the notion that the pastors are influenced by a certain stripe of church growth theologians with their particular view of ecclesiology, to wit Munger, McGavran, etc.
2. There seems to be more emphasis on reaching out than on pastoral care within the congregation. (See interviews with church members on tape…)
3. With regard to movements and influences from outside the church that could undermine the Reformed faith there has been very little warning. One example is the appearance of a certain Marvin Schmidt, a faith healer. Very little guidance and direction has been presented to lead the right way.

Another concern dealt with the gift of prophecy which was present and had been troublesome for us too in the earlier stages of our charismatic renewal. Though our Council gave clear and biblical guidelines as to how that gift could be deployed in a Reformed church, these guidelines were not always followed. The church visitors, in response to some members of

First, wanted Council to state categorically that the gift of prophecy had ceased with the closing of the Canon of Scripture, and thus all prophecy was spurious. Their solution was simple: Forbid it! Period! Though that would have been the easier route to go, we could not do so with a clear conscience, especially when a 1973 denominational report on Neo-Pentecostalism stated that there was no *biblical* evidence to indicate that certain gifts had ceased after the "closing of the Canon of Scripture." As Council we were in harmony with what Synod stated; we could not forbid with integrity the use of any of the spiritual gifts just to keep peace. But we were under intense pressure to go that way.

The Classis committee summarized its concerns:

> *Something must be said about the soil out of which the spiritual and numerical growth in First Church has developed. We are thankful for the growth in the church, both numerical and spiritual... The charismatic movement has crossed many denominational lines and has given much of the impetus for a new awareness of the Spirit and His gifts. There is within the CRC today a real lack of Biblical discernment. The faith of many, although very genuine, is also very shallow. Much of the literature that people read today is very simplistic and superficial.... We feel it is this Pentecostal, fundamentalist literature that is feeding some of the lead personalities in First Church. The soil in which the growth is planted is not truly Biblically Reformed.* (Page 4 of report)

In short, the committee presented this critical report that encouraged the "concerned members" to continue their criticisms. (By now they were known as "concerned members" as the church visitors referred to them. To others they were "aggrieved members." To Council and to the delegates at Classis, that became their title. They even referred to themselves as "the aggrieved members").

As Council, we challenged the report at the Classis meeting. So did many Classical delegates, so much so that it became obvious that their recommendations were not likely to pass. Instead of making a decision or taking action on the report, Classis decided to thank the committee of six and release them. They worked for a year but had been of no help. For us as elders and the congregation it was an exercise in frustration; it didn't help us at all, it provided nothing to unify us, and the aggrieved members felt that we hadn't "heard" them at all.

We had. We simply didn't agree with their concerns.

The storm continued to ebb. It seemed to revolve around the question as to who *owns* the church and *who* sets her direction? The aggrieved were convinced that Council was clearly on the wrong track and saw us departing from the way of the fathers. It was their God-given duty to do all they could to stop the deterioration. We pastors and Council were equally convinced we were on track in becoming more of an outreaching church with deeper, fruit-bearing roots in our Calgary community. We lived with constant tension balanced for many of us by the joy of seeing changed lives and growth in spiritual vitality. If this was the price we had to pay to help people grow, just as messy diapers come with new babies, and slobbering and spilling are part of any family blessed with preschool kids, so be it. We were just trying to grow up.

Conflict, Discouragement, Division

Tensions grew. Unhappy groups of members met, sometimes with a neighboring pastor or with the church visitors. We often learned about these meetings after they had been held. It became obvious; the goal was to get rid of me. They thought once I was gone, they could deal with Council. (They were so wrong about that.) The aggrieved church members were building support among people even outside of First Church, especially among people who might be delegates at a future Classis meeting. Some of these people started coming to me suggesting that for the sake of peace I should do the sacrificial act of resigning. Some of these suggestions came wrapped in icing sugar, others were bathed in lemon juice.

It was a tough time. Quitting looked attractive, and I offered it more than once to the elders who strongly advised against it. They were convinced it would not solve anything except leave them vulnerable. Each night I went home from church more discouraged than before. I began to wake up in the middle of the night with fear and darkness surrounding me. Sometimes I managed to go back to sleep, but many nights I tossed and turned from around 2:00 AM till about 6:00 AM. When it was almost time to get up, I'd fall asleep again. This went on for several months. I realized I was becoming depressed.

I was deceiving others that I was fine. I thought that since God continued to use my preaching, I must be okay. And, strangely, I never lacked passion and I never ran out of Scripture topics to preach about. But I wondered how I could be in such pain every night yet function so well during the day? Am I turning schizophrenic, bi-polar?

Sometime later I concluded that perhaps the Lord loves His church too much to allow one hurting preacher to mess it up. That was weird comfort. Many nights when I could not sleep, at 2:00 or 3:00 AM, I would go downstairs and sit on a couch in the living room, look out the front window, and see the light on top of the Calgary Tower blink on and off 51 times a minute with a steady rhythm. I wondered how long can I continue like this without collapsing? I was in contact with enough counselors to know that extensive periods of sleeplessness carry a price tag. I began to fear the ultimate: a nervous breakdown requiring intensive therapy with medication or, worse, hospitalization. Near Lacombe, Alberta, where I lived as a youth, was Alberta Hospital in the town of Ponoka. It was a large provincial hospital for people with mental illnesses. I knew it well since one summer between school terms I worked there doing gardening, lawns etc. with patients. I loved the work and my co-workers!

But all Albertans knew about Ponoka! As kids, we made fun of the place and jokingly teased each other, "You're ready for Ponoka," something not funny at all. The one place I did *not* want to go was Ponoka. It still had that stigma for me.

As low and fearful as I was, my pride and self-image were still high. If I left, the aggrieved members could use that and say, "See, we knew all along that he was..." I couldn't stand that thought. Early one morning while I was wrestling on the living room floor (again), I realized it was pure pride that was controlling my spirit of fear. I also remembered a statement by Job (3:25), "What I feared has come upon me." Fear of Ponoka was bigger than God. I wrestled, "please don't send me there! Please..." It was as if God was there with a spirit of peace and said, "If you go to Ponoka, I'll be there too." My response was, "Okay God, if you want me to go to Ponoka,

I'll go, and since you said you'd never leave me nor forsake me, if for some reason it honors you that I go there, let's go!" I meant it! At that moment I surrendered the fight, let go and gave up. Doing so broke the fear and I knew from that moment that if I had to go, I was not going alone; we were going together, God and I. For the fear to be broken I had to learn that *nothing* in this world is so big that it would separate me from the love of God (Romans 8:39). My call is to stay close to Him, and draw from Him, only then can I do all things! Enabled to be ruthlessly honest with myself, I soon began to improve, quite rapidly. I was relieved that I didn't have to go.

A Petition

At the April 10, 1980 meeting of Council, we were made aware that two young men were circulating a petition through the congregation. The petition in essence stated that the signers were withholding financial support from the church's general fund until such time that unity was restored "by Council in dealing with all Neo-Pentecostalism in First Church."

The elders knew that the two men were not the creators of the petition. Who was behind it? We had our suspicions. We appointed two teams of two elders to visit each of their homes. When the elders called to set up the meetings, the men asked us to meet with both of them at one home along with someone else. They also wanted me to come.

We made the visit on April 23, 1980. As we arrived, I noticed that one of our members, I'll call him "Joe," was also there. Before we even sat down he addressed us:

"I told these fellows, if you want a response from Wildeboer and the elders, just hit them in the pocketbook. That always works, see! We hit you with money and within a week you come running."

He went on for several minutes in a loud tone and with anger; when he stopped, one of our elders answered softly and graciously but firmly with a response I will not forget:

"Joe, the Bible clearly teaches that to attack God's anointed is a dangerous thing to do. As elders and pastor we are far from perfect; we have made mistakes but I tell you we are God's anointed. When you attack this way I believe you dishonor the Lord. It is a risky thing to do."

The words of the elder and his expression of them made me shiver. It was now quiet in the room. Joe and the two young men recovered quite rapidly, though, and made more similar vituperative comments.

We tried to respond. To argue seemed futile, so we did not stay long. We did quote a rather amazingly appropriate Synodical decision adopted by the Synod of 1864, stated under Church Order Article 80. For those desiring a traditional approach, a document from 1864 certainly qualified.

g. Withholding financial support

Members able but unwilling to contribute to the support of the church and the poor are to be admonished; and, upon continued delinquency, to be ecclesiastically disciplined.

(Minutes of June 1 1864, Article 12. See Manual of Christian Reformed Church Government, (2001 Revision), under Church Article 80, 4, Specific Cases, f, 4, g. Page 444.)

We read the statement to them, they understood it well. One of us led in prayer and we left. All of this was fairly brief but very much to the point.

Since a number of people in the congregation had signed the petition, we decided to place this synodical statement in the bulletin and the petition mysteriously disappeared in only a few days. The anger and criticism did not. The aggrieved members were now openly expressing that my time as pastor in First Church was over. They were angry and determined, it stung. Their criticism was giving me sleepless nights but I dared not weaken or break in front of them. I was reminded of my boyhood farm days. If a bull knew that I was afraid of him, he'd have me out of his pasture in no time flat. He could smell my fear! That's how I felt with the critics -if they knew I was fearful, I'd soon be looking for another pasture. Instead, I continued to try to communicate with them, but it seemed that every discussion ended with them telling me that they couldn't see why I couldn't see that it was time to go. And they truly believed they spoke for all. And they did, for all the people *they* spoke with. By now we were quite divided. It really hurt.

Another Check-up

It was no surprise that the 1980 spring Classis meeting appointed a new committee (I believe it was the third) of two pastors as church visitors and a third person Classis called a "consultant," a retired Free University professor who had moved to Calgary. Their mandate was broad: "to meet with First CRC to investigate the various movements." We should have strenuously objected to the appointment. Again there were no charges, protests, or appeals of any kind, so why another investigation? Our desire to be cooperative led us to go along with it. We shouldn't have. *We* ended up doing un-church-orderly things under the rubric of trying to be cooperative. Somewhere in that endless investigative process we should have loudly said, "Stop, enough!" We didn't. This was one time when we, trying to be nice, ended up with bad compromises.

By fall 1980, the committee had met with Council once. They had also met with the aggrieved members of the congregation and asked them to prepare a: *"discussion paper and submit a list of some of the reasons why they were disappointed in the quality of leadership given to the congregation."* It was another open invitation to a self-appointed group to rummage through past events, worship services, and meetings to find and compile a list of grievances and complaints, all with the church visitors' blessings but with no Council awareness or involvement.

The concerned church members responded with a nine-page, single-spaced, unsigned document listing their grievances. This list of complaints was dropped off at the church office. The church visitors asked Council to appoint three elders to serve on behalf of Council on what would then be a committee of six to seek unity. The list was to serve as a discussion starter for a meeting to be held on October 6, 1980. We appointed two elders and Pastor Breisch to meet with them.

The introduction made clear what to expect:

> *It is difficult to pinpoint a reason or group of reasons that led to this conclusion but it is more of an atmosphere that fosters the perception that the opinions and sensitivities of a large segment of the congregation are considered to be irrelevant by the leaders.* (Page 1, Discussion paper for meeting of October 6, 1980)

Following the introduction was a list of rather trivial things slanted and given negative interpretations. I'll quote only a few examples:

Some youth elders appear to have a defective view of what it means to be a Christian. In the spring of 1978 when discussing a lukewarm inquirer at a meeting of youth elders one of them said, 'I'll take him skiing and he'll be a Christian before we get to the top of the hill. The attitude appears to be man glorifying rather than God glorifying... (Page 1, paper, Oct. 6)

Their list continued. As pastors, we were criticized for laying hands on an elder at his installation service. Pastor Dean Dyk ended a service with an altar call without prior Council approval. After many discussions as elders, and even with the congregation, the decision had been made to serve only grape juice at Communion rather than grape juice *and* wine. We knew we had both, recovering and closet alcoholics, whom we did not want to tempt or offend. The aggrieved members objected and cynically asked, "What about an open plate for the offering? Does that not bring a prospective thief into temptation?" They also pointed out: "So many people are upset with the direction of the congregation that only a few now attend evening services." When Pastor Breisch responded with actual numbers that about 73% of the families and youth were present in the evening (really an amazing number, even then), their response was: "He seemed quite satisfied with such a poor attendance."

At about the same time, just before a worship service on Sunday morning, one of the sons of "Andy Brown" (changed name) reported to me that his father had gone into a Calgary hospital with "abdominal" difficulties. I knew I often had trouble with that word, so I was super-cautious with the announcement, so cautious that what I feared happened. I mentioned that the father was in the hospital with "abominable difficulties." The minute I said it, I knew what I had done. I was embarrassed and apologized immediately. But too late, the congregation chuckled with laughter. To add to the problem, I became more flustered and repeated the mistake, now totally convincing some that I was just having fun at the expense of poor brother Andy. Following the service, I sincerely apologized to his family members. They said they forgave me, but I think they thought I had done it intentionally. This too showed up in our discussion paper.

> *In a church where 'love' is preached Rev. Wildeboer announced that "Andy Brown" had undergone abdominal surgery (if only I had announced that!) He then proceeded to turn his announcement of a seriously ill member of the church into a joke by saying he did not mean abominable, but … and then he could not pronounce abdominal correctly again. The congregation either burst out laughing at his joke or else all the members who know Mr. "Brown" were tempted to walk out of the church because of this man's insensitivity.* (P.8, paper for Oct. 6)

Preaching did not come off well either. There had never been any protest or challenge to any of our messages. They were biblical, practical, and challenging. Most church members and visitors loved our sermons. But apparently not all:

> *Much can be said about the preaching in our church, and since we are not theologians, we find it hard to give a solid critique. Every sermon is taped so perhaps these tapes could speak for themselves….. It is not often that a scholarly sermon is given in the Christian Reformed tradition which is a grammatical-historical-theological interpretation of God's word. When we go to another Christian Reformed Church we are deeply touched by the depth and richness of God's word which is brought out by the minister's preparation and reflection.*

> *Especially Rev. Wildeboer's sermons are often the same. A sort of psychological explanation, then how he personally struggles with whatever it is he is preaching about, and in the end he tried to fit it in with the text. There is no explanation of the texts, just an endless stream of words which after so many years still sound the same.* (P. 8, 9, Paper for Oct. 6)

The "discussion paper" was dropped off at church on Friday afternoon, October 3, where it came to Pastor Frank Breisch. I had left earlier for Lacombe for an evening wedding rehearsal for Ruth Salomons and Kees Krabbe whose wedding was scheduled for the next afternoon. Frank came to the wedding the next day and showed me the paper. He was angry. It was really the only time I ever saw him lose his cool. He had read the paper and prepared a reply which he showed me saying, "Henry, this is ridiculous! I've had enough of this! Here is my response." And he gave me his response, already sent.

140

4 October, 1980
The Church Visitors
The Consistory of First CRC

Dear Brothers,

I trust that I have made clear in the past my desire for reconciliation of the groups within First CRC and my willingness to work toward that reconciliation. However, the document which I received yesterday entitled "Discussion Paper for meeting of October 6, 1980" makes it impossible for me to continue.

Because that paper contains outright untruths; because it takes statements out of context and thereby misconstrues them; because it indulges in judgment of motives and imputes the worst possible motives to given acts; because it brings up matters which have been discussed and explained in our meetings as if they have never been explained; because it breathes a spirit of unwillingness to accept the leadership of those whom God has appointed as rulers in this congregation; and because it reflects a neurotic rummaging in the garbage heap of the past, I cannot and will not dignify it by discussing it.

Therefore:

1) I hereby tender to consistory my resignation from the committee elected to meet with the committee representing the dissidents. (I have studiously avoided using that word before; I can do so no longer.)

2) I respectfully request the Church Visitors to urge the dissidents to bring charges according to the Church Order, against the ministers and/or consistory of this church for any heresy, sin, or neglect or abuse of office they think they are aware of. I request this course of action with complete confidence that we shall be totally vindicated.

3) I urge the consistory to declare, by word and deed that all protests against actions of the consistory must be made according to the Church Order and that protests in any other form will be dealt with firmly.

Brothers, I am willing to lay down my life in any constructive effort to advance the church of Jesus Christ. But I am convinced that this document displays an attitude which is both self-destructive and destructive of all who allow themselves to be involved. I cannot spare any more of my limited emotional energy in efforts that are doomed to futility.

May the Lord our God deal in mercy and grace with this part of his church,

In Christ's name,

Signed Frank Breisch

Struggles Continue, On and On

The meetings between Council and the aggrieved were never held. Instead the "dissidents" (as Frank now called them) and the church visitors were offended by Frank's response. They accused us again of being uncooperative. They were convinced that if we could reconcile these issues, everything would be all right. We did not agree, the issues were much bigger than that.

I recall this as a time when I was frustratingly angry. I tried to contain my anger, but others became aware of it. I was "short" at home with the kids, unusual for me. There were times when one of them was talking to me and I would not hear them until Jan would say, "Henry, Doug (or whoever it was) is talking to you." I apologized more than once for being absent while present. It was at such times that I started checking *Banner* ads for vacant churches and the *Calgary Herald* for possible positions. But that did not happen often.

On the positive side, the church was still blessed with many energized, generous people. We had an enthusiastic staff, and we enjoyed inspiring worship services where we met new people every week. Every service had visitors. Some came from other CR churches in our Classis, some to check to see if things were as they had heard. I recall that at the end of some services, visitors would shake my hand, introduce themselves and tell me what church they were from. With astonishment they would add, "I really enjoyed the service," with an obvious problem written on their shocked faces, "What do I do now?" They had expected to experience something more upsetting. Instead, they were blessed and inspired, an unexpected surprise after all they had heard. It was like they were saying, "Now how do I go home with that?"

Through 1980 and into 1981, other changes, not just charismatic ones, were occurring in First Church. Issues like sanctification, holiness, and spiritual growth and change as the result of the Holy Spirit's empowerment became more important to many. Members became more determined to find ways and ministries to better fulfill the Great Commandment and the Great Commission. They spoke more openly about their love for the Lord.

These positive changes frankly were a strong factor that kept me from obliging those who wanted to see me wave goodbye from the back of a moving van. In fact, one man in the moving business even offered me -and told others this as well—that he was willing to place an advertisement at his expense in *The Banner,* the church's denominational magazine, to provide a free move to anywhere in North America to any church willing to call me. It was supposed to be a joke and we all laughed heartily like it was funny. I too did publicly, but it stung.

How did this ministry become so nasty? I had occasionally heard the statement, "Watch out for the people who welcome you at the train station," but wasn't sure what it meant. Now I did. The *very* people, who are instrumental in bringing in the pastor, are often the very ones who also play leading roles in controlling the direction of the congregation. *They* tend to pick a pastor who fulfills *their* goals and desires. As long as he does what they desire, he can stay, he can even challenge them –sometimes- but woe to him if he see things differently and no longer dances according to their agreed, corporate tunes. It sets the stage for a Church Order Article 17 separation. We were there. But I still had a deep conviction that I was where God wanted me, as did most of our elders. I simply couldn't walk away. Unless a good number in Council support the pastor, parting of ways is inevitable sooner rather than later.

When we met as elders and leaders of the congregation they informed me quite frankly that if I "threw in the towel," as one stated it, so would they. I told them regardless as to what happened to me, they couldn't! They responded that they were ready to start a new church and wanted our family to come with them. Though it was tempting, I wasn't comfortable with the idea. Peter Wagner, a well known church leader, states it well, "It is often easier to birth the new than to raise the dead!" I know a number of people stayed because I did, and I stayed because they did.

By the fall of 1980, we became aware that the aggrieved members and the church visitors were meeting again, without Council being informed or invited to be present, again contrary to the Church Order of the CRC. When we asked the church visitors why they went outside of the prescribed Church Order in their dealings with us, we were told that our problems were so serious and unique that they were beyond the normal scope of the Church Order and they felt justified in making these exceptions. Because the church visitors did not follow Church Order, they also lost the support of a number of pastors and elders in the Classis who otherwise might have agreed with their recommendations.

As Council members and especially as pastors we made sure to follow CRC polity. Frank Breisch and I strongly insisted on this. We knew we were in harmony with Synod's decisions and that the church visitors and the aggrieved members were not. Among ourselves we said (but very quietly!) that it was not us "who troubled Israel." (I Kings 18:18).

The struggles continued through the winter of 1980 and spring of 1981 when the church visitors again came to Classis with another negative report about us. We were not surprised, but we did wonder when this would stop. We were wearing out. Little did we know that things would get worse. We didn't think they could.

Chapter 9

From Storms to Hurricanes

Calgary, 1981 - 1982

A Breath of Fresh Air

In March of 1981 we experienced a unique event which I believe God brought to us. A number of Evangelical churches in Calgary had decided to sponsor a community "Festival of Praise." The plan was to bring in an entire worship team, including musicians, dancers, and a drama group all accompanied by their pastor, Canon David Watson, who would do the teaching. The group was from St. Michael-le-Belfrey Anglican Church in York, England, a congregation that had gone through beautiful Scriptural, spiritual renewal. Because of our turmoil and ongoing conflict I was not going to endorse this but quietly invite participation by those who were interested. We were cautious. Plans called for the week-long event to be held at Grace Presbyterian Church a classic congregation with a large, older facility seating about 1,200 people and located close to downtown.

Before committing his team to coming, David Watson and his executive assistant were in Calgary to get "a feel for the spiritual climate," as David put it, to meet some of the church leaders, and to explore how open we were for renewal. I was part of the planning team and with four others spent an afternoon with Pastor David and his partner. We included a visit to the planned facility. It did not impress them. They asked if any other facilities were available, so we visited a large, newer Baptist church and got a "not bad." Now what?

One member of the team suggested we show them First Church. I was reluctant. Though I was eager for us to have opportunity to participate in the festival, I was afraid to have it at our facility because I knew it would give the aggrieved members and the church visitors another item for their list of grievances. I knew David well since we had done some team teaching at Fuller Seminary in the D. Min courses; I also knew David would like our building. First was blessed with a member named Marius Van Ellenberg who was a highly creative decorator. Sports stars, top business execs, and a number of movie stars who had homes in Calgary called on

145

Marius to decorate their homes. He had livened up our worship center with an avocado green interior offset with salmon-like orange in perfectly matching long curtains. It's hard to imagine now, but it was striking at the time.

We drove to First Church, walked into the recently redecorated narthex, and I heard, "Oh, I like this," and my inner reaction was, "Oh no." As we walked into the worship center, I remember David, in his clipped English accent, saying, "This building bespeaks renewal. We must have it here." Although we could only pack in 600 at most, our facilities and stage lent themselves excellently for the Festival of Praise. The decision was made.

A Needed Boost

The festival provided a great boost for the Christian community in Calgary. It came at a time when many people at First including me were at a low point spiritually. It included enthusiastic times of praise. Their praise team taught us new renewal songs popular in the UK, and we sang them along with Psalter, Fanny Crosby and Wesley hymns. We used organ, piano, guitars, banjos, and drums. We had dancers and dramas that David's team worked into his nightly messages. All of it was creatively biblical but not yet common in CRCs at that time. It was coming! We heard testimonies as to what God had done in individuals' lives. We celebrated and felt a sense of release. For many, the festival was life-changing. The fresh breeze of the Spirit blew away some of the smog of tiredness, controversy, criticism, and conflict. It truly was a gift from God to First Church. I remember walking into the church that week with a zip in my steps with no fear of worry, only a feeling of anticipation. It was liberating for many of us.

To some others these worship services were undignified and were signs of "work righteousness" said our church visitors. As expected, we were criticized for a lack of sensitivity to the aggrieved members.

The Pain of Change

In the spring of 1981, Frank Breisch received a call to become pastor of the Presbyterian Church in Banff. He was drawn to it partly because the Presbyterian Church was his background but more so because they were open to women in ministry, as was he, and we were not. I also believe he was tired, like I was, of the fruitless hassles. In addition, he was committed to the mission of the church but found it difficult to focus on it because there was always another seemingly more urgent issue. Frank decided to accept the call, and though I understood his decision, I was very sorry to see him leave. We saw things differently at times, but we shared a deep love and respect for each other and we were both diligently committed to the authority of the Scriptures.

The aggrieved members were not that happy to see Frank go, he was not really their target. I knew, however, that he was far more dangerous to them than I was. He was a strong theological thinker who was not easily swayed by what others thought or wanted. He was tenaciously biblical, logical, and articulate. He was difficult to refute theologically. (Note his letter to "the dissidents" quoted in the previous chapter.)

It seemed like we were in a time of experiencing losses and defeats. I understood Frank's decision to accept the call from Banff but I personally felt it as a loss of a strong support; his leaving added to the shakiness of an already wobbly ride. Had I received a call to another church at that time, I too would have left, I think. But because by now our struggles were known throughout the denomination, for several years I received no invitation from other churches. I think I couldn't *buy* a call if I wanted to. I was labeled "unreformed" (there was no worse insult in the CRC at that time), "Pentecostal," or "charismatic" (not much better).

In times like that we would sometimes receive a surprising "lift." I took that as a token of His love and a reminder that He had not abandoned us. Two such boosts came our way in August 1981.

Coincidence (?)

The first started on Friday morning, August 21 when I came to church and chatted with Dean Dyk. We had both seen on Thursday evening's Calgary TV news that Billy Graham had arrived in the city to begin a Crusade on Sunday. He was surrounded by police and security. It was obvious that the City of Calgary was not going to let anything happen to this highly respected Christian leader as had occurred rather recently when someone attempted to assassinate the Pope. And Calgary certainly did not want the

Dallas, Texas fame as related to former U.S. President Kennedy. We both remarked on that and then I jokingly suggested that we call Billy Graham and take him for lunch. We didn't call but concluded the conversation with me saying, "I would really like to meet that man some day."

About 10:30 that morning I received a phone call from Don Chevey, (his common Real Estate name for Chevaldayoff) asking me if I had the night open and wanted two tickets for the evening's Calgary Stampeders' football game. I called home to see if any of the kids wanted to go and Judy was eager so we gladly took the offer.

We were early for the game but the stands were filling up fast. The "Stamps" - as they are lovingly called by Calgarians- were approaching play-off time and each game counted. As Judy and I were talking, she suddenly said, "The guy next to you looks familiar." She saw him as she was talking to me. I had been looking at her while we were chatting. So I turned to look at him and saw a man in a trench coat with the collar turned up and wearing a hat covering most of his face. He looked at me and I saw that he was attempting to go incognito, so I softly asked, "Are you who I think you are?" to which he responded, "probably," with a heavy Carolina accent. It *was* Billy Graham who had come with his friend and long-time ministry partner Grady Wilson to enjoy the game, but equally important, to get a feel for McMahon Stadium, the place for the week-long Crusade

We spent over two hours together, side by side. I explained Canadian football (as well as I could!) to him in comparison to the American game. He liked our three downs better than the American four, believing it created a more active game. He in turn spoke extensively to me about the wonderful relationship that he had had with his mother who had died only 6 days earlier, August 15. He was obviously grieving and in speaking to me quoted long sections of various Psalms that she and he had memorized and which they had prayed together as she was dying. It was a holy moment for me as he repeated the experience by retelling it; it was a privilege to let him minister to me, and I to him as he expressed his deep and tender love for his mother who was now "with Jesus." I received a rare glimpse as to how a godly son can deeply grieve coping with the death of his godly mother all in the context of celebrating a life filled with joy. I think that is the way God would have us part ways when one's time has come. It was an uplifting experience. The following week Judy and I received a short note of appreciation for our time together, signed with his typical "Billy" sign-off.

An amazing coincidence? I would have classified it as such, if it had not been for my morning comment, "I would really like to meet that man some day." I now see it as a beautiful portrayal of God's amazing sense of humor. The Holy Spirit obviously overheard my comment, took it as a prayer request and went straight to my Father with it, who -I think- smiled and said, "Now how shall we work this out in a surprising, fun-like way?" The "us" (Genesis 1:26) of the trinity surely figured it out. I smile and become comfortably warm inside when I think of it. He showed up, totally surprised me, and lifted my downcast spirit of defeat and discouragement. I can't imagine how He could have done it any better. We know God delights in giving us the desires of our hearts. Occasionally, like any parent, the Father enjoys spoiling us. This moment of spoiling was for me an oasis in the desert.

Whoops

The second boost came also in August when seemingly out of nowhere, our Council received a letter which totally surprised us and lifted our spirits. It was a copy of a letter sent to our Classis church visitors by the Rev. William Brink, General Secretary of the CRC, and Dr. Richard DeRidder, at that time, Professor of Church Polity and Church Order at Calvin Seminary, both in Grand Rapids, Michigan. Apparently, the church visitors siding with the aggrieved members had become frustrated in dealing with us and had written these two respected church leaders for advice. Before responding to them, Rev. Brink and Dr. DeRidder had requested copies of all the information pertaining to the struggles of First Church with Classis. They had read the materials and responded to the church visitors in writing and, as is common practice and courtesy, sent our Council a copy of their response. Their copy to us was our first clue that they had been consulted.

Their response did not turn out the way the church visitors had expected. I quote from Rev. Brink's and Dr. DeRidder's letter on Calvin Seminary letterhead, dated 5th August 1981 over the signature of Richard R. DeRidder.

1. It appears that the church visitors exceeded their lines of responsibility as outlined in the church order by:

> *a. Becoming an investigatory committee*

> *b. Conducting hearings with persons who have not officially and in writing presented their grievances to the consistory. The church order does not permit by-passing a duly constituted assembly.*

2. There is no evidence that the concern of Classis Alberta South is based upon fully processed appeals or protests of members of First Calgary.

3. Providing services to "the aggrieved" (cf. 4c) imply that the authority of the church visitors supersedes the authority of the duly constituted assembly (the consistory). Note: it is assumed that the consistory may be by-passed or that it is derelict in its duties.

4. The advice and decisions of Classis Alberta South appear to encourage "the aggrieved" to continue their complaint without following the proper ecclesiastical procedures...

It backfired on them. The letter was a relief for us. Finally, people with credible authority and integrity in the CRC were saying what we as Council had felt all along. Someone–other than us—was actually telling the aggrieved members to stop complaining and put their case in writing.

Protests

The aggrieved members quickly decided that the only way to officially address the situation would be to write protests to Council challenging Council's and/or the pastors' actions, preaching, theology, or morals. (Note: Proper process called for members who were aggrieved to present a protest -with grounds for the protest- to Council, to which Council would respond. If Council's response was unsatisfactory to the protester, and we suspected it would be, he could then appeal to Classis.) This meant the protesters had to charge us and prove that what we were doing was either unbiblical or immoral, contrary to our Confessions or Church Order, or in conflict with Synodical decisions. Since the church visitors had been reprimanded for being too available and helpful to the aggrieved members, they backed away from helping them at a time when they needed it most.

By October 1981, Council had received a flurry of eight protests. We appointed a committee of three younger elders to prepare responses on our behalf. We knew that whatever our response was, it likely would not matter much to the dissenters. They were eager to appeal the responses to Classis. We were well aware we were writing responses for the Classis meeting and that the delegates would read the material to decide whether the charges were valid. The aggrieved members hoped to have adequate grounds to remove Council and me. At the regular mid-October Classis meeting, Classis was informed that things were tense at First CRC and protests were in the making. Classis began to plan for a "special meeting to deal with First CRC Calgary's concerns" which would be held sometime in December 1981 or January 1982.

Where are we going?

So, in late 1981, with elders preparing responses to protests and a special Classis meeting pending, we were busy. In preparation for this event, Council appointed four Council members and me to update a previous year's vision-mission paper entitled, "Where are we Headed?" for the 1981-1982 Season. We produced a four-page, single-spaced, thorough statement in which we carefully articulated who we were and what we believed God was calling us to do at *that time* and in *that community*. Although we were accused of "making too many changes," this vision-mission statement showed a clear consistency and focus. (I think this was 15 years ahead of the time when vision-mission statements would become common in many congregations. I helped churches in Ontario do this when I served as a consultant with Home Missions.)

The vision-mission statement shows that our church was essentially what would now be called "a mission-focused church." Note, for example, on page 2 we quote from a paper written the previous year, setting out Council's perspective:

Council continues to endorse what we summarized last year. The church is placed in the world by Christ to continue the ministry of service to the world, and all of the activities of the church must contribute to the task which He has laid upon His church… and though the church does many ministries for the nurture and growth of her members, all of it is done in the context of 'equipping God's people for ministry and service.' (Ephesians 4:12).

The rest of the paper outlined plans for worship. Our Sunday AM services would be more formal, teaching-oriented, emphasizing the God-people relationship under the theme of "We are not our own" (Heidelberg Catechism, Lord's Day 1). The evening services (which we had every Sunday) would retain the preaching and teaching of God's Word but our overall theme now was, "We are not alone." Those services had liturgical freedom, variety, and included the sharing of blessings and pains in prayer times. We would focus on themes like youth, children or elderly, including testimonies and interviews, or we might address an important ministry area; we encouraged active participation by members. The summary comments were:

In short, we expect our services to usher in the Kingdom in all aspects of life and to all aspects of creation….We expect phenomenal growth as we joyfully praise and serve God.

Subsequent sections explained our vision for pastoral care, education and fellowship, service and outreach, youth and singles. The concluding statement indicated that First Church was a church involved in "Church Renewal." Exciting indicators of renewal were seen in conversions, changed lives, growing concerns for others, and investment in others' needs. Growth in ministries was supported by giving that had increased some four-fold between 1971 and 1981 especially for ministries reaching beyond our local congregation. We were blessed.

We shared the paper "Where are we Headed?" at two open congregational meetings with time for questions and responses in fall 1981. Ten days later, on a Sunday morning to achieve maximum participation, we asked every professing member to endorse and support the overall direction with the option of signing their ballot vote to indicate "I am on board." More than two-thirds of the membership did.

As elders we felt strongly affirmed but we were also puzzled by the results. Though *not one person* had expressed any reservations or objections why had

152

25% voted no or abstained from voting? How *do* we bring the congregation into unity when a clear vision-mission statement with specific plans had been summarily rejected by a quarter of the congregation? We were discouraged and frustrated. We tried to unify the congregation but our efforts had failed again.

Shortly after the congregational vote, the rumbling started again. I learned then that if a church has continued irrational opposition, visionary leaders lose patience, give up, and either become docile and passive maintainers of the status quo, or quietly leave to go elsewhere. That was happening to us. Elders who had long been supportive now started coming to me asking if they could resign. They were tired. (So was I!) With more than a two-thirds majority, we should have thanked the congregation for their (strong!) support, praised God, and moved forward with the implementation of the plan. Some of the elders -mostly younger ones- felt strongly that we should still do this. Had Classis and the church visitors not been breathing down our necks, we would have. I was hesitant and fearful but I was wrong. I deeply regretted later that we had not heeded the elders' advice.

We're not On-Board

Soon after the vote Council learned that six of its 22 members (the typical 25-30%) had voted no or abstained from voting. As Council executive we decided to meet with the six who had voted no to ask them what the reasons were for their no vote. Would they reconsider so we could move forward on common ground? Could they *abide* with the majority decision without compromising their convictions –whatever they were- since none had objected to any part of it earlier? ("Abide" simply means that though I do not agree with the decision, I will go along with it.)

They would not. Instead, all six resigned, as they put it, "with protest, under duress" stating that we had no right to ask them to support the vision-mission statement since they had already signed the form of subscription. "Isn't that good enough?" The church visitors agreed with them.

A Spark of Light

This was a low time for me, so much so that I seriously thought, "I am done. I have nothing more to offer." Earlier Jan and I had decided that we would use two tests to determine when it was time for us to fold. The first test was an earlier ulcer. In Seminary I spent a day, at -what was then-Blodgett Hospital, for tests checking whether I had a stomach ulcer. I did, not a major one but significant enough so that with some prescription medicine, lots of milk and Maalox it was controlled and created no further trouble. My test was that if the ulcer started acting up we would see that as one of God's signs that it is time to review our "calling." Through the entire ministry experience it never appeared again.

A second "fleece" was our two older daughters. We had decided we would check with them periodically to see how they were doing in all this. If they indicated that it was damaging them seriously or they felt *they* had had enough, we would see that as God's sign to review our present calling. During that part of the Calgary journey they were in the vulnerable teenage-high-school years. At times they were reminded by friends that due to *their* dad some of the friends' families were *pushed* out of their life-long church. Though they heard it, they did not always tell us, but at times I did check with them. On one such occasion when we had been through some tough days, I was taking Judy to school. We were alone in the car so I asked her, "Judy, what do you think of all this that's happening in church?" I remember exactly where we were on our route to school. She was quiet before she responded and then she said, "I don't know, dad, but one thing I *do* know. You're for real." That was the highest compliment I received while in Calgary. I just looked straight ahead, hoping she could not see the tears in my eyes. In my heart I said, if that's what it takes, I am ok for another year! A few days later I asked Barbara, also in high school, "You know what's happening, Barb, should I quit and go do something else?" I thought of the two girls she might be more fed up with it all, so I wanted to make it easy for her to say, "I think we have had enough, let's do something else." Not so, her answer was short: "Dad, a Wildeboer never quits." That was it. We stayed put.

A Bigger Battle

I wondered many times, why is all this happening to us? I believe we were pure in heart, had openly laid out our plans, and had moved forward with integrity, but our efforts for unity had failed. We became aware that the battle was bigger -much bigger- than theological disagreements. I could not comprehend the tenacity and pride that refused to admit that the church was obviously experiencing growth, vitality, and renewal. They probably could not understand how we seemed equally stubborn. But it was bigger than that; it was more than a conflict of wills. It seemed like we were in struggles dealing with issues of life and death. We found ourselves in a debilitating, depressing, spiritual power conflict that we could not resolve, no matter what we tried.

Besides affirmations from our kids, the church amazingly, in the middle of these trying times experienced beautiful assurances that God was with us. He would bless us with signs of his love exactly when we needed it most. Without that I am not sure we could have gotten out of bed to do it again day after day. He provided encouragement to continue. We had a wonderful group of fervently praying people including elders. It was the worst and the best of times all at the same time. Painful conflicts and deep moments of joy often came together. In the middle of a bad conflict, "out-of-the-blue" I would get a phone call from a mother or father (often in Ontario) thanking me for what the church had done for their son or daughter. (At times I didn't even know who they were talking about.) Sometimes a young couple -one a Christian, the other barely interested- would *both* start attending services and the spouse was converted. When that happened, especially through a specific sermon, we praised God even when we couldn't understand how that happened through *that* sermon. The born-again experience surely is the work of the Spirit of God and a wonderful experience for the whole church! These events so inspired and empowered me that I would jokingly say, "If this is what it takes, ok, so be it! Bring it on!" But it wasn't always that way.

Appeals and Responses

In the meantime, we prepared responses to the eight protests we had received from the aggrieved members. Though we carefully answered the protests, they summarily rejected our responses and sent them as appeals to Classis Alberta South against Council. The Classis executive called a special meeting to deal with them to start at 1:00 PM on Monday, November 30, 1981. All delegates were informed to expect to stay through Tuesday, December 1.

I remember our Council meeting before that infamous Classis session. We began by spending a time in prayer. Then a young, rather new elder, Frank Van Ginhoven, who had been involved in preparing the responses to the protests, said that as he saw it, none of the protests would likely be sustained. At the meeting he looked at me and said, "They will be hard on you; they want you out." I knew that, still it was shocking to hear him say it so crassly.

The Classis meeting started with devotions followed by an update from our church visitors and their consultant. They painted a picture of frustration with a Council who was uncooperative and out of touch with many good, concerned, lifelong members of the church. The tipping point occurred when in a time of much tension, Council came up with a "revolutionary paper" titled, "Where we are headed?" which deeply offended the concerned members. They stated that the paper had alienated a "large part" of Council (6 out of 22) so that a number of elders and deacons were left no option but to resign. For anyone uninformed, it sounded terrible.

1. "Where are we Headed?"

We then began the procedure of dealing with each appeal. The person whose name was attached to the appeal was given the floor to explain or defend it. In the first appeal, we were charged with presenting a "very controversial and unacceptable mission statement," which though credited to Council had supposedly been written by me. Out of that came the demand that "you as consistory herewith start proceeding to remove Rev. Wildeboer from the office of pastor of this congregation." Classis quickly decided not to sustain the appeal.

2. Pastor's Leadership

The second appeal objected to my leadership. It stated that "an intolerable situation exists in the congregation" and that I should be removed as pastor from the congregation according to Article 17 of the Church Order. This is the article, referred to earlier, that provides a Council or pastor the opportunity to request approval for severing the pastor-congregation relationship for "weighty reasons" if either or both deem it best for the well-being of the congregation or pastor. It can be initiated by Council and/or the pastor, *but not by a Classis*. The CRC, having a Presbyterian form of governance, believes that the pastor is primarily accountable to the elders of the local congregation. This appeal was not sustained primarily because it was out-of-order.

3. Asking Elders to Endorse goals
One objected to our paper outlining goals, direction, and the request to have elders endorse these goals with their vote of cooperation. Not sustained.

4. Worship Informality
Another appeal protested the growing informality and flexibility present in our worship services indicating a loss of dignity, especially in the evening services. It became obvious that what we were doing was done in many other churches in Classis. It did not take Classis long to vote not to sustain it.

5. Teaching of "Perfectionism"
The next appeal charged me with the teaching of perfectionism, a teaching they claimed was closely related to the charismatic movement (not really so, hw) and by participating in teaching in sermons and in a series entitled, 'Growing the New Life in Christ,' I was charged with being unreformed. "This was also shown by First Church's involvement with interdenominational activities when David Watson, an English Anglican pastor, and his worship team came to Calgary to lead a Festival of Praise" and preached several nights for us. Because we had emphasized the importance of sanctification and growth in love and obedient service, the appeal felt we were teaching a "work righteousness" which in turn contributed to teaching perfectionism. The appeal was not sustained.

6. Lack of Dignity in Worship
Though it was a separate appeal it really over-lapped with the two just before it. Because it was written by someone else it came separately. Our response indicated that the festival's emphasis had been upon serving and worshiping God with our total beings. We had expressed praise with a

157

variety of musical instruments, including drums, guitars, banjos, and brass, and we had communicated the gospel in sermons but also in dramas, readings and dialogues. By now Classis was aware that the appeals were weak and they were obviously getting tired of dealing with them. Rather quickly it followed the others as it too was not sustained.

By now it was Monday evening at 9:30 PM, so we adjourned for the evening. Six appeals so far had been discussed and considered, and each one was "not sustained." It was tiring and frustrating, especially for those who had worked so hard to prepare and present them. We began to feel that we might spend two full days going through all eight appeals, sustain none of them, and then go home having accomplished absolutely nothing.

7. Elders had not Resigned

The next morning, the seventh appeal was presented. It protested that Council members had not resigned in the spring when the Classical Investigation Committee had recommended that all elders resign and a new Council be selected. Council had discussed it and declined the committee's advice. Now it was challenged. Again rather quickly Council was sustained and the appeal was not.

Seven appeals had now been presented, and none were sustained. All the appeals had been weak with unsubstantiated charges. Frankly, Classis dared not sustain any one of them. Apparently, some Classis delegates privately supported some of the appeals. However, they felt that if they supported a weak appeal, we could take it to Synod, where we might well be sustained, thereby embarrassing Classis before the entire denomination. Synod was like a stick behind the door. (Synod is the highest body of the CRC which through various boards directs CRC ministries throughout the world. It is also the final court of appeal in adjudication of matters in congregations or Classes.)

8. Charismatic Experiences

By Tuesday afternoon, we had one more appeal. This one was different; it became the major one. It was based upon a sermon I had preached in First Church following an earlier instruction from the church visitors, "that the pastors clearly teach on the Holy Spirit and spiritual gifts in the church today in line with the report and recommendations adopted by the Synods of 1973 and 1974." One member took one of my sermon tapes, transcribed it word for word, flaws, repeats and all, printed it, and charged me with teaching "second blessing theology." Though not intended, this would prove to be the most humorous highlight of the entire Classis session.

In the sermon, I had stated that CRC people could -and did- have charismatic experiences and receive gifts such as healings, speaking in tongues, interpretation, and prophecies. Though these gifts are often referred to as "spectacular" or "manifestation gifts," they are listed right alongside the more common gifts of mercy, generosity (often called, liberality), teaching, leadership, etc. There is no distinction between gifts; they are all spoken about as equal. In the sermon, I had repeated what Synod 1973 stated: "There is no biblical support to say that these gifts have ceased." Historically, we in the CRC adhered to the "cessation" position but we never really biblically substantiated it, even though some gifts have not been as visible during certain times in history and certainly not in the CRC. Though Synod of 1973 had adopted a more open stance on the gifts, many CRC members still held the "cessation" position.

In First Church, some long-time (Reformed!) members experienced the gift of tongues and used that gift regularly in their times of personal prayer. They reported a deep sense of trust and peace accompanying that gift. One 68-year-old elder expressed it like this: "When I pray in tongues, I sense that the world and certainly my wife and I are wrapped in the arms of the Lord and surrounded with his love, no matter what happens." He said this while he was fighting cancer. He radiated with love, had a warm smile and gentle eyes that warmed me every time I visited with him. Even now, I can picture his face and smile when I think of him! We experienced some amazing miraculous healings, more commonly experienced by Pentecostals and Charismatics, perhaps because they expect them. Yes, Christian Reformed people were having "charismatic experiences." It is true that we struggled with some prophecies which were not edifying, but we were also blessed by others. We could not deny the presence of the gift of prophecy, and we could not in good conscience forbid it at First CRC .

During this time, these gifts were also appearing in other churches of the denomination, and few now denied their existence. Because I held that all gifts could be manifested in the present day, I was charged with teaching second blessing theology. In short, the appeal charged that I was in conflict with the recommendations of Synod's 1973 report. What did that mean?

Pentecostal or Charismatic

I have had to explain this often. *Pentecostal* theology teaches that when a person is regenerated and converted, he becomes a Christian; the better goal, however, is to become a Spirit-filled Christian. This occurs when "the baptism of the Holy Spirit" comes upon the person involved. It is viewed as an experience *distinct from* and *subsequent to* one's conversion. The hallmark sign of this "baptism" is usually the gift of tongues. Thus, the question is asked, "Have you been baptized in the Spirit (yet)?" This is usually viewed as a one-time experience identified with a specific time and place. We then end up with two-stage Christians: one, those who are regenerated and converted by the Spirit of God, and two, others who have been "Spirit-baptized" and have the gift of tongues. I never believed or taught this second blessing theology as understood in the classical Pentecostal tradition.

Charismatic theology is more flexible but also acknowledges prayer for the filling of the Holy Spirit as Paul instructs in Ephesians 5:18 where God's people are commanded to be filled with the Spirit. The present passive verb tense indicates that it is an ongoing action performed in people by the Holy Spirit and is directly related to surrendering oneself to Jesus Christ as He is revealed in His Word, the Bible. In fact, the parallel passage, Colossians 3:16, replaced the phrase "be filled with the Spirit" of Ephesians 5:18 with "let the Word of Christ dwell in you richly." Charismatics, and now also many Reformed and Evangelical churches, perhaps influenced by the charismatic movement, teach that "ongoing filling" must continue to occur not just for a second experience but for a tenth and twentieth and a hundredth, etc. It is *ongoing and essential* to sanctification. Without the activity of the Holy Spirit, no one can live the Christian life. We taught this at First Church and we knew we were in harmony with the denominational position adopted by the Synod of 1973. We had been challenged on this many times. I was clear about that in my mind and was not afraid to be tested on that again, should that happen.

At the Classis meeting, we went around and around as to whether CRC people could have charismatic experiences without being Pentecostal. A number of delegates aligned with the traditional CRC position that miracles occurred *before* the Canon of Scripture was completed and *no longer after that,* period!

Equally ardent was the alternative view: that, yes, CRC people can have charismatic experiences. But *how* those are interpreted makes all the difference. Both Frank and I had carefully taught the need for and the possibility of "ongoing filling." We emphasized that people are converted by the Spirit and equally important, the Christian life can *only* be lived in the power of God's Spirit (See Galatians 3: 2-3). It is not in us to produce Christian character without the wooing, molding, and shaping of the Holy Spirit. At other times, the very same Spirit with outbursts jolts and tosses us into repentance and confession and leads us into giving up resulting in a new humility.

If the cessation position prevailed after a vote, I would be considered a heretic, and Classis would have to decide how to deal with me. Though I realized this might be problematic, I wasn't worried. I knew I could appeal that decision at Synod and would be sustained. But I was weary of battling and arguing and did not want to go through this again. I was tired of having to defend First Church's ministry. We were biblical and those opposing us were not. I know that sounds arrogant, but I believed it with all my heart.

By this time it was nearly 3:00 PM on Tuesday afternoon, and Classis was ready to vote on the last appeal. The chairman declared this to be an important decision and led us in prayer. He then stated the heart of the appeal, that "by declaring that CRC people could have charismatic experiences, Rev. Wildeboer was in fact 'teaching second blessing theology.'" I whispered to elder Al Meyer sitting next to me, "This is going to be close; I may just be a heretic after this vote."

The chairman continued, "All in favour of sustaining the appeal say, 'aye'". Al Meyer and I were totally stunned when not one sound was heard in the room! "All opposed, same sign," and a resounding "aye" rang out.

Al Meyer leaned over and whispered, "We just had a charismatic experience." It would have been humorous were it not so tragically sad.

"The appeal is not sustained," declared Chairman Ken Verhulst. I was in the clear. He then announced it was time for a 15-minute break.

Non-Charismatics Became Charismatics?

Right after the break, the truth of Al's statement became clear. One of the pastors was on his feet immediately and called out, "Point of order, Mr. Chairman, point of order."

The following dialogue ensued,

Chairman: "What is your point of order?"

Reply: "Mr. Chairman, during the coffee break some of us were talking and we would like to call for a revote on the last appeal and we'd like to vote by *ballot.*"

Chairman: "Why is that?"

Reply: "Some of us wanted to vote in favour of the appeal, but we couldn't make our voice come through our throats."

By now a number of delegates were chuckling, and Al leaned over again and this time whispered, "I told you! Isn't that something? The most outspoken, non-charismatic person here, insisting that CRC people do not have charismatic experiences, has one and doesn't even realize it?" It was surely a most unique way for God to show up.

The chairman refused the revote. He was challenged but was handily sustained by Classis.

I would not believe this had I not been there. Every time Chairman Ken Verhulst and I meet now, before we say anything, we chuckle over that moment and then remember it as a humorous moment in a very sad time. Several times during that long session of Classis, it seemed to me that God would let things go just so far and then intervene. This time He showed up with an amazing sense of humor. His guiding hand was always there.

By now, all eight appeals were not sustained. We were exhausted. "Depleted," is the better word. Where do we go from here? We had been meeting for two days with some 40 people and had absolutely nothing to show for it. Since there was no other business, we should have adjourned the meeting and gone home.

Now What?

But our problems were now public and many were watching. During many of the sessions we had a number of visitors who came to see what was happening, especially for evening sessions. Had we gone home then, the delegates would have been asked, "Now, what did you do with First Calgary's situation?" An honest response would have been, "Well, we dealt with eight appeals against their Council and/or pastor. We sustained none of them, so after that we adjourned and went home." But that would be hard for people to swallow. Shouldn't something more be done? Shouldn't somebody be fired, or at least reprimanded?

I felt that way a bit too. Is this all? There was no resolution for us either. Are we to let go of our ministries and our exciting life-changing worship services or should we continue to do whatever it took to win youth into the service of the Lord and into His church? We were tired and scarred, but we did not want to take the no-risk, safe route. I, for one couldn't after tasting what I had tasted.

By this time it was 8:00 PM on Tuesday evening, so it was decided to end for the day. We delegates from First CRC moved to *adjourn* the meeting but received no support. Had we not been so tired, we should have firmly insisted on this. Instead, Classis voted to meet again the next morning at 8:30, hoping to finish by noon! To do what?

This meant that some kind of agenda would have to be created overnight. Classical rules would need to be stretched again to allow that procedure, but somehow neither I nor our elders were alert enough to realize that. I think we were emotionally spent.

We returned the next morning, and after devotions, a fresh, new proposal appeared as a motion on the floor of Classis. Some people had done some late night work. A document was circulated, "Motions of Classis Meeting,

December 2, 1981." It was obvious that frustration had precipitated the proposal.

In short, the document proposed two motions preceded by some introductory comments including the necessity to take decisive action. The two motions were:

1. *that we must ask each individual member of the present Council to resign and*
2. *that we must ask Rev. H. Wildeboer to seek actively a call within our denomination in order that First Church may make a new and fresh start.*

.

It was the Classis actually attempting to sever the pastoral relationship in the tone of Art. 17. Since neither the elders nor the pastor of First had asked for this, Classis was simply out-of-order. And they knew that. They indicated that they were *not instructing* First Church to do this but they were (merely!) saying *"must ask"* in each request. What they wanted, they could not really do but by using "ask" they were safe. First Church delegates challenged Classis that this material was out of order. Classis does not initiate this kind of action. Classis is called to listen, evaluate, and adjudicate what councils, churches, or members present. This proposal was initiated to deal with the general frustration of trying to resolve a lengthy church conflict which was at a stalemate. It was strongly supported by a group of traditional, unhappy people who were frustrated because they had lost control over their church. Our attempt to have the motion called out of order was voted down. So we resigned ourselves to the fact that we were in for another challenge.

After some discussion, Classis voted by ballot on whether to ask the First Church elders to resign. The count was 16 yes votes and 17 no votes. It was defeated; Council stays.

The second part of the motion to ask me to actively seek a call within the denomination did not take long to discuss. By then, I had been in Calgary First for 10 years, and a number of delegates sincerely believed that no pastor should stay longer than seven or eight years. Since ten years is beyond that, it was relatively simple. Others felt that a change was needed so that the church would come to peace. Still I was shocked when the votes were read one at a time, "yes, no, no, yes..." and then I heard the total -17 yes and 16 no. I went numb. I am being fired! That's how it felt. I looked at the elder who was with me and he looked at me. We both said, "Now what?"

Ten years earlier, I had been a young, 31-year-old pastor who had been called to serve all kinds of congregations in both the US and Canada. Now, the message handed me was "the majority of Classis Alberta South thinks you need to go elsewhere." I felt they were saying you are good enough to stay in the denomination but go somewhere else. It was a hard blow to my already brittle ego.

By this time, it was Wednesday afternoon and Classis decided to write a pastoral letter to First CRC, modeled after letters the apostle Paul wrote to his churches. The delegates from First Church were dismissed until the evening. We returned after supper, the letter was read to us, and we were asked for our immediate response. We didn't say much of anything. We were numb and had no energy left. We hardly cared anymore; we just wanted to get out of there. "Do whatever you want."

By now I badly wanted to go home and spend time with Jan and the kids to discuss this strange situation. I especially dreaded telling the kids. Jan had not been present at the Classis when the vote was taken, but she had been informed by Deanne Dyk, the wife of our youth pastor. It was hard to tell two teenage daughters and three younger sons what it all meant. After more than 10 years there, Calgary was all they knew. I feared a barrage of questions from them, and a bit later from many in the church and community. The word got around fast. Where are we going? How soon will we be leaving? Can we finish the school year? I didn't know the answers to these questions. I was "fired," but I really wasn't fired. We were to leave the congregation, but not the denomination. We didn't know where we'd go or when. Could I, or the elders, decline Classis's request to "actively seek a call within the denomination?"

The Paradox

After talking with my family, I went upstairs and took a long shower. I felt absolutely filthy and tainted, as if I had been sitting in a bath of poison, and I wanted to wash it off. But I couldn't scrub it clean. This still stands out as one of the worst experiences of my life; but not as hard as when many years later our 25 year-old son was diagnosed with life-threatening cancer. I would not choose to go through it again -not even for a million dollars. It took a while to sort out what possible good could come out of this. I realized:

Though this was a nasty experience it was also formative. Some things I learned:

The Christian Reformed Church Order is often criticized. I experienced that adherence to it provides justice for an individual based on the Scriptures, Confessions, Synodical decisions, and basic godly morality. It makes room for any individual to challenge the system or status quo and be assured of a fair hearing. It does require that *all involved* adhere to it.

- I had a need to be a popular preacher admired by his colleagues, but I also wanted to be godly. I needed to be tested by God to see who and what is really number one. That proved to be a long and painful examination.
- It was a major shift to learn to think biblically instead of institutionally or traditionally. Taking a biblical stand is tough, is learned over time and takes a courage that only the empowerment of the Holy Spirit can supply.
- The feeling of walking alone through a long major struggle with minimal support from colleagues and denominational leaders made a deep impact on me. The pain of those memories caused me to make myself relentlessly available to support and help other pastors especially through tough times. Mentoring and coaching (younger) pastors became a passion for me. I didn't –and still don't- want anyone else to go through something like that alone!

When the congregation heard the decision of Classis, some were angry as could be expected; some were happy. It divided us even more. Within a few days, different groups of people came to me with a long list of names of those who were ready to start a new congregation. A nearby vacant Safeway store had been checked out and could be rented. They wanted a "Spirit-filled" fellowship where they could freely worship without constant criticism and complaints. We have had enough of the CRC.

I sensed a spiritual superiority attitude in a setting of exhaustion and frustration. I think spiritual superiority is more dangerous than spiritual deadness. I had read -more than once- that church splits are ugly blights on the annals of church history leaving deep scars on all those involved. They are also a terrible witness to a watching world. I believe John Calvin, a 16th Century Reformer, stated he would cross seas to avoid a church split. The idea of a new Spirit-filled church was liberating, but it also sent a shiver up my back. It was really tempting because it would allow us to stay in Calgary. At that moment the only option seemed to be that we were to seek a call, anywhere but Calgary. I wanted to say "yes" to a new church but I felt I could not lead a church split. After a few days I declined the invitation.

Wise Advice

About 10 days after the Classis meeting two elders and I arranged to go to Grand Rapids to meet with the two men who had previously written the letter to the church visitors to "butt out," the denomination's Executive Secretary the Rev. William Brink, and the Professor of Church Polity and Church Order at Calvin Seminary, Dr. Richard DeRidder. Both were wise, experienced, respected churchmen. Before coming they asked us to send all the available written materials, including the decisions made at the Classis meeting and the letter from them to First Church. We were looking for some encouragement and some advice as to our possible options.

When we were ushered into Rev. Brink's office, Dr. DeRidder was already there. Both men had read all the materials and were well informed. They frankly extended their sincere love and sympathy to all of us for going through such an ordeal, "most of it done quite un-Church-Orderly," stated DeRidder categorically. They advised us to forgive and forget the nasty things that were said as quickly as possible and to help the congregation do the same lest we become bitter. They sensed our anger and hurt and spoke openly about it. They were refreshingly candid. Their love and compassion for the church and for us felt like fresh rainwater falling on a parched desert.

Now, what about the motions that were passed and the written material? With that, they went directly to the final letter Classis sent to First Church. I distinctly remember Dr. DeRidder saying to all while looking at me:

> *Henry, you've got to see what they said! They said you are Reformed in your preaching and ministry. That's a strong affirmation. The biggest 'flaw' they focus on is your desire for healing, which the letter indicates you may not be able to bring about. A bit later when they address 'the concerned' it becomes clear why the healing will not likely be accomplished when they are told (-and he read from the letter,) 'to open wide your hearts to the ministry of pastors and consistory'… and more, 'We urge you to examine your hearts to see if there is need for you to make confessions and seek forgiveness from any in the congregation whom you may have hurt. Finally, we urge you to avail yourselves of opportunities to become actively involved in the life and the ministries of the congregation.' In short, Henry, it is easier to ask you to move than to discipline them, but we wonder whether that is just or helpful.*

We were stunned with his blunt comments. As he was speaking, all three of us were taking notes, which we later combined in a report to our Council. Rev. Brink looked up and said, "Wow, Rich that is strong. Are you sure?"

His response was similarly frank,

> *Yes I am; that's why they ask Henry 'to actively seek a call within the denomination.' They obviously feel they have no ground to discipline him. In fact they want to keep him in the denomination but, like the concerned, just get him out of Calgary. That's what they asked and that's all they want!*

Then he stated something I will not forget, He looked straight at me and said:

> *Now Henry, if I instruct you to meet me for coffee at Arnie's at 10 AM tomorrow and you don't show up, you are disobedient! But if I ask you to meet me for coffee tomorrow and you don't show up, I can only be disappointed! They only asked you to seek a call. Had they instructed you to do so, you, or your Council, could have appealed to Synod and there is no doubt in my mind that Synod would have sustained you strongly, and likely rebuked the Classis. Classes simply can't tell ministers to move or seek calls. A pastor's Council may ask for the pastor to be released but only if they have 'weighty reasons' and only with Classical approval and*

then only with the 'concurrence' of three synodical deputies. After that a Council can declare a pastor to be available for a call. Even then a pastor doesn't seek a call! Someone has to declare him available. A Classis can't ask a pastor 'to actively seek a call within the denomination.' It is not in our Church Order.

We were taken aback with this blunt but accurate assessment of our situation. I looked at Rev. Brink for his reaction. He looked at me, nodded his head, and said, "I think Rich is right, that's kind of how we see it." He added, "There is nothing Classis has said that should force you to go. However, I really wonder if for your own sake, and especially for your family's sake, you would be wise to consider a move." I informed him I had been open to that. However, after our long conflict, I was viewed by some as a hero, by others as a troublemaker. I took too many risks for some, was too stubbornly biblical for others. The upshot had been that few, if any wanted to risk calling me. I had not received an invitation for a call to another congregation in at least three years. I felt like I was marked. This was still difficult for me; I know I had asked the Lord to check me out as to whether recognition and popularity was more important than His approval. Now that He was doing that, I didn't like the feel of it one bit!

Where to Now?

Both men emphasized that we as elders and as congregation needed to pray and seek what was best for the congregation as well as for our family. DeRidder again repeated, "Henry, Church-Order-wise, you cannot seek a call. Churches seek pastors, not the other way around. Furthermore, should you get a call, before you can accept it you need your Council's approval."

One of the elders asked, "And what if we think for whatever reason that he should *not* accept it?"

"Then you may state that. You may even forbid him if you as elders deem that a pastoral change at that time would seriously harm the congregation." He then gave an example of a pastor who had accepted a call and then had to reverse his decision when his elders insisted that he needed to stay and resolve some issues before he could leave.

The elder smiled and replied, "I think you just answered our question." DeRidder responded with, "In fact, if Henry left because of this, it might

169

set a bad precedent." And he listed the reasons: 1) If you're unhappy with your leaders, and if you complain long and hard enough, you'll eventually get your way. He saw this as rewarding bad behaviour. 2) Worse to him was the fact that a small minority can dictate to and control the greater majority. They can create enough problems so that the majority eventually goes elsewhere. 3) His greater concern was the damage my leaving at this time might do to the larger part of the congregation, but also insisted that the elders together had to weigh this.

In closing the meeting, our counselors urged the elders to meet both with me and without me. They advised that any decisions they made needed to be clear, decisive, and clearly communicated to the congregation. They prayed with us and we were on our way.

Looking back, I see that we received excellent ecclesiastical advice. They were wise "church lawyers." I clearly understood what my options were. The future was in God's hands who had entrusted it to the elders. We also had a better understanding of the last few years. We realized that we had tried so hard to please that we had lost sight of our calling and responsibility to lead a large and vibrant congregation. Our struggles had changed our focus, and we no longer led effectively. Instead of searching for ways to make the gospel more relevant in the language of the day for our church and the greater community, we had been busy trying to keep peace and quell wars. Although we knew the importance of being authentic and relevant, we had been preoccupied with fixing "squeaky wheels."

On our way home, we knew that era was now finished. When our resolute little group left Grand Rapids to return to Calgary, we felt a fresh courage. We became excited about celebrating Christmas. One elder stated, "I can't wait to start the New Year. We need to get on with it!"

As Christmas approached, I too felt a resolute determination to be the church of our Lord. I tried hard to celebrate the Christmas season, but I found that trying to be happy was hard work. I was tired and anxious and was sinking to a low emotional state. I stayed up late, often sitting in our front room looking out the window at the Calgary night skyline. And when I did go to bed, I couldn't get to sleep. Sometimes I'd pray, "God, since you never slumber or sleep, why should I stay awake? You promised to build your church, so why am I getting so tired?" The uncertainty about my future weighed on me and made me into a zombie for about three weeks.

As a Christmas greeting, I sent a letter to our elders. I shared my pain and hurt and asked them to pray for the church and for our family's future. I trusted them and felt fully confident in putting my future in their hands. If they felt it best for the church to make a new start with a new pastor, I would not stand in their way. If, however, they felt we needed to pick up where we had left off, I was also willing to give that my best shot. I wanted to know clearly what God desired, and I felt I had no way of finding that out without the elders taking a strong leadership role. I felt a quiet spirit of submission, and I sensed a great relief and peace the night of December 31 when I knew that 1981 was finally over. Never have I enjoyed more the turning of the page from one year to the next.

Finally, the Year Ends

Every winter in early January starting in 1977, I had taken two weeks of classes at Fuller Seminary in Pasadena, California to complete courses in my Doctor of Ministry program. January is a great month to leave Calgary and spend two weeks in California. This new year, 1982, I left Calgary on Sunday afternoon, January 3, and returned 12 days later on Friday evening, January 15. When Jan picked me up at the airport, she told me that the elders had met the previous evening for their regular meeting. Then she surprised me by informing me that they had made a number of decisions, which were already printed in Sunday's bulletin. It made me anxious since they had done all that without me, and without even consulting me! It was scary and unnerving. I told them I trusted them and I had put my future in their hands, hadn't I? They had taken me up on it, and now I wasn't so sure I liked it. Giving up control is hard. When I got home, I read the elders' response to the congregation to the recommendations from Classis. Ingeniously, they addressed the congregation and in so doing addressed Classis, obviously utilizing the advice from Dr. DeRidder and the Rev. William Brink. The bulletin stated:

Council Response to the Recommendations from Classis Alberta South meeting of Nov. 30, Dec. 1 and 2, 1981

After much prayer, discussion, and reflection with regard to the decisions of Classis at its last meeting on Dec. 2, 1981, Council hereby wishes to communicate the following response to the congregation at this time:

1. *Council declares that it is pleased and thankful to God with the decision of Classis endorsing the leadership of this Council and affirming the preaching and ministry of Pastor H. Wildeboer as Reformed.*
2. *Council declares that healing and reconciliation is of the essence for First CRC and desires it intensely. It deems that Biblical healing and reconciliation requires the participation and ministry of Pastor H. Wildeboer. Council unanimously endorsed the pastoral leadership of Rev. H. Wildeboer at its meeting on Oct. 15, 1981 and will continue to uphold that decision until such time that God makes it clear to him and this Council to do otherwise. At this time Council strongly urges the congregation to do the same.*
3. *Council furthermore declares that normal Church Order polity shall prevail concerning the calling of our pastors, including Pastor H. Wildeboer. Our pastors are always available for calls and should a call be extended to one of our pastors, then the pastor concerned in consultation with Council, shall seriously seek God's will.*
4. *Council asks any member who disagrees with decision 2 above… "Council deems that Biblical healing and reconciliation requires the participation and ministry of Pastor H. Wildeboer," to submit reasons and grounds for their objection either in writing or in person to Council on or before its next meeting.*

The Fight is over

That was a bold demonstration of clear, godly leadership on the part of the elders. I was totally surprised and utterly blessed by their declarations. Each statement felt to me like an affirmative godly decision oriented towards healing. All four points were unchallengeable within CR church polity. The response was never challenged either by Classis or any member of the congregation. The concerned had given it their best shot. The battle was over.

During the next 6 to 9 months, more than 100 members of First Church transferred to neighboring churches, mostly to Emmanuel CRC. Many who left made sure that I knew they had been lifelong members of First who, thanks to all the changes, now felt displaced and had no choice but to leave! Few young people and singles left. Although a number of people left us, our membership numbers stayed the same; new people joined at the same pace as others left. Our budget surprisingly never fell short.

For Jan and me, it was an uncomfortable time. It was difficult to go to public areas or activities, such as a local Christian School activity, a mall, or other places where we would run into former members of First. In a shop where my wife went regularly, one woman, formerly from First, would head for the back whenever Jan came in the door. We had decided earlier, though, that we were not going to cross any street or duck into any store to avoid anyone. It was sometimes hard to keep that commitment. It was also hard at times for our daughters especially at the Christian High School. The younger boys seemed to be fine.

Though the "wars" had ceased, I know it took a year for "the spirit of peace" to return. Healing came slowly. Forgetting the past and pressing on took even longer. We were wounded deeper than we realized. We had become super-cautious and fearful of any kind of criticism; simple questions created cautious responses. Even my preaching had become cautious. If I said anything that could possibly be misunderstood, misconstrued, or misinterpreted, I provided thorough explanations covering all possible angles. After a year of this, a young doctor invited me to meet with him in his office. I found his request a bit unusual but did not hesitate to set a time. When I came in, I sat down on a chair. He intentionally chose to sit on a higher stool looking down at me. Without much chatter, he started right in. He said he wanted to meet with me on his turf and time because he was concerned about me. He looked me straight in the eyes and spoke words I can still hear in my mind: "Henry, the fight is over!" I didn't say anything, so he said it again, "Henry, I said the fight is over."

He asked if I knew what he meant. I wasn't sure and said so.

Then it came:

> *Henry, I am tired of watching your defensive posture shown in almost everything you say and do. I feel when you preach you are scared of us and frozen with fear of being misunderstood. In order not to make any possible mistake, you cover everything from every possible angle! I feel you preach like you think we are just waiting to pounce on you. You don't trust us. We are your friends who love you*

and want to grow with you in godly discipleship. So please don't treat us like skeptical critics. We love you and we don't distrust you.

That did it. Oh, he hit a really painful chord. I have tears even as I write this. Everything let go inside of me and the tears just poured out. He wisely sat quietly and let it happen. When I finally looked up, he just smiled. He put his youthful hand on my shoulder and said a brief prayer thanking God for what had just happened. He asked Him to help me stop fighting internally, heal me, and allow others to love me.

I was stunned, but I knew he was right. It really stung, though. I realized that I had developed a defensive pattern of speaking and preaching. In hockey terms, I had become puck shy. When a goalie is puck shy, he is scared of the puck and is useless to his team. I realized that because I didn't want to get hurt again, I had built a protective wall around myself.

In the weeks that followed, I often thought about what the doctor had said, especially when I was preaching and very intentionally when he was in church. When I slid into the pattern again, all I needed to do was look at him. When he grimaced or smiled, I knew what he meant. I could smile at him and go on.

Gradually, I was becoming aware that God was trying to get me to face some long-standing painful issues and inner wounds that likely preceded the conflicts at First Church. I thought I was done with the pain, so this was disconcerting. I realized then that some of my past buried deep inside me needed to be stirred up and addressed. It appeared that this might happen sooner rather than later.

Chapter 10

One More Battle to Face

Calgary, 1982-1984

After the classical difficulties faded and the members who had left were settled in their new places, the rest of us felt like we were in a vacuum. The length and intensity of the struggles had sucked the life and energy out of us. Instead of being "free to soar," we were too tired to crawl and too sad to celebrate; we grieved the loss of family members who had left us. As a church we needed a time of rest, reflection, and recuperation. I was given a six-month sabbatical to finish up my doctor of ministry dissertation at Fuller Seminary, dealing with -of all things- charismatic renewal from a Reformed perspective.

Now a Doctor!

My work at Fuller was approved in the fall of 1982, and I received my doctor of ministry degree. With the degree and the battle at First finished, I should have been ready to go back to work with fresh life, fire, and zeal. But something felt unfinished. I felt like God was saying, "The church struggles are over, but I am not finished with the changes I want in you." For years I had been in deep water dog paddling, trying to keep my head above water for all I was worth. I had been so busy doing church stuff that I had spent little time or energy cultivating and weeding my own inner garden. The result was a spiritual drought that caused many of the flowers of life to wither and die. I knew I needed to do something about it, but I didn't know what.

But also a Patient!

Emotionally I entered a low time. Over a period of about a year, I realized I was becoming more depressed. I lost self-confidence and began to be afraid, without knowing what I was afraid of. I was doing the work of ministry, including a lot of preaching and counseling, but passion and power were missing. I felt like an eight-cylinder car firing on six pistons. I don't know how long it took before friends began to notice and gently probed to find out what was happening. Others weren't quite so gentle!

Gradually, I began to realize I needed help. That was hard to admit. I had little idea what was wrong or where to get help. I had always been in control and ready to help others, but now I was the one who needed to be on the receiving end. I shared my feelings with Jan and a few others, but they too were puzzled. What was happening? Was I experiencing some kind of emotional breakdown?

At our elders' meetings, we usually opened with a share and prayer time. We would break up into small groups and pray for each other and our families. We were refreshingly open and honest. We knew we needed vibrant hearts if we were going to shepherd our diversified congregation effectively. At one such session, I shared that I was not functioning well. Things that I used to do with minimal effort now took everything I had to finish. A couple of elders -shocking to me- admitted that they had noticed this and were concerned. In fact, it became clear that they had spoken with each other about it. As we talked some more, they agreed that I needed help and urged me to get it as quickly as possible and to take whatever time I needed.

A few years earlier, some of our Calgary churches, CRCs, Reformed and Presbyterian, had sponsored an excellent three-day conference with John and Paula Sanford from Coeur d'Alene, Idaho. The Sanfords led a counseling ministry that dealt with inner healing and especially helped Christians address long-standing emotional wounds. A number of us had read their book, *The Transformation of the Inner Man*. During their time in Calgary, we had become friends; I felt free to call John. When I explained my situation and the elders' comments, he suggested I come to the counseling center in Idaho for a week to 10 days. I decided to do so. With minimum preparation time and planning, lest I chicken out, I drove to Coeur d'Alene and found their home. Just the drive through the Canadian Rockies was refreshing.

The counseling center was located in their bungalow home. It had living quarters on one side; some extra bedrooms on the other side had been converted to counseling rooms and an office. It was nothing ostentatious. They had made lodging arrangements for me at a nearby motel, and since it was hot, I was happy to have an air-conditioned room and a swimming pool. John suggested I check in at the motel and come back around 3:30

PM. When I returned, he was wearing a suit, a bit unusual for John, and in the front hall were three suitcases. That's when I learned that he and Paula were leaving an hour later for the Spokane airport to head to Pennsylvania for a five-day teaching conference. I was shocked and immediately thought, "But what about me? I came for help, ready to do business to get my stuff out in the open, address it, and get some help. And now you are leaving!" But in the same breath, John mentioned, "We have arranged for Jean (name changed) to work with you and help you."

My First Lesson, Pride

I felt like Naaman with Elisha (see II Kings 5). Naaman was utterly disappointed when Elisha sent out his servant to tell him that if he wanted to get well, he had to dip into the River Jordan seven times. That was all - nothing more, nothing hard. It shocked him; it was an assault on his pride. Naaman thought that Elisha would come out, gush all over him, wave his magic wand, and with a nice performance -with everybody watching- heal him. But there was none of that. I thought John himself, and if not John then Paula, would work with me. After all, they had led a conference with a lot of registrants from various congregations and denominations in our church that I helped organize. I felt entitled to his help! I only realized much later that at that moment I was getting exactly the help I needed. It was my first "therapy" session from God Himself. My spirit of entitlement needed deflating, and God apparently had made that number 1 on His agenda.

I was introduced to Jean, an overweight, 65-year-old woman who had been married and divorced three times. She was the opposite of what I anticipated, yet she was the servant Elisha sent out to me. What I needed, God provided in Jean. Jean had learned to walk close with God later in life through her own pain about which she was not very transparent. In bits and pieces, I learned that her tough journey had made her cry out to God. In sheer desperation she had discovered that He had not abandoned her, even though it often felt like He had. She knew the importance, the process and the power of repentance, confession, and forgiveness.

Jean began by patiently and carefully walking me back to the beginning of my life as I recalled it. Gradually, some of the more painful experiences came out, like the war times when we only had the bare bones minimum of food, or when I woke up in the morning in the potato cellar, having survived the night-time bombing raids. I relived the pain of immigration and leaving good friends behind, and especially my grandfather's death on the very day of our departure for Canada. Those experiences were so intertwined that I had never really dealt with the grief of his death. Frequently, Jean would pause, allow both of us to sit quietly for a while, and then invite me to lay all that at the feet of Jesus. She would speak His grace, comfort, and very much be His presence with me. She brought a certain closure to the brokenness in each section of my life and then did not allow me go back. If I did, she would kindly but firmly stop and remind me that that part was now finished. Jesus had forgiven, and when He does, he also forgets.

Over the next five days, Jean sat with me for some 25-30 hours, just walking back page after page through my life. She asked questions about my siblings, my uncles and aunts, cousins, and friends, every now and then stopping to ask more questions, to reflect in silence for a few moments or to tie events or relationships together. She would ask me to put a load of "my life junk" in my hands. Sometimes she would tell me to hold it up, look at it and own it. Only if I would confess that it was my stuff of my own making could I be freed from it. Then she would tell me to hand it to Christ, by turning my palms down and bringing down my arms, all the while urging me to picture myself putting it all in His hands and leaving it there. At times I wondered where all this was going, but I had decided to submit myself to the process and let Jean lead me—this time I was not in charge. My explanations, excuses, and rationalizations did not stop the process. Jean quietly kept saying, "You need to deal with that, Henry, not excuse or explain it. Lay it at His feet."

I began to notice that little by little the fog was lifting and my mind was beginning to feel more at rest. It was a revealing and healing process. It was a unique experience in that I looked at my life more and more as one line strung together with many commas and fewer periods. I began to feel that all my life had been lived under the guiding eye of the Father who had held my hand for the entire journey, even though many times I had not been aware of it. It really was the fulfillment of "I will never leave you nor forsake you." I learned a lot during the process.

The Release of Confession

I know now this was a time of confession. I was in the confession booth and Jean was the priest behind the curtain. After a time of confession, Jean would lead me in prayer and lay it -and leave it- at the foot of the cross. She then would take on a priestly role and declare forgiveness for the specific things that had been confessed -nothing vague or general. I am now much more aware of the need for and the value of confession, very much in the CRC but also in the broader evangelical Christian community. In this important area the Reformation "threw out the baby with the bath water." We need to find the lost "babies" and wash them anew in the cleansing water of Christ's shed blood. A vague confession of "forgive us all of our sins" at the end of a prayer may sound pious but hardly qualifies as an authentic confession that liberates. Since my experience with Jean, I have become more available as a "priest" who hears confessions from church members and pastors. Once I went through the experience myself and allowed myself to be open to offer it to others, the practice was requested more often. It is a wonderful privilege to be used by God "to set the captive free."

Introspection

Jean also took me through a time of introspection. I felt no stone was left unturned. I knew that First Church had gone through renewal and had grown deeper in spirituality with a new hunger for worship, prayer, and Scripture reading that was energizing and refreshing. But I knew that if I were to continue to lead the congregation, I too needed refreshing and renewal. After the church struggles ceased, I stagnated spiritually and felt I was being left behind. In one of my sessions with Jean, I felt guilty and dirty over stuff that she had pushed me to face. Into my mind flashed the thought, "I am not as bad as all that!" Almost instantly, I was overwhelmed with the thought, "You are much worse than that, but I love you anyway." It was distressing and comforting at the same time.

What Happened?

I believe I experienced inner healing as I faced my painful wounds one by one, many of which I saw as of my own making. To be sure, some were inflicted on me by others. But it really didn't matter how I got them; dealing with them was important. I noticed I had developed some patterns to avoid pains that were destructive: short-fused anger, defensive explanations, closing up or sulking with self-pity. Some of these started innocuously enough but grew into addictive patterns. I never used alcohol or drugs. Rather, I escaped into periods of withdrawal; silent, sinful thoughts or daydreams; occasional glances or winks of inappropriate flirtatiousness. I know now these started as momentary relief -a little fix for pain and turmoil. But if repeated, a seemingly innocent fix subtly and silently grows and grows, until what was a form of relief from pain becomes an addiction. Over time, it roots deeper and deeper into the heart and psyche and then holds ground tenaciously giving up the gains reluctantly.

I often lacked the brutal honesty to handle these addictive nudges and patterns. I was in denial. Denial is a powerful tool that keeps us quietly enslaved. God nudges us quietly, often first through Word and Spirit. If the quiet nudging of God's patient love and tenderness is not heeded, God loves us enough to embarrass us with "caughtness" and shame, rather than letting us destroy ourselves. He may well send someone who asks as innocent question as, "What's happening to you?" We are blessed if we have someone who will ask the hard questions and insist that we respond.

The longer we continue in our destructive patterns, the more painful it is to get caught. Shame plays a huge part in keeping us from seeking help. The choice becomes clear: denial, avoidance, and dying; or ownership, repentance, and living. The first leads to hiding, withdrawal, and depression. The second allows for a new start with a fresh, authentic humility which lifts the load.

My time of healing with Jean prepared me later to help others in their confessions. Those like me who make this new start become valuable in the kingdom to help others who are also hiding behind walls of secrecy and fear, longing and crying for liberation that is possible only after an honest, humble, face-to-face encounter with God. The joy of leading such confessions and mediating such encounters is inexpressible. My time with Jean helped me to realize that many in our churches coddle addictions, often undetected because we have become professional at veneering them into our lives so that they are invisible most of the time. We sometimes do see them in each other but we have unspoken agreements not to ask any questions.

Jean also helped me to recognize my "nice" escapes. I often covered the pain of inner failure by working hard and accomplishing a host of good things. As a youngster, I learned early that good performance earned affirmation and praise. Another nice escape for me moved in innocently and unnoticeably. My business interests were stirred while I was still a teenager. I learned that saving money was harder and smarter than spending it. While serving in the Sunnyside congregation, I became aware that I needed to save for our future. At 65 I would receive a steady -but meager- pension. Housing, the costs of which were continually rising, would be a major problem for us if we lived in parsonages all our ministry life and did not purchase our own home. I learned that if the opportunity came, it would be wise to buy a house. So I invested to try somehow to get a down payment. Though I was sure God would provide, I was not sure how we would manage the costs of Christian education for our children from kindergarten through university on one salary. With some encouragement and help from others, we began to save and invest. I quickly discovered that I loved business ventures and found them energizing, especially if a venture brought some success. My adrenalin kicked in with risks and adventurous investments. In 1977, after being in Calgary for six years, we did purchase our own home.

Business became an attractive escape when ministry was disappointing. It was fun to be involved in business, so much so that offers to go into it full-time became temptations. But I dared not leave pastoral ministry because I could not shake the conviction that God had called me and had not given any indication that He was releasing me. I know honest business in itself is neither wrong nor sinful, I just knew that for me it was a distraction since God had given me another assignment. I see both business and pastoral ministry as ministries to which God calls. He just hadn't called me to a business ministry. For me, the business outlet held an addictive power. I was always aware of that and have had to ask good friends to keep an eye on me and alert me if they see me sliding.

Seeking Dad's Approval

My father was a hardworking farmer, but he was also a sharp businessman. Both, some of his farming and business genes came my way. I mostly deem them as assets. The farming background has helped me understand the Scriptures much better. I know the deep love for animals and several times I spent hours looking for a lost calf (we never had sheep). I understand the adrenalin rush of bringing in the harvest when it is ripe and ready. There is urgency about getting the crop into the bin before the snow flies; that's not the time to dilly-dally. I know the challenge of separating good grain from useless chaff and trying to figure out how to take a good crop of oats and get rid of the wild oats, a hated weed mixed in with the good stuff which hurts harvest volumes and sales. Farming and business were intertwined. I remember suggesting to dad that we could reduce seed costs by sowing more sparingly by using maybe a third less seed. Dad responded by telling me in no uncertain terms that that was a stupid way to save. "Skimp with seeding and you'll get nothing; the weeds take over and choke out the good stuff."

But the business temptation was strong. When I was involved in it I experienced energy and passion. Jean suspected that I was longing and seeking for my father's approval and blessing. I knew dad had hoped that I would go into the agri-business, and when I didn't I felt like I let him down, although I don't know whether I did; he never mentioned it.

In one session, Jean helped me understand the brokenness in my father's own journey. As a child and young teenager, Hendrik Wildeboer lived in a strong, conservative, legalistic community called Staphorst, still known today for its rigidity. When he was a teenager his family moved some 15 kilometers away but took the rigid community spirit with them. My father struggled with family challenges, the place of God in his life, and what to do with his church experiences. Additionally in November 1936 dad was in a very serious motorcycle accident which killed the driver, his best friend, and left him, the passenger, with a badly broken leg. By mid-February 1937, the hospital released him and shortly after that he married my mom. Jean pointed out that his upbringing; the accident, marriage, and fatherhood – shortly after that- were too many major changes in too short a time. I think it created confusion and inner conflict that was heavy to carry. He was a man who longed to be godly. I am not sure my father ever sorted out the tension between a legalistic church culture and the conviction that by grace he was freed from perfectionistic rule keeping. I believe he did but I do not know how or when that came about.

When my parents had three children, they moved to the city of Zwolle so that dad could be closer to the office where he worked and where he and mom developed their own values. He was articulate with his words but closed with his feelings. He would not talk about the war; he said very little, if anything, about his relationship with God. He probably told me he loved me, if he did, I do not remember it. That was all very private with him. I suspect it had a lot to do with his painful experiences. I believe at heart he was soft and tender, but he never learned to express these feelings without becoming emotional or weepy. So he bottled them up rather than appear "weak" or vulnerable.

I didn't know all that. Once Jean helped me understand my dad, much of my own hurt and anger dissipated. I wept because it became clear to me that I had made life even more difficult for him at times. I thought he *didn't want* to communicate more openly. I thought he was tough and stubborn and refused to talk about many of the things that I wanted to know and learn from him. So when he closed up, I assumed he was blocking me out and I reacted with frustration and anger. I made an already-hard life even harder. I regret that now and wish I could redo some of those times. I'd love one more conversation with him even now! But it is too late. He died seven years (1975) before I met Jean. Jean helped me work through these things, and I found considerable relief and peace.

Finishing Up

On Monday afternoon after the weekend, I went back to the motel feeling cleansed and pure. I felt like all the viruses, poisons, and garbage had been burned on a pyre of God's grace and love. It seemed like everything was out of my system. I had had no idea what was inside me and how it had dragged me down. For the first time in years, I felt healthy and clean.

It was a hot day, so I changed into my swimming suit and sat by the motel pool reflecting and praying for some time. It suddenly dawned on me that I had nothing left to confess. I said out loud, "It's all done." I stood, and looking up I said, "There is nothing left that I am not willing to face." I raised my arms and said, "God, you have nothing against me anymore. I did all that you told me to do. I now accept your forgiveness. I am done and I am free, period!" I stood on the edge of the pool and stated, "In the name of the Father, and the Son, and the Holy Spirit." I dove in, thinking, "This is the beginning of the rest of my life. No more condemnation."

I came out of the water, went to my room and phoned Jean and said, "We're done, I am going home tomorrow morning," wondering what she would say. Her response was, "You're ready. I am not surprised." We met for about an hour that night, and early the next morning I was on my way home.

Returning Home

I came home a changed person. Others soon remarked that I had a deeper spirit of peace and trust and a more genuine sense of humility and less stubborn feistiness. They liked it, as did I. As a consequence, the church, my family, and I were able to have a good period of healing and blessing. Finally, we settled into what seemed to be a more normal pastoral ministry (if there is such a thing). My defensiveness lessened, conflicts ceased, and Council meetings dealt with pastoral issues pertaining to the congregation rather than combative questions and endless arguments. It was a time of peace after eight long years of discord.

But though on the surface things in the church appeared to be going well, at the deeper level we were still grieving the pain of loss. Our energy level was way down. We were tired and beat-up. We missed many of the individual members and families who had left; they had been good friends for many years. We missed the power and joy of a unified worship that caused the building to ring with praise or cry with the pain of the illnesses of family members or friends. We did not know how to handle the broken relationships of a long feud involving long-time friends who now rarely spoke to each other. We did not know how to repair friendships that had been ripped apart. It took time for many of us, especially the leaders, to complete the grieving process and release the pain. Although we didn't realize it, we had closed our hearts to those who had earlier closed their hearts to us. We had to forgive those who had hurt us. And we had to ask for forgiveness from God and from others. We were not guiltless or innocent. I had always hoped there would be a united worship communion service for the Calgary CRCs that acknowledged the brokenness of the past, in which we owned and confessed our involvement and could thus bring a proper closure and a fresh start for all.

At the time, I think I was settling in for a new stretch. We anticipated a quiet period of growth and rebuilding. We needed some new staff help. Jake Ypma came for about a year as an interim pastor and served us well in the area of pastoral care. He was followed by Dave Tigchelaar, a new co-pastor who shared the congregational ministry with me. He had been a mission pastor, and we deemed his church planting experience would help us move forward and outward in our commitment to community service. It felt like the church had gone through a painful divorce, and now like a couple that has parted after a divorce, we needed to recuperate individually. It took time to adjust accordingly and learn to walk on a new road. In short, we had to rediscover our identity. We knew we were a community-oriented church; that was now firmly ensconced in our DNA. Our ministries like the Sonshine Center, evangelism, new member classes, discipling others, and small groups were still in place, but many of them needed to be restarted.

Without the constant questions as to who we were and what we were all about, we were no longer doing important introspection. We no longer asked questions like: "Is what we are doing really serving God? If it is, how can we do it better or more effectively?

I still felt like the pastor of the previous church. Perhaps I too needed a fresh start. At times I did wonder whether all the things I had experienced and learned could be more effectively used in another setting. But where would such a setting be?

I had no idea. But God did.

Chapter 11

On to Oshawa

1984 - 2000

It was a cold Sunday in Calgary in January 1984 when, just after getting home from leading two morning services, I received a phone call from a man named Abe Wamsteeker, chairman of Zion Christian Reformed Church in Oshawa. It was totally unexpected. As an Albertan, the first question that popped into my mind was, "Where is Oshawa?" Their Council, without talking to me had nominated me as the pastor to be called by the congregation. They wanted to let me know in case there were "any valid binding reasons" why I could not prayerfully consider a call to their church. My response was, "No, I guess there is no binding reason, but it is highly unlikely that I will move." Things had settled down, I was making a fresh start in what now had become a more pleasant place to work, and good things were beginning to happen. I was starting to enjoy ministry again, something I had not done for a long time. New people were coming, new ministries were starting, and new young adults were checking us out. I had no intention of moving, and if I did, I would not pick Ontario as my first choice. I was a thorough-going Albertan, maybe even a bit of a redneck, at least when it came to Eastern Canada! I told him to let the congregation know this before they held their vote.

Come and Help Us

He let me say all that and said little in reply. About three weeks later he called again on a Sunday afternoon, with the news that Zion Church had voted overwhelmingly that morning to extend an official call to me to become their pastor. My first reaction was one of anger: "Didn't you hear what I said a few weeks before?" I told him I was honoured but reluctant to think hard about it. It just didn't seem right for me, or for our family. I had told him all that three weeks earlier. Rather quietly, he replied that their Council had received that information, talked and prayed about it, shared it with the congregation, and then voted. The result was that 95% voted in favor of extending the call to me. Council stated that they had decided to lay the challenge before us. They added one request: that I would visit them at their expense to meet with their Council and congregation. And, if it was at all possible, would I please come and preach at a Sunday morning service? Their Council wanted to present their needs to me face to face. If after that I was convinced that I should decline their invitation, they would accept that as God's decision and that would be it. "No hard feelings whatsoever. No pressure, but please do come and visit us." That was pressure!

A few days later, I had an elders' meeting and openly shared that I had this call which I was reluctant to consider; in fact I even found it hard to pray about it. The elders strongly expressed their desire that I stay. However, one of them got to me. He said, "Pastor Henry, they have done this prayerfully and they feel God clearly led them to call you. Should you not at least honor them with the visit?" I decided to do so and left about eight days later on a Friday night red-eye flight from Calgary to Toronto, arriving Saturday morning about 7:30 AM. I rented a car and spent part of the day looking around Oshawa affirming strongly in my mind that there was no comparison between Calgary with the majestic Rocky Mountains on its western horizon and Oshawa with the GM smokestacks on its south side.

In the afternoon, I met some of the church members and for the evening, they had scheduled a meeting with Council. I soon discovered that their journey was similar to First's in many ways. Zion had been through some painful theological conflicts revolving around the pastor and a contingent of elders. Some of the leaders had struggled with a pastor regarding his biblical orthodoxy. Unable to resolve the conflict, the result had been a parting of ways. That pastor was followed by a new pastor, Rev. Peter DeHaan, who had served well for five years and brought much healing and reconciliation to the ruptured congregation. Once the church was healed, he felt his task was done and he accepted another call to a church with a similar history. When I spoke with him, he told me frankly: "Zion is ready to move forward with servant ministries to the community, and they need someone like you to inspire and lead them."

Zion CRC Oshawa had started in 1963 with a creative, forward-looking bent. Like many other Canadian communities, Dutch immigrant groups moved into the Bowmanville, Oshawa, and Whitby area during the post World War II years (1948-1952). This resulted in two larger Christian

Reformed churches in Bowmanville and Whitby but none in Oshawa, the biggest city of the three. It was decided that, "Oshawa needs a Christian Reformed Church, rather than have every Oshawan drive to Whitby or Bowmanville, besides those churches were full. They were also encouraged by the Whitby pastor, Rev. John Van Harmelen, since Oshawa, as the larger city warranted a Christian Reformed Church. I later learned the real reason. The Oshawa church started with a more free-spirited group of people who wanted creativity and flexibility in worship and ministries. They knew that to be mission-focused required a fresh approach. These priorities showed in their choice of pastor and in the very design of their facility.

Similar Journeys, Different Places

I, like them, had also finished a journey of conflict and pain in Alberta, trying to make disciples who served God in a secular world. I was impressed with the honesty and humility in the way these people expressed their need and longing for a pastor who would help them reach a deeper level of spirituality and who would model a passion to serve others. That became obvious in the next day's worship services. The church was filled with an enthusiastic and energized crowd of worshipers ready to respond. Since the acoustics were excellent and the enthusiasm was high, when they sang, the building resounded with life and vitality. I preached a nontraditional, unsafe message on David dancing before the ark as it entered Jerusalem (II Samuel 6). (Note: The Calgary elder who urged me to honour Oshawa with a visit also urged me to preach that sermon, which I had preached in Calgary just a few weeks earlier. He commented, "If they still want you after that, we are in trouble.") As I moved through the message, I was touched by the people's response. "Amen" sounded in various corners of the worship center and people at times uttered "yes!" They even clapped several times to indicate support. I was used to a responsive congregation who participated in the preaching in Calgary, but even there I had not experienced anything like this. (Much later, I learned that many of those responding were not members of Zion at all but ex-CRC members from area churches who had left during recent years for Evangelical and Pentecostal congregations. They had heard that I would be there that Sunday morning and, for whatever reasons, they decided to come as well.)

After the evening service, we had a dialogue time in which the congregation asked me various questions about worship, ministries, and especially about reaching out to others. I noticed an authentic passion in them to minister to a broken world. I was profoundly touched by it and could not shake it off. Neither I nor my family wanted to move to Oshawa, but I was starting to feel that I couldn't decline the call.

When I got back to Calgary, Jan picked me up. She looked at me and said, "We're going, aren't we?" She could see it on my face. And though I managed to say, "I don't know," I did not convince her. The very next day I went to another meeting of Classis Alberta South, and then I knew with certainty. It felt like the same argumentative spirit all over again. My era in Calgary was finished.

A Fresh Start

I believed God wanted to bring together a congregation which had been through much pain and learned from it, and a pastor who also had been through pain and learned from it. On my daughter Judy's 18th birthday, March 14, 1984, we accepted the call and told the kids that after 13 years in Calgary we were moving east. Because life in Calgary was all they knew, this unleashed buckets of tears, and once they started Jan and I ended up joining them. Judy remembers this as her worst birthday ever.

Once the decision was made, though, things came together as if "Someone" were moving the pieces at just the right time. We wanted to move about the end of July or early in August. But we would have to sell our house in a market which was absolutely disastrous for house sales. We listed it immediately after we accepted the call to Oshawa. We prayed for God's guidance to sell the house and added that somehow God would bring a price fair to the buyer but also to us. I had no idea how He might do that, but I prayed it audibly at a family meal and I meant it. I believed He would do it.

There was no interested party in April, May, or June. Our friend and realtor, Don Cheveldayoff, held open houses, advertised the place and did all he could to promote it. Even though we knew the market was bad, we began to feel like the house was jinxed. We had no lookers, until about mid-

June when Don finally got an offer. The asking price was $145,000. The offer of $142,000 was close enough to be acceptable, but the buyers' down payment was small which meant that they wanted us to take back a second mortgage of about $15,000. We were reluctant to do that. Then Don pointed out something else. He said, "There is something I think you should know. It appears the two people making the offer are living together but are not married. Should the relationship end for any reason, I don't know how secure your loan would be. You may end up with the house back in your lap." We declined the offer. By now it was nearly July, and we were scheduled to leave Calgary for Oshawa in mid-August. I thought, "Come on, Lord. We have put our trust in your hands, but this is pushing it."

But We Need to Sell This House!

The next morning at breakfast I prayed and thanked God for the six wonderful years that we had experienced in this family home. On the spur of the moment, I asked Him to bring another Christian family with at least four children to enjoy it. It was a brief but specific prayer. I remember Jan saying, "Do you have to be that particular, wouldn't just a sale be satisfactory?" I had heard that God wants us to be concrete and specific in our prayers, so this time I was. I don't know why.

A week later we left for a two-week vacation on the Washington and Oregon coast. Judy and Barbara, now 18 and 17, stayed home since both had jobs and they would look after the house and yard. On Thursday of the second week of our vacation, we phoned the girls who told us that Don had taken someone through the house for a tour and he had returned for a second look. The man was a psychiatrist from Montreal who was moving to Calgary to work at Holy Cross Hospital, located only a few minutes from our house. His wife was coming from Montreal for the weekend to see the house. I remember one of the girls saying, "We're going to sell the house before you get back. We cleaned it inside and out, we washed the windows, cut the grass, and even weeded the garden and flower beds!"

When we called the girls on Tuesday to see how things had gone, Don had just asked them to tell me to contact him since he had an offer. They had asked him what the offer was. When he told them the offer was $144,000 cash to the first mortgage, they knew it was better than the previous one we had been ready to accept. Their response was, "We'll accept it. Just take it to dad's lawyer, Bryce MacDonald, and tell him it's okay." The girls were right; it was a deal.

A week later we phoned the buyer to invite him for a visit so we could show him the electronic furnace cleaner, fireplace stuff, and other aspects of the house. Since his nights were open, we invited him to join us for supper. He readily accepted.

A few days later, Dr. Aldous came a bit early. I had not arrived home yet, so Rob, age 8, was chatting with him. "Do you have any children?" "Yes I do, I have four." Upon that, Rob ran into kitchen, "Mom, can I ask him if he is a Christian?" Jan said, "Why?" His immediate response: "I want to know if God really answers prayer." Jan deemed that a psychiatrist should be able to handle that, so she gave her okay.

Just then I happened to come in the door and heard Rob's question, "Are you a Christian?" I also heard Dr. Aldous's answer, "Yes, I am, I love the Lord very much." We learned he was born in a parsonage in Oshawa -of all places- and as a doctor had spent some years doing medical work in Nigeria, along with a number of CRC doctors and missionaries. We are still amazed and chuckle when we reflect back on the sale and the price! The ingenuity and humour of God never ceases to fascinate.

An Amazing Trip, "His Banner over Us"

Our Farewell Sunday, August 12, 1984, was very difficult after more than 13 years of intense living, struggling, and growing. We were deeply invested in the life of First Church. Our lives were intertwined with the hearts and lives of the people. I had performed more than 200 weddings, baptized some 300 children, and saw many lives changed in major ways. Because it was a young church, I had done only a few funerals.

We also loved the community. It was hard to leave! We had planned to leave early Monday morning. Two cars were all packed up - we had seven people! One was a large, tank-like 1976 Chrysler Town and Country station wagon, pulling a 24-foot, 20-year-old Airstream trailer that we would use for meals and sleeping as we traveled across the country, some 4,000

191

kilometers. The other was a 1974 Volvo which the girls would take turns driving.

After the Sunday evening farewell service and social, we arrived home about 11:30 PM. We had also said goodbye to some of my siblings and their families who had come from Lacombe for the farewell service. Finally, when we were on our own with our adrenalin still flowing the girls said: "Let's go now, we don't want to get up in the morning and still have to drive out of Calgary."

So the few things we still had in the house were packed up. We turned out the lights for the last time, closed the door, locked it, and dropped the key through the mail slot. We were finished. By now it was after midnight. We stood on the dark driveway by the two cars, joined hands, thanked God for our amazing years in Calgary, and asked for protection, safety, and a trouble-free trip. It was a moving moment -never to be forgotten. We left a dark, quiet city that was peacefully asleep by now.

The two girls drove the 1974 Volvo, often accompanied by one or two of the boys, who preferred their music over that in mom and dad's car. Jan and I and one or two kids rode in the station wagon with the trailer. We drove about four hours until we were about 80 kilometers east of Medicine Hat where we decided to stop. The adrenalin rush had faded and we were now exhausted. We stopped at a wide area along the road and parked the vehicles, one in front of the other. When we woke up the next morning, we noticed we were right at the Alberta-Saskatchewan border. One car, the Volvo, was still in Alberta. The station wagon and trailer, just ahead of it, were in Saskatchewan. We were on the way but we had many miles to go.

The trip went smoothly. We had decided to go to Grand Rapids first and arrived there on Thursday. We visited with Jan's parents for the weekend and celebrated Jan's 42nd birthday on Sunday. On Monday we drove the last seven hours and arrived in Oshawa about 4:00 PM. I made a bad mistake by taking both cars directly to the church. That route led through the older, dilapidated, industrial district, which was the family's first view of Oshawa. It's not impressive and certainly not pretty! Later the girls told us that while driving up Ritson Road, both of them had cried hard and wondered whether they could turn around and go right back to Calgary.

Daily Manna and "Shoes"

It is still amazing to me that our prayer for safety and a trouble-free trip was answered perfectly by God. For the most part, the two cars stayed within view of each other and were never separated from one another for more than 15 minutes. We never replaced a light bulb, touched any of the 12 tires -even to add air- nor did either car require one additional drop of oil in the entire 4,000-kilometer journey. We had asked God to confirm that we were doing His will by moving to this "distant land." We felt He did, from selling the house through the entire preparation and trip from Calgary to Oshawa. Everything came together. All needs were amply met. He provided daily manna and our cars' "shoes" did not wear out. This was comforting for a family which was still very reluctant about the move.

We arrived in Oshawa in mid-August, and the installation service was planned for a hot, humid Wednesday evening. A good number of the church members were either on vacation or had decided that a swim in a cool pool was more attractive than a long, (fairly dull?) service in a sweltering, humid, church. I found it hard to blame them. The attendance was poor. The only noticeable thing that stands out -and we only learned this later- was that our now son-in-law, Edwin Van Schepen, was cajoled by his mother to call a few of his high school friends to attend. "After all, the new minister has some teenage children and it would be nice for them if some youth showed up." Reluctantly they left their pools, pleased mom and came and sat in the back of church. When Edwin saw Judy, he told his friends, "I am going to marry that girl." Some six years later he did.

Also unknown to us at the time, but something we learned later, was how Judy and Barbara really felt. Jan and I had gone to church early for the service with the three younger boys. The girls remained home and were to come later, just in time for the start of the service. While at home, they had a serious discussion about taking the Volvo and heading back to Calgary. They wondered how far they'd be able to get before they'd be missed, and how we would handle the situation. The main problem with their plan that stopped it all; they had no money. Instead, grudgingly they came to the service where I made things even worse by introducing the family members to the congregation and asking them to stand. Imagine two 18 and 17-year-old girls being asked to stand up in church to be "gawked at by all" as they put it. It was not an auspicious start.

A New Congregation

After that "grand opening," we were received with open arms and soon learned that in many ways we as church and pastor really complemented each other. I was more convicted than ever about the reality of the gospel and the importance and the urgency of it for our lives. God was good to us in bringing us as a family into a fresh time of joyful ministry, one free from tension and conflict. We started the fall season by taking an early September trip to Grand Rapids to enroll Judy in Calvin College. The boys seemed to be fine in their new schools but missed their Calgary schools and friends. It was far harder for Barbara who had to start her grade 12 in a new school, community and make all new friends. If we had to do that again we would explore various alternatives.

The congregation was ready for change and responded well to us; the church started to grow. Members started to invite others to come to church with them. The church grew through the addition of regular visitors, many of whom were either former members of Zion or members of other churches. I noticed a pattern: the first visitors were Christians from other churches who visited to check out what they had heard. They would come to our evening services after attending morning services in their own churches -many felt they had done "their duty" and earned the right to go somewhere else in the evening. Next, we noted that people from the community with minimal- if any- church background started to visit more regularly.

Oh No, Trouble Ahead?

We were there only a few months when a major challenge came our way, so similar to what we had faced in Calgary, that it scared me. A 51 year old man, Adri Oudyk, a long-time Zion member came to me. He was thin, could barely walk and told me he had been unable to work for about eight years, since 1976. He said:

I understand you and the elders in Calgary anointed people with oil and prayed for their healing. I have been struggling with multiple sclerosis (MS) for 17 years and I would like to ask you and the elders to anoint me with oil and pray for my healing.

I suggested he put his request in a note to the elders and get it to us. I was buying time. I am a new pastor in a new congregation and this "anointing with oil" is new here. I know it is fully biblical, have no question about that, but for many churches, because they haven't seen or done it, it is divisive. Am I heading for my first major conflict? I was cautious, but not very long. Our next elders' meeting had Adri's request. The elders agreed to fulfill the request and suggested that we do so the following Sunday morning. What happened is reported as a story in a study book that I wrote for CRC Publications in 1995 dealing with miracles entitled, <u>Miraculous Healing and You.</u> Adri tells the story as events transpired.

My illness started in 1967 when I was thirty-four years old. I was enjoying my work at General Motors, supporting my wife and three children, the oldest of who was nine years old. Numbness in my leg and blindness in one eye led me to my doctor. He suspected a possible blockage in my spine, but wisely had me hospitalized for tests. They discovered that I was afflicted with the debilitating disease multiple sclerosis, commonly called MS.

I was unable to work for about twelve months. From 1968 to 1976 the MS continued its course of depleting my life and energy. I experienced periods of paralysis of my limbs and loss of coordination. I would work a few months, suffer another attack, lose more work time and return until the next bout. Each attack meant further loss of strength and stamina. In 1976 I came to the dreaded moment when I -and others- realized that my deteriorating condition precipitated an early retirement. At the youthful age of 43 I was retired and put on a disability pension. Though no longer working the disease continued to drain me. I was regressing. I realized it would only be a matter of time. The longest distance I could walk was 200 feet, and then only with the support of a cane. In 1981 I suffered another severe attack which left me very weak and tired.

In the fall of 1984, after much thought and prayer, I asked the elders of my church to anoint me with oil, lay hands on me, and pray for my healing as James 5 instructs. They responded positively and did so at the conclusion of a Sunday morning worship service. The entire congregation was made aware of the request and most of them stayed for a time of prayer while the elders fulfilled my request and prayed over me. It was an up-building experience for all. I felt very much affirmed and loved. I felt nothing dramatic nor did anything change at the moment; however, since then I have never had another attack.

Nearly two years later, I was still using a wheelchair regularly, but I was improving ever so gradually. Over the extended period of time my strength and stamina returned. Coordination began to improve. I began to swim, take longer walks, and began cycling with great regularity, even in the winter when at all possible. In fact, I had two cycling accidents in two years. The first resulted in a broken arm, the second left me with a shattered leg. My recovery in both instances was remarkable.

I continued to improve. By now I was swimming 30 minutes, five times a week; I was walking 2 kms and cycling about 8 kms per day. I believe God healed me and so gradually that it was hardly noticeable at times. Only when I looked back over longer periods of time did I most clearly see the improvements. My family, my church, and I are deeply thankful for what God continues to do in my life.

It was amazing how God worked this out. When the request came I was a reluctant fearful participant. The Calgary turmoil now almost five years old was still fresh in my soul. The wounds though addressed, were not fully healed at all. I needed the encouragement of the elders to move forward and "get over it." The gradual healing was perfect this time. No one was threatened by it and no one questioned it. God honored His Word. He did exactly what He promised in James 5:13 ff. Adri was healed and immensely blessed. He is now eighty years old.

Growth

The church grew and after 18 months our 10:00 AM service was full; the elders suggested we initiate two morning services. This quickly created the first wave of resistance. In its 25 years of existence, Zion's membership had been stable with about 100 to 115 families for a total of about 300 people. In the minds of many, the present increase was just a temporary blip, and they felt that the church would soon return to "normal." Instead, I suggested that we pray and plan for further growth and blessing. This was annoying to some who asked: "Who does he think he is to believe we are actually going to continue to grow?" For some, it was not in their scope of thinking that their church could increase. They had never seen it and did not expect it. Others were excited and prayed for continued growth. It

196

seemed to me that no matter where one is located, growth comes with pain and fear. The two AM services were started, and after a month or two the resistance was minimal. It was now necessary. Changes in Oshawa came easier than they had 15 years earlier in Calgary. By this time, other churches were also making changes, especially in the areas of music and worship. Most congregations were not opposed to change. In fact, they were quite open to it; they just hadn't experienced much of it.

More things changed shortly after we arrived at Zion. The church had no overhead projector, so for evening services when we wanted to sing some of the new hymns, Jan or I would go to the Christian school late Friday afternoon and borrow an overhead projector. We had a small screen with three legs which we "wonkily" set up on the communion table. We soon received the complaints we were hoping for -the overhead was fine but many in the back couldn't read the words because the screen was too small. The church had earlier decided -even set aside funds- to revamp the stage area in the worship center. Council decided to add funds for "a good-sized projection screen" in the project. One elder carried the day in the Council discussion when he said, "I am a carpenter and I need tools to do my work. I don't let others tell me what tools I am allowed to use. We brought this man all the way from Alberta, and he needs tools to do his work, so let's get them instead of telling him how to do his job without them." That was the end of that discussion. The motion was passed by all; we bought a 16 x 10 foot screen electrically powered for lowering and raising it. Thanks, Cor!

Drums and guitars became more common. Greater participation by men and women, children and youth was much more readily accepted than it had been in Calgary. Members and visitors alike were eager to participate. Now, I rarely felt alone in any congregation if I raised my hands in praise to God during a hymn.

Nice Try

In the summer of 1986, two years after we arrived, a large (83 acres!) piece of land became available on Taunton Road between Wilson and Harmony for about $700,000. We were entering a recession in Canada; in spite of that, it was a bargain. I saw huge potential and my entrepreneurial bent kicked in immediately. I mentioned at an elders' meeting that we should explore buying the land as soon as possible. I already had someone who offered to fund half of it. He wanted to see the church do something major and community-shaping. Besides the possibility of a sizable church building with ample parking, we would have enough land to build a number of badly needed affordable housing units. We had room for a senior housing complex; there would be space for a new Christian school and more for other projects as well. Any unneeded land could be sold, with the proceeds paying for part of the church and school buildings. It was a great idea for a prime site perfectly located for future growth, but it was too early.

Some elders thought I had delusions of grandeur or I was on an ego trip. With a condescending smile, they shook their heads as if to say, "How can you be so ridiculous?" I was still too new, even after three years; I had no "chips" of trust in their bank, so the idea didn't go anywhere. Somebody moved that we explore it, and that's where it died. We couldn't even get a second to put the motion on the floor so Council could discuss it. At the end of the meeting, one elder came to me and commented that he thought it was "the right thing to do but these guys just can't see it! And they have never had to." Growth thinking was not part of church thinking.

Subsequent time has confirmed all of the above. In the next five years, the property was sold and resold several times for values more than ten times (!) the cost quoted to us. In the meantime, a group from area CRCs organized to build a senior housing complex. They bought five acres of land for much more than we would have paid for five acres had it been part of this project.

A 25th Anniversary

In 1988, Zion Church celebrated its 25th anniversary. On the Sunday night of the anniversary celebration, I preached that God was calling us into adult maturity and servanthood as He does with any 25-year-old. The days of immigration were over; fewer Dutch accents were heard in conversation, and more Canadian accoutrements were appearing in our homes and schools. Most of us didn't lack for a thing. Rather than being preoccupied with our own needs and desires like kids are, I said it was time for us as a church to recognize our age of 25 and shift our focus to helping others.

We challenged the church's membership to adopt some significant outreach ministries, and they did. We had a special thanksgiving offering for 25 years of blessings to be used to start new community ministries that would require sacrifices of time, talents, and finances. They were intended for ministries that would bring no benefit to the congregation directly except for the joy of serving and blessing others in sheer gratitude to God. Two big social needs were obvious in the community: one, an affordable housing complex for families and singles, and two, a counseling ministry to help those who were facing personal, family, social, emotional, or financial needs. The offering was big enough to excite us with the many possibilities. It was obvious that the congregation was eager to reach out and serve people in the Oshawa and Durham Region. Even visitors donated and volunteered to help.

New Hope Housing and Gate 3:16

We appointed two task forces. The first, in conjunction with other interested churches, was to explore options to create a housing project to provide subsidized shelter for low-income people, especially single parents. This was promoted as a justice issue. Everyone needs a roof over their head, and with much poverty and many people with disabilities, we simply had to help. It was our Christian calling. With some capable people from various Oshawa churches undertaking the project, some five years later a beautiful, functional, interdenominational 118 unit apartment complex called New Hope Housing was opened. It was accomplished without a lot of fanfare.

The other project was Gate 3:16. People with physical or emotional challenges in the recent past had resided in homes and care centers that were no longer available due to provincial budget cuts. Suddenly, the Whitby psychiatric hospital reduced its patient load, leaving some patients without care or homes and some employees without work or income. Both were out on the streets. Likewise, group homes and hospital support were reduced on very short notice.

Oshawa, being a city with GM factories, had many GM employees. When they came to work they would enter the factory grounds through one of several gates. We named the project with the obvious reference to John

3:16, "gate 3:16" or "the gate" for short by which one comes into fellowship with God. A downtown storefront was rented and opened with coffee and donuts, usually donated by coffee shops in the area. The drop-in center started with Zion's initiative and funding and rapidly became a welcome place to sit, chat, enjoy a cup of coffee, play Scrabble, cards, dominoes or other games. Volunteers and support soon came from other churches to help staff it. Congregations worked together to raise enough funds so the interdenominational board could rent a facility and hire a part-time director.

In the meantime, God was preparing a person. George Witvoet came to Canada as an 18-year-old immigrant. He was the oldest of several siblings who came with their mother from Holland in May 1950. (They happened to come on the Volendam, the same ship and in the same month as did my family.) Shortly before his family was to immigrate George's father died, but that did not stop his mother and the family came anyway. George as the oldest was called upon to help the family survive. George practiced the only trade he knew, hairdressing, which he had learned from his father. He had a shop in downtown Oshawa with which he had supported his mom, his younger siblings, and later his own family.

It struck me shortly after our arrival in Oshawa that George had a yearning and passion for worship and a desire to serve others. As soon as I dared, I asked George if he would help me in leading worship. He welcomed the opportunity. God had gifted and prepared him. Within a few years as he spent more time in ministries, he phased out the hairdressing shop and became coordinator of ministries and evangelism for Zion Church. Both his credibility with the congregation and his long-time involvement with the community resulted in a warm welcome by all. When Gate 3:16 started, George became involved, and not long after that the Board asked him to become its director.

Since its beginning Gate 3:16 ministries has been located in a number of sites in downtown Oshawa, often determined by rental costs. It has continued for many years and is faithfully supported on a monthly basis by members of various Durham region congregations. George served as director until 2001 when a heart attack took his life. Others, including Martin Van Harmelen, a long-time member of Hebron Christian Reformed

Church, have provided faithful, sacrificial leadership to this much-needed ministry.

These were two very good ministries which stand out as living tributes to the greater community of a church's 25th Anniversary Celebration.

Worship Conferences

About this time we started receiving requests from various area churches asking for assistance in worship related matters. We were exploring flexible ways of worshipping God involving gifted members. We found an eagerness for a participatory style of worship. Members wanted to share in the planning and contribute *their* thoughts and talents.

Worship services were changing in Christian Reformed churches and in other denominations as well. There was a common hunger for creative liturgies; many wanted a greater variety of music besides the organ and piano. To respond to the increasing number of requests from individual churches and in order to better help a larger group of churches at the same time we decided to do a Friday night – Saturday conference with worship, workshops, and sharing of resources. We announced it, Marie Broersma, our office administrator, formed a small team of workers to arrange for publicity, registration, food and many the other details. She made that conference –and four other subsequent ones- happen.

The response was surprising to us. Registrations came in quickly from as far away as 250 km. We used speakers and workshop leaders who were doing these things and we immediately struck chords of appreciation in many hearts and with the church leaders who came. It was all hands on stuff. It was exciting and inspiring to us at Zion to see some 150-200 people from all over Ontario come together.

We began Friday evening (about 8:00 PM to allow travel time) with a worship service led by our gifted *lay* leaders including praise teams, banners, instruments, drama, dance, and concluding with a key note message. Each year we had one main theme on which we focused such as prayer, evangelism, or small groups. The following morning we opened with a brief time of praise and a plenary teaching session followed with a workshop till noon. After lunch we had one more workshop session.

We had a variety of workshop topics from: prayer to praise teams, blended music to banners, dance to drama, sound solutions to song selection, evangelism to enfolding, leadership, healing, and worship. We were blessed with members gifted in these areas who humbly shared their love of God through the various mediums and they were willing to do it in a workshop. Because they were local members without special training, that in itself gave the encouragement to others to say, "If they can do it, maybe I should try." This was a big "permission giver".

We ended every conference Saturday afternoon with a final challenge given to the entire group. I usually led it and based it on what had transpired the rest of the day. It was a time of commitment, prayer, commissioning and empowerment. Somehow we always ended on a high note, with final words from many being, "please do it again next year." We still meet people who tell us they came and were blessed. We were thankful to be used by God to bless others.

One or Two, Where?

By 1988 Zion had outgrown its building and was struggling to decide whether to move as one congregation to a larger site or to divide and start a new congregation in another area of the city. Both options had strong proponents and opponents. The greater majority by far wanted to move as one. In either case, we would need a piece of land for another site. But by now land had become prohibitively expensive compared to a few years earlier. For many, it was simply too expensive. We looked at a number of sites and noted that as the economy declined, so did land prices. One site that was available was near the one we had considered in 1987, a 3.1 acre property on the corner of Taunton Road and Harmony. To me it seemed the perfect location for a vital church, "smack-dab" on the main corner in the center of the next major commercial development in the northeast end of the city. The property was listed for $950,000, well worth it because of its choice location. But it had one down-side, it was too small for a larger church and therefore too costly for only 3 acres. In order to build a large church facility with ample parking, we needed more land. We reluctantly let it go. Contributing to our reluctance was the fact that we had been trying to sell the present Zion property on the corner of Central Park and Adelaide with no success. The building was too big for a start-up congregation, too small for a growing church; the site was only one acre. A few parties showed some interest but at prices less than land value even though it had a modern and attractive facility. The congregation decided that before proceeding with the new facility we needed a sale commitment for the Adelaide property.

Recession Blessings

In 1989, a recession set in. Properties were not selling and prices were dropping rapidly. In mid-1991 I received a phone call from the owner of the property on the corner of Taunton and Harmony, the piece that we had tried to buy a few years earlier. I had met him before. He had come as a German immigrant and still had a strong German accent -so much so that the minute I heard his voice on the phone I knew who it was. He wanted to know if we were still interested in his land. I told him our interest -like the recession- had declined, especially with our inability to get a buyer for our present property, I told him that our motivation "ist nicht gut!" (is not good).

He chuckled and asked if I would stop by his office "sometime soon." I offered to come with another member of the church, but he did not want that. He wanted to sit down "just mit the two of us." A week later I stopped at his office in Markham where he warmly welcomed me -with coffee at that- something he had not done before with me. We had a fairly good relationship by that time, and my Dutch background seemed to combine well with his German heritage -historically that certainly wasn't always the case! After a bit of chatter, he came right to the point. He wanted and needed to sell the land. He had built a number of Petro-can gas stations and he had bought the Oshawa property to build another one. However, to do so he needed a zoning change, something the city of Oshawa had now refused three times. He had concluded that it wasn't going to happen and he was not going to fight city hall any longer. Instead, he decided he would sell us the land for "the very good price of $600,000." I told him frankly that I could not sell that price to Council or the congregation. In fact, I wouldn't even take that back to them. Just like that, he dropped the price to $500,000 -the quickest hundred grand I ever saved, but never saw!

I knew then that he was open to an offer of some kind. A few weeks later after meeting with Council, we met again, and I presented him with an offer. With some help from a realtor and a professional appraiser (both from the church), we decided to present a firm written offer for $375,000 about which he groaned and moaned. He said we should be ashamed of ourselves for insulting him. But he and I both knew it was all a game, and I kind of enjoyed listening to him sputter. A few days later he accepted our offer. We closed October 29, 1992.

Once the land was bought, we had two issues to address: one, our move was coming, and, two, the site was not large enough for future growth. It was big enough for our present needs, but for any future growth we would need more land.

One or Two? Or a Team?

When we had decided earlier to relocate as one large congregation, we decided to do so with a diversified, gifted staff team. When we bought the land, we were well on the way to adding staff. In the mid-eighties we started a second position with a youth pastor. For three consecutive years we had one-year interns who were students at Calvin Seminary. Rob Hogendoorn came in 1985 followed by David Feddes in 1986, who was followed by Karl House in 1987. Karl's year of internship concluded his responsibilities at Calvin Seminary, so at the end of the year he became available for a call. In 1988 Zion called him as associate pastor and pastor of youth. He accepted and after being ordained we worked well together for another six years, after which he moved to Peterborough to be the pastor of Living Hope, a new congregation. In February 1988, shortly before Karl was ordained, George Witvoet became part-time minister of evangelism following Rudy Heezen who had previously served in the position. Herman VanderBurg, former counselor with us in First Calgary, moved to Oshawa and served with us as counselor on staff until he retired five years later. We had some capable people who developed and served us well as worship coordinators. George Witvoet, Glenda Hull, Sharon Bradimore and Yolanda Brouwer - each made unique and valuable contributions in this area.

Tyndale Seminary and Teaching "Leadership"

My role was also changing. In the later eighties, I had become acquainted with what was then named Ontario Bible College and Seminary (now Tyndale College and Seminary), an energetic, evangelical, interdenominational college and the largest Protestant (Evangelical) seminary in Canada, located in Toronto. The dean of the seminary, Dr. Ian Rennie, had asked me to speak at the combined college and seminary graduation ceremony in 1987. As our friendship grew, he noticed my interest in leadership development, and since I had a doctor of ministry degree from Fuller Seminary, he asked if I would develop materials to teach a class in that area. Ian saw a growing need for leadership development and with my interest and passion for it offered an adjunct professor position in that area. I liked the idea, Zion Council did too, so I began by teaching a three-hour class every Monday afternoon for 13 weeks. I loved it, and end-of-semester evaluations showed that the students loved it as well. It was an enriching opportunity for me to integrate the practical aspects of pastoral ministry at Zion Church with the academic community of a seminary. It was a win-win situation for all, the seminary, the church, and me. I was nourished as I nurtured others.

The teaching at Tyndale and the experience as pastor at Zion made me deeply aware of the importance of godly leadership and integrity. Churches, organizations, and ministries all rise and fall with leaders who are intentional about character development and integrity. Christian leadership requires Holy Spirit empowerment which provides the impetus to believe what God has said, and act upon it. This is faith! We then discover that God *means* what He says. This in turn provides the courage to be prophetic causing one to dare to go upstream from common cultural practices.

An Amazing Diversity

I continued the church and teaching combination and added two more courses later. "Revitalizing the Older Church" was a summer course primarily attended by a variety of evangelical pastors serving older congregations mostly throughout Ontario, with some coming from the states of New York, Michigan, and Ohio. "Advanced Preaching" was a course I was asked to teach during the tough, brittle years of 1995-97 when the institution teetered on the edge of bankruptcy and was really short of faculty. The seminary could not afford more than a few full-time faculty members, so for several years many courses were taught by adjunct or associate faculty members. They consisted mostly of experienced pastors, hopefully with doctorates, who could be hired to teach a variety of courses for minimal pay (and no benefits), since they already had church salaries to provide basic incomes. And because almost all of us were busily engaged as pastors with a total of many years of church experience, the courses were down-to-earth, totally practical, and most helpful for people who went directly from seminary into pastoral work, counseling, youth work, or mission service as about 90% of the graduates did. I loved the place for various reasons: it had a tender, gracious spirit; it had both an interdenominational and international flavor. An ecumenical tone was enriched with a diverse cross-cultural makeup. Presently more than 50% of the students are women and about 45% are non-Caucasian. I found that class discussions were never boring due to this vast diversity. Imagine a discussion about baptism, infant and/or adult, or about the return of Christ, with a variety of dispensationalists, with pre-mils, post-mils and a-mils with each group astutely placing the rapture and tribulation in the time slot when it would surely occur.

When teaching courses in leadership, I faced all kinds of questions about organizational structures and gender issues from men and women who were involved in pastoral work. Authority structures were diverse, from total equality of men and women as in the Salvation Army where husband-and-wife teams are fully equal and either leads and/or preaches, to denominations where only men are eligible for preaching and pastoral leadership roles. It was challenging and I was stretched through it. From a Tyndale class I would return to the congregation for pastoral work which either confirmed what I was trying to teach, or result in revisiting what I had taught due to confrontations with reality.

The Trial of Illness

One of my joys while teaching at Tyndale was the presence of my son John who was an M. Div. student at Tyndale. He had graduated earlier from Calvin College and he and His wife Grace felt God was leading them to Tyndale Seminary. In 1995, while in seminary at Tyndale, John had developed a serious itching problem and was constantly scratching himself. Between 1995 and 1998, he saw a variety of specialists, many of whom believed that he had picked up some kind of tropical disease in 1993 during a five-week ministry project in Nigeria. Dermatologists examined his skin and tried different salves, lotions and pills, each for three to six weeks with no improvement; internal specialists tested his "insides," nothing unusual; two psychiatrists spent time dealing with what they thought was depression or obsessive compulsive behavior (OCD) because he was scratching himself ad nauseam. Other doctors tried other tests, all to no avail. The itching continued; the scratching never stopped. He tried antidepressants which slowed him down and made him groggy so that he would fall asleep in seminary classes, but as soon as he woke up he was scratching again.

After more than two long years of trying to find the source of the problem, John was seriously ill. By the time he graduated from Tyndale in 1998, he was weak and obviously failing. The seriousness of his illness became most obvious to Jan and me when we saw him on the stage for his seminary graduation. Later that year he was admitted for tests through the University of Toronto under the care of Dr. Jay Keystone, said to be the most knowledgeable tropical disease specialist in Canada. He surmised that it was not a tropical disease that was plaguing John, in fact he fairly quickly determined that John had a tumor in his chest that was squeezing both his heart and lungs, resulting in shortness of breath and an accelerated heartbeat. The tumor was cancerous, associated with non-lymphoma Hodgkin's. For us as John's family, it was an extremely anxious and distressing time especially for John and his wife Grace.

God used six months of nauseous chemotherapy and a month of radiation treatments to heal John. We are deeply grateful for his healing, and the subsequent blessings of a family with three healthy children. Though our Calgary trials were tough and draining, nothing was as painful as seeing a son suffer and approaching death while we were completely helpless outside of ceaseless prayer. Since then, John has been given a new lease on life and is passionate about the good news of new life in Jesus Christ. When he is asked why he is so urgent about Christ, he answers with, "When you have had the privilege of looking death in the face at the age of 26 and get to walk away from it, everything changes." It has been an inspiration for us to see him enjoying a close relationship to Christ and to his family, and now see them happily serve the Rehoboth Christian Reformed Church in Bowmanville as pastor. God is good!

Leadership Training

Through an invitation of John Van Til, Regional Director for Home Missions in Eastern Canada, and with some financial assistance towards travel expenses, I received training at bi-monthly meetings in Chicago with a group of pastors from the Midwest, all with strong leadership gifts and passions. Terry Walling and Bob Logan, associated with Fuller Seminary in California, led us for three years of courses in, "Refocusing Leaders" and "Refocusing Churches." For me they were years of development of practical leadership, an area that laid dormant in me but was just waiting to wake up. The training combined wonderfully with my teaching ministry at the seminary and my pastoral work at Zion. That's when I realized that I took to leadership issues like a duck takes to water.

This was energizing and came at a time when I was ready for it. These experiences proved to be life-shaping for me. I sensed that God was preparing me for the next phase of my ministry. I just didn't know what it would be or how I would move into it. My passion for leadership development was high and whenever I was given a chance to deal with leadership issues, I would go for it. I also began to realize that my heart for congregational ministry was changing in that I longed to do more training, equipping, and mentoring. I became passionate about being available to younger pastors who were struggling with leadership issues; especially when opposed by a few "power" people. I had been on a lonely trip, and I wanted to spare others that pain.

More Equipping, Less Doing

Desiring to be open, I shared my heart's interests one night with my elders who quickly picked up the implications. One elder, Ray Rodenburgh, looked at me and said, "I think your priorities are shifting and I wonder what that means for us?" When I responded with "I don't know," he suggested that Zion's elders needed to look hard at that. We did so for about two months and decided to seek a younger co-pastor who could join

208

us and in two or three years take over the leadership of the team and church. In the summer of 1995, Pastor Arlan Koppendrayer joined us. Shortly after his arrival, I began a six-month sabbatical. I needed the break, and it gave Arlan the opportunity to become acquainted with the church.

Because of my faculty connections with Tyndale, for the sabbatical I was offered a faculty position as pastor-in-residence at Regent College in Vancouver. My responsibility was to mingle with students and especially with those searching for clarity in the area of vocational direction. The sabbatical from June to December 1995 stands out as one of our best learning experiences for Jan and me. We were invited to sit in on any and all classes, including an intensive summer school program, led by faculty from all over North America. As part of the faculty, I was invited to attend faculty meetings. The school also had small groups made of four faculty members and spouses who met twice monthly. Jan and I were invited to join Bruce and Elaine Waltke (Old Testament), Eugene and Jan Peterson (Spirituality), and Paul Stevens (Christianity and the marketplace), a group which met every other Sunday evening. They were people who wanted to make their lives count for God. The Regent experience was refreshing; the small group was the highlight of it all.

I remember the last Sunday night meeting before our return to Oshawa. As we were leaving the meeting, I said to one of the faculty members, "Do you have any advice for me as I get ready to go back to the church?" Since he was a contemplative person, I was not surprised with his response, "Yes, I think so. Let's talk Tuesday morning. I'll share some thoughts." I nodded, "Okay, I'll find you Tuesday morning."

Between Sunday and Tuesday, I wondered what he wanted to say that he couldn't have said Sunday night. I knew him as one who rarely stated anything off the cuff but I wondered what he might come up with.

Tuesday morning came. We met, got our coffee, found a corner in the atrium, and sat down. I looked at him and said, "I am curious to hear what you want to say." He looked at me and said, "Good." Smiling at me, he went on, "I think you should get out of the church's pastoral ministry." And he stopped to let it sink in. I was a bit stunned, so I responded, "Can you say some more?" to which he nodded. "You're not bitter yet. You love the church, and I find that many pastors tend to become bitter and disillusioned when they get to your age" (I was 56). He went on, "I think you should spend the rest of your ministry years training and raising up the next generation of church leaders."

I was floored. It was a prophetic word, and when I heard it, inside rang a loud, "Yes! That is exactly what I long to do." I didn't know how I would do it, but what he said touched my passion right down to my toes! After talking a bit more, I thanked him, we shook hands, and a few days later we began our trek across Canada back to Oshawa in our trusty 1984 Volvo.

I came back home with a fresh vision. It was not entirely new but it now had a new urgency about it. I had renewed enthusiasm and some fresh new ideas. I soon realized that the sabbatical had changed me but also the dynamics of the church had changed. Things just weren't the same. I didn't know what was next.

As congregation we were still trying to decide how to move forward. All the plans for a new building were in the makings. But we needed more land for additional parking. Along Taunton Road were a number of one-plus acre lots with smaller, older homes that abutted our new site. We began to explore whether one or two of those homes could be available for purchase. The time to buy them was now. The area's zoning as residential would likely soon change to commercial which would inflate prices significantly. We also knew that when other owners became aware of a likely zoning change and that a church was interested in their properties prices would go up. After some patient negotiating with one of the homeowners, Roger Bouma, a good realtor in the Oshawa area and a member of the church, helped us buy one of the homes with 1.3 acres of land for some $220,000. The back of the new property adjoined the back of the church property, now giving us a total of 4.6 acres. This was adequate for extra parking, especially when we learned that directly across the road from us would be a large mall with ample parking. In fact, plans called for a corner traffic light and pedestrian walk lights. It looked great!! We rented the house and held onto the property.

Back Home in the Meantime

Shortly after the purchase of the first piece of land, we had appointed a planning-building committee that had worked with an architect to prepare a full set of working plans for a functioning and attractive facility at the new location. The new property of nearly five acres was still considered on the small side for the facility we were planning. Roland Jonker, a Toronto architect, spent many hours with our building committee led by Henry DeWolde. Together they came up with what seemed like a great plan with a facility appropriate for worship, and yet practical and attractive for many community functions. The building would serve well for our present ministries but would also have enough space for future growth. It would be attractive on this very visible and accessible corner, and we put up a huge sign reading "Future site of Zion Christian Reformed Church," with the motto "Moving Together in Harmony," a wordplay with our hopes - Harmony- which also happened to be the name of the main road.

Our property on Adelaide was still listed but no offers came our way. Our hands were tied with a congregational condition stating we would not start construction until we had a firm sale of our present property. Some felt this was a wise, prudent, and stewartly decision; others believed it was a decision based on fear rather than faith. Some church leaders strongly stated, "We need to trust the Lord and start construction as soon as possible. God will provide as we step out in faith." Some even felt we should keep the Adelaide site to develop as a major ministry center close to downtown. The non-decision was crippling us. We had spent thousands of dollars developing a complete set of working plans, and we were ready to build. Many leaders and members urged us to call a congregational meeting to ask for approval to proceed. It was time to move forward. Not to do so was perilous to the vitality of the congregation.

We called a congregational meeting where we explained the plans, costs, and answered questions. We indicated we were ready to do a major fundraising campaign, borrow the needed balance, and build.

Council also recommended a proposal for congregational approval, calling for a 65% vote in favour that we would proceed with construction even though we had no sale on the Adelaide property. After much discussion, we voted on a Sunday morning and received 63% positive vote. We were short by two percent.

Some felt we should vote again, especially since some of those in favour of the plan had been away or had neglected to vote. Others felt the vote was a sign from God to drop the plans and stay where we were. Some felt that God had put us on our present site, and if it was His will that we not be there, He would not have put us there in the first place. To some, our inability to sell the property was God making his will obvious to us. I think that fear and a lack of faith held us back. We should not have stopped since we anticipated no more than about $500,000 out of the sale of our current building anyway. In comparison to the costs for the total project that figure was quite minimal.

By now, though, other dynamics were in play, including the lack of a unified vision within the church and what was worse, within the leadership. Because we were already facing accusations of "manipulation," we decided not to revote. We should have re-voted; it was too important a decision to lose so closely. That was a major mistake for which I take responsibility. I think I was not clearly focused at the time and did not provide the cutting-edge leadership that the project needed.

Inner Turmoil

I was in turmoil. After the damaging 63% vote and our inability to sell the present property, we felt we needed to drop the relocation plans. Arlan had been with us for about three years and was eager to take over the lead pastor role. After all, we had picked him with the goal to do exactly that so I could step back and increase my teaching, coaching, and mentoring. I really felt the time had come for him to take over, but I was reluctant to let that happen. Some church leaders felt he was not ready to lead the church. I felt the same way, but I wondered if that was because I did not want to let go of my pastor role. I was accused of being a leader who says he wants to develop other leaders and let them take over but who at heart was a "control freak" who really didn't trust others. I don't believe that was the case this time.

I felt called to move into the next phase of ministry. That was my goal. I had no plans to move out of the Oshawa area. I wanted to remain a member of Zion, perhaps as an associate pastor who could be a helpful resource to the congregation. Maybe that was unrealistic. I wanted Arlan to take a greater leadership role. He had indicated to me a desire to lead the meeting and the vote, so I had intentionally attended a conference in B.C. on the weekend of the decisive vote. Later I knew that was a mistake. Arlan simply did not have the confidence and trust of enough of the people. In my own leadership journey, I learned that when crucial decisions are at stake in the life of a community, the leader needs to be visible, model confidence, and blow a clear trumpet sound. In case of doubt cautious people vote no. Perhaps the fact that I was not there added enough uncertainty to make the difference. There was indecisiveness in the air that if I had I been leading the meeting, I probably could have helped reduce it enough especially since the vote was very close. We failed again when we didn't go right back and revisit the decision.

After that, we entered a time when many including me became discouraged. We had prayed and worked and now it seemed like all the air was out of the tires; for many the heart and momentum for relocation had passed.

Loss of Vision Leaks

Over time, the situation began to change. Those opposed to relocation became more vocal. More people questioned whether more space was really needed or whether it was just a pipe dream or an ego trip for a few leaders. Several years earlier, we had added a portable building with six small classrooms. In view of the growing costs and divided opinions, a number of members began to say that the present building was satisfactory and with some revamping would be adequate for many years to come. Some also clearly indicated that they would not move, regardless what others decided. They wanted to stay on the Adelaide site.

A large number of younger families, however, felt strongly that we should plan for the future and make the move so we could have a larger impact on the city of Oshawa and Durham Region. The prime location of the area was begging us to build and serve. We would have impacted a huge population corridor in a rapidly growing region. Everything since then has affirmed

213

that. Fear, the very opposite of faith held us back. Every suggestion to proceed was offset by opposition from a smaller group which opposed the move, was shocked by the cost, and had an aversion to debt. By now the leadership was no longer united in her vision and passion.

We worked hard at trying to keep things together, but it wasn't happening. Those of us who had worked on the previous vision, "Moving in Harmony," began to realize that one new building for all would not likely happen. The resistance was entrenched, and the team wanting to see the vision materialize was no longer strongly committed to it. I and others, were tired and losing heart. I no longer felt the strong support to lead the transition, it was time for the next generation to take over, but I wasn't excited about that either.

In the meantime, I had spoken several times with both John Rozeboom and Dirk Hart, leaders with CRC Home Missions, about the growing need to revitalize older, established churches. All three of us felt many of these churches lacked spiritual vitality, were ritualistic in worship, weak in outreach, and in many instances were losing members who were either dropping out or going to other churches. I challenged Home Missions to put more energy, resources, and finances into older congregations. I was not opposed to new church plants. I just did not see putting so much effort and resources into a small group of church plants was good stewardship. We needed to create new life in churches that already had long histories, excellent reputations, great facilities, and good leadership and ministry teams. Most importantly, these churches' members were imbedded into their communities, which allowed them to be effective "fishers of men." For 25 years I had maintained that "We are putting too many eggs in the wrong basket. Can you imagine the outreach and growth that could occur if our churches' members were released and became empowered for the mission of God? Why not put more resources and energy into that?"

In a meeting requested by John Rozeboom, then Executive Director of Home Missions, John looked at me over the lunch table and said, "Henry, go do it! We'll support you financially. Let John Van Til, (another Home Mission employee in Ontario), work with church plants and campus ministries and you spend your time to energize and serve the older established churches of Eastern Canada."

A Ministry Change of Focus

In 1997, I resigned as pastor of Zion CRC, a step long in coming but traumatic nevertheless after 32 years of being a pastor in rather exciting church ministries. I had no definite job at the time although there were some options on the horizon. The CRC of Canada was looking for a new director of Canadian Ministries. I gave them my resume, had an interview, and was dropped from further consideration. By then, I guessed too that I might not fit well into an administrative bureaucracy. Dirk Hart again spoke to me about working with established churches, and we agreed that I would give CRC Home Missions 50% of my time, leaving the other 50% to continue teaching at Tyndale Seminar and help start a Doctor of Ministry program in conjunction with Fuller Seminary. Since that too was primarily an administrative position and did not challenge me, I stepped back from it after some eight months and increased my work with Home Missions to 80% full-time (which really *is* full-time.) With regular Sunday preaching requests and frequent Friday night and Saturday workshops, I was busy and I enjoyed it.

Scenario of Choices

In the meantime, discussions continued at Zion church. It was at a stalemate. Since I was no longer the pastor, I avoided meetings and even pulled away from the leaders in an effort not to influence the direction of the church. It was hard for me not to say anything; most of the time, amazingly, I didn't. With the help of Dirk Hart from CRC Home Missions, a congregational process called "Scenario of Choices" was started. This is a process in which leaders of the congregation and members would meet with Dirk's facilitation to discuss options for the future. A commitment was made up front that whatever option received the strongest vote endorsement by the members of the congregation would be accepted and implemented. Those who differed were expected to abide by the decision. I think many church members did not realize the significance of the process.

A variety of possibilities were presented to us. After reviewing all of them, we decided on two basic ones: One, we would all move to a new location and a new facility, or, two, we would divide into two congregations and

215

divide all assets proportionately on the basis of the percentage of members that went with each congregation.

In September 1998, we adopted the option to "multiply" (not "divide") into two congregations. In reality, it would be more of a mother-daughter relationship. After the vote, time was granted for members to indicate which group they wished to join. We now knew our vision of one large congregation with a staff team in a new facility at a great location was gone. It was hard to accept for many because it was the loss of a long-time vision and dream. Arlan indicated he planned to go with the new congregation. I had already resigned as pastor since I did not want to influence who went where on the basis of the pastors. In the end, 53% went to the new congregation which soon named itself Hope Fellowship; 47% stayed with Zion at the Adelaide property.

In November, Council agreed to ask a committee of three outside people to evaluate all Zion's assets and propose how they could be divided equitably and proportionately according to the number of members in each congregation. In one transfer, 53% of Zion's members became Hope Fellowship; accompanied by 53% of the property value and funds which made for a beautiful start for this new congregation. It was a big sacrifice for the older congregation to give up so many members and pay such a huge dowry. The loss was many of the younger members and much of their vitality and life since most of the worship leaders and musicians moved to the new church. It was not surprising that Zion's members were mostly older since a number of them were charter members who had resisted the move. Zion had been debt-free for many years; it now had to borrow funds to address a dated building in need of significant repair and updating. Those who resisted the move as one paid a dear price. Hope Fellowship received resources of people and funds to give them a tremendous boost for a great start. I do wonder whether they appreciate enough the price Zion paid. Hope Fellowship paid the price of being homeless for 5-6 years and had to meet and worship in rented facilities and schools that required resources, mobility, and hours of "setting up" time. But it was an amazing way to start a new church; they were blessed.

Subsequently, the land was sold for $1,250,000, (we had paid $375,000) with the funds divided between the two churches. The house next to the church on Adelaide was turned over to Zion and the extra house and lot near Harmony was sold for about $650,000 (we had paid $220,000) with these funds going to Hope Fellowship. We had surely been right about one thing -the land had become a valuable asset.

After two years, the new congregation parted ways with Arlan, its pastor, and, after a short vacancy, Pastor Peter Slofstra came from St. Catharines, Ontario. Since then the church has been blessed with the purchase of a vacant school and additional land. In 2008-9 they build a large new worship center and other needed facilities. They are well poised for the future.

Helping Churches

During the years of church multiplication in Oshawa, I served with Home Missions helping congregations, mostly in Ontario and at times in Manitoba and the Maritimes. My work was often with struggling churches and consisted of listening and helping them with tensions and conflicts, often within the leadership. One cannot develop a vision for the future when leaders are scrapping. Some churches wanted help to change their orientation to become mission-focused rather than maintenance-oriented. Many were aging and declining. Unless they made significance changes, I knew they would die; it was only a matter of when. If I told them that some members became incensed and defensive. They could not believe that God would allow their church to die. Now some of these churches have closed; others have merged with neighboring congregations.

I also led retreats and workshops in areas of leadership, or I would help with the process of developing a vision and/or mission statement and follow that with the planning of concrete strategies. I found that after taking a church diligently through a good process, I did not have the authority to hold them accountable to actually *do* what they believed God wanted them to do. I would repeatedly follow up with visits, phone calls, or emails, many of which were not welcomed. I often felt helpless. I learned that if no steps were in place with specific mandates, people assigned, and time lines in place, little, if anything would happen. In many instances, churches later confirmed that their plans and goals were sitting in a binder on a shelf somewhere or in a closet in the Council room. Often they couldn't even find them.

In these instances, I became acutely aware of the inadequacy of our church's authority structure. As a pastor serving in a regional capacity, I had no way of holding any group of leaders, a Council, or a congregation accountable to do what they said they were going to do. I sometimes wished I was a bishop with the authority to make things happen. I would see that action steps needed to be started now but the best I could do was try to inspire or "charm" them into action; nothing more. It was frustrating for me and disappointing for them, especially since *every* congregation has some key people (often younger ones) who are eager to move forward. They would often contact me and share their disappointment in not having the "clout" to proceed. Regretfully, I'd have to admit that I had no more clout than they did. Our structure is not helpful to address these issues. Often a few outspoken people could block the setting of goals, the planning to reach them, and resist subsequent changes. After I went home they simply shelved what we had done and stayed with the status quo.

There were instances when the key leaders clearly understood the value of what we were doing but there was another issue. Somewhere in the process a few would pull me aside and quietly whisper, "What do we do with our pastor? He just doesn't get it." In one visioning workshop, I spent a long Friday evening and most of a Saturday till about 3:00 PM working hard at visioning, planning, and setting specific, manageable goals, and we laid out some energizing concepts. It was really quite exciting and Council members were well invested in the process. When we were done, it seemed like Council and Pastor had a fresh enthusiasm with some good plans. I was encouraged.

Imagine my surprise when I met with the pastor and his wife sipping a glass of wine to celebrate the completion of a great planning time. While sitting in their living room, the pastor looked at me and calmly informed me that he had been talking with another church and would likely leave that summer to start in another congregation. All through the workshop he had "pretended" excitement about giving leadership for a refreshed vision and new plans. At the end he coolly informed me that he was not going to be around to implement any of it! And he wasn't. By fall, the church's priorities had completely changed from the important to the urgent -get a new pastor! Another set of good plans ended up on a shelf; I suspect they have not seen the light of day since. I was angry because I felt that not only had I been deceived and used but worse, so were all the church leaders. It seemed that all of us had just wasted about ten hours of time.

Traveling

During this time, I continued to teach a regular course at Tyndale Seminary. I enjoyed the seminary setting immensely. It meant driving back and forth about 55 km each way from Oshawa into Toronto. I was also driving across the entire city of Toronto with increasing frequency. I found myself attending various meetings at our Canadian CRC offices located in Burlington, some 100 km. It was hard to know when to leave home to be in Burlington for a 9:00 AM meeting. Traffic was often unpredictable. Sometimes I got there an hour early, sometimes an hour late, occasionally right on time. I would plan for a 90-minute trip which in normal traffic was very do-able. One snowy day I decided to count the accidents between Burlington and Oshawa. That's when I concluded that if I kept up this travel schedule on the busy 401, especially in the winter, sooner or later it might well be my turn. By then, Jan and I also felt it would be better for us to get out of Oshawa. We were uncomfortable in each of the two congregations, especially when unhappy people in both wanted our input on what was happening. It was time to move to a more central location after living in Oshawa for over 16 years!

Once the decision was made, we began to look for a house around Burlington, Oakville, or Mississauga. We soon found something in Oakville that attracted us. The previous owners had built a nice office in the basement which would be ideal for my work with Home Missions and churches. The home was functional for us and the price was right! It was located in an older area of tree-lined streets in East Oakville on a ravine lot with Joshua Creek right behind it. Location wise it was much better for my regional road work. From Oakville I could go north and west quite readily where most of the churches that I visited were located. To head east meant driving across the city, but that happened not nearly as often. In November 2000, we left Oshawa and moved into our house which we thoroughly enjoy. Since we need daily exercise, it is an ideal spot for walks, including a 30-minute round-trip walk to a local mall with a well-stocked grocery store.

We make many trips to the store walking; we rarely use a car. We are starting a new phase of life and find ourselves abundantly blessed.

Chapter 12

Moving into Convergence

Oakville, 2000 ff.

Our move from Oshawa to Oakville was a short move but a big change. Over the years when we had moved from one church to another, we faced the pain of difficult farewells, especially after five years in Sunnyside, 13 in Calgary, and 16 in Oshawa. We were part of many people's lives and they were deeply intertwined in ours. The pain of leaving Sunnyside and Calgary was soon replaced with new friends and new joys in a new church. But leaving Oshawa put us into a new community where we had to find and choose a church -something we had never done before. This was also the first time we didn't have children at home, so we didn't have their help in making connections with other families. And we lacked the obvious strong Christian school connection. We had to "grow" into a new community, like every other person who picks up and leaves one place to go to another. In my consulting work, I had preached and facilitated a number of activities at Clarkson CRC, so I had met a number of their members and leaders. We felt we would fit into that congregation because it had a contingent of people our age. This was something new for us since prior to this move we had served congregations with a predominance of younger people. We now had different criteria for choosing a church. We soon found ourselves attending Clarkson (now ClearView CRC since its relocation), which was also the nearest CRC to our new home.

As more churches became aware of the value of outside assistance, my work as a consultant to congregations increased. I was more urgent about the work and could say what needed to be said and would be heard -not because it was new, but because someone other -and now usually older- than their pastor was saying it. And because I showed some signs of "wear and tear" along with grey hair I was heard by those who by virtue of their age tended to be cautious and conservative. I was also working more passionately and with greater urgency and boldness. Time is short! Some people were offended or angry with my frankness, while others nodded assent and afterwards sought me out to thank me for what I had said. In many instances churches lived with buried issues; I just named the obvious elephants in the room.

Time Moves on

As I moved into retirement I felt my sense of urgency was increasing but it was accompanied by a decline in energy. I no longer liked 12-hour workdays. I faced my mortality more honestly, not in a morbid kind of a way, just realistically. I became more convinced of the importance of empowering others to lead, and that meant changing some of our attitudes towards leaders and leadership. In the CRC, we have been hesitant to encourage the gift of leadership; we fear it will create dictators or tyrants. Leaders with clear vision and focused determination are more often viewed as threats than blessings. We have not commonly understood that leadership is *not* about power but about releasing, blessing and employing the gifts of others so they are used in ministries that serve the church and the world. We are so afraid of counterfeit power and abuse that we often quench the gifts of leadership.

Inside of me I sensed a passionate, lifelong desire to lead and see others encouraged to flourish in ministry. But I too was reluctant to lead for when I had done so in the past, I had been criticized. In our early years of ministry, I was regularly reminded by some elders, "We, the elders are the leaders. You are the preacher and pastor. We lead and make the decisions, you preach." I felt they were the board of directors and I was the employee who worked for them. I was rarely encouraged to be a godly, prophetic, mobilizing leader.

The seminary faculty at Tyndale seemed to be aware of these challenges earlier than other seminaries, so much so that they became intentional about leadership and started leadership development courses, first as electives in the early eighties. Shortly after that, as they realized the value, they made leadership development a basic required course for every seminary student, whether they were heading into pastoral, youth, counseling, or mission work. The effectiveness of the entire church and her ministries are enhanced through leadership development -all boats float higher.

Convergence

After settling into the Oakville community, I continued my work with Home Missions and various congregations. I continued to teach and enjoyed both roles. I began what Robert Clinton in his book, *The Making of a Leader*, calls the "convergence stage of leadership." This happens when a leader, approaching the age of 60, enters the stage in which everything he has learned and done begin to blend together to provide a wisdom that comes from the journey of growth and a measure of spiritual maturity that flows out of the years of life and experience. I became energized and comfortable teaching, mentoring, counseling, and facilitating all kinds of troublesome situations. I developed some "handles" to process conflicts and tensions that brought out the best in everyone, including myself. I was no longer afraid of new problems or situations; in fact, new situations were new challenges. My ministry became more effective with much less energy and stress. It was a good time for both Jan and me.

I turned 65 in July 2004 but continued my work as before. I thoroughly enjoyed what I was doing and planned to continue it. I had been on 80% of a full workload and salary with Home Missions. The remaining 20% of my time was used in teaching. I loved teaching, and between the two jobs our needs were amply met, so much so that we were saving and able to help our children with some Christian education costs. Life was good.

Retirement

In November 2004, I called the executive director of Home Missions to chat with him about my future, including part or full retirement. We agreed that I would officially retire on January 10, 2005. This was fine with Jan and me; it was also helpful for Home Missions since they were running in the red on the income side. I shifted to the CRC ministers' pension Fund and started to receive my monthly pension cheque. I also knew I would enjoy a more relaxed pace and fewer hours. It began a new phase of life but I wondered if I would be bored.

On January 12, 2005, we began a seven-week trip; we called it "our transition journey," first by heading to Florida for a vacation and a visit with Jan's dad. After a few weeks there, we traveled all across the southern

US through Texas, Arizona, and into California. From there we went northeast through the Grand Canyon over to Denver and from there to lead a winter pastors' retreat in the Minneapolis, Minnesota area. From the retreat, we went to Chicago to visit son Rob and his wife Christine before returning home. During the entire seven weeks, we eluded all snow and we had no icy, snowy roads anywhere! It was a wonderful trip for both of us. When we arrived home, we felt we had transitioned out of the Home Missions role and out of the work routine.

I did continue the same work but now as a volunteer. I taught some courses at Tyndale, mentored and coached pastors, worked with some churches, and preached most Sundays. There was one noticeable change: I did it at my own pace. I was gradually learning to say no.

I also recall the first year of retirement as one in which I felt lost. My worth simply had been too closely tied to my work and accomplishments. All my life I felt best when I came home tired. Changing my pace of life required major adjustments in values. Continuing to preach regularly helped. I received invitations asking whether I could "fill the pulpit" for a particular Sunday. My standard, rather corny, reply was, "well, depends on the size of the pulpit." I sometimes felt like that's exactly what they wanted -someone to fill that 30-minute preaching slot, hopefully entertainingly. I would answer that if *they* would tell me what *needed* to be addressed in their church, I would consider their invitation. That resulted in some interesting discussions. Most of the people who invited me thought I would have a generic package of sermons that could be preached anywhere at any time. I do, but I preferred that the elders ask me to address a specific issue or topic. I could then preach with the authority of their leadership. I found it extremely helpful if I could start a sermon by saying, "Your elders have asked me to speak on this topic, or Scripture passage." I found that the congregation listened better and was more invested in the message.

Affirmation of the Past

A unique request came my way in May 2005 from a committee planning a special afternoon service in conjunction with the coming summer's across-Canada CRC bike tour. More than 200 members of various Canadian Christian Reformed Churches were spending 10 weeks biking as a group from Vancouver, British Columbia to Halifax, Nova Scotia, some 5,000 kilometers in conjunction with the celebration of the 100th anniversary of the CRC in Canada. The theme chosen for the service was: Helping our churches look forward: What would the next hundred years look like for the CRC's in Canada? Each biker was sponsored by and represented his or her congregation. The funds donated for this endeavor would be used to plant new congregations across Canada. Well over a million dollars was raised.

Wherever the bikers were on Sundays, they would take a day of rest and a local group of churches planned a special afternoon or evening worship service with them. The services were well announced, and as the tour traveled across Canada, the crowd grew in size, especially if the service was held in an area where there was a larger number of Christian Reformed churches. Sunday, August 14 would find the bikers in southeast Ontario, and the worship service was scheduled to be held in Guelph. Since this was an area with more churches nearby than any other place in Canada, the planners could expect a big crowd but they had a difficult time predicting just how many people might show up. It would be held at the peak of the vacation season when many were away. If it was a hot, humid day, would those not away on vacation come or will they choose to enjoy their pools and nearby lakes? How big a venue do we need? If we acquired a big place that seated thousands and only a few hundred showed up, it would feel awful. But if we did the opposite -rented a small place- and thousands came, we would have to turn away hundreds of people, many of whom had probably driven a good distance to be there. What should we do?

We decided to go big! We signed a contract to rent the entire Guelph ice arena which would seat 6,500 people! We prayed for a big enough crowd so that it would look, feel, and sound "respectable" in this huge arena.

We advertised the service. I was to preach and I was told, "Preach something to challenge us to face the next 100 years." Both the event and the topic excited me. Grace and Colleen, well-known worship leaders from the Meadowvale area, would lead the music and praise. We wondered right up to the time of the service how many would show up. Participants were urged to come early, no later than 2:30 PM with the service starting at 3:00 PM. We arrived about 2:15 PM and already people were streaming into the

225

arena from all directions. Many came early to make sure they found seats. Just before 3:00 PM, the bikers came in with their bikes, wearing their helmets and biking gear: all very impressive. Some rode in, some walked. As the bikers entered the auditorium, people in the audience started to clap, then stood up and cheered the entire time it took the 200 or so to file in two-by-two. When we were ready to start the service, every seat was taken, all 6,500 of them! Fire marshals ordered us to close the doors; we were full and adding more was dangerous. Later we learned that none were turned away! An amazing answer to many prayers!

The service was filled with energy. Praise rang through the arena; I wondered if any hockey game surpassed the enthusiasm present that Sunday afternoon. The singing continued for 30 minutes. I preached my message on facing the challenges of the next 100 years; I indicated that unless significant changes occurred in the next 10 to 20 years, the CRC would be in deep trouble. Unless major life-transformational -not just incremental- changes took place in many of our congregations bringing revival, a good number of them would be gone in 20 years or less. Some would need to merge with nearby congregations to survive. The glue -much of it was Dutch culture- that had held the denomination together was no longer able to do so as the CRC in Canada was now acclimated to her surrounding culture.

Survive or Thrive

To survive is not enough. We need to thrive. What will that take? Though the harvest of Dutch immigrants is now minimal, immigrants are still coming but now from other places. Can we see the new Harvest? We need a fresh vision that looks outward rather than inward and that serves our present world and communicates the good news. More church plants are needed, but just as importantly, the older established churches need a fresh outpouring of God's Holy Spirit. They too need a "baptism" of God's Spirit that empowers younger and older to see new Kingdom possibilities. It will include a fresh reading of His Word and prophetic preaching that dares to say "thus says the Lord" to our culture, but that also addresses the compromising practices in our churches. It requires a Holy Spirit boldness that dares to call for repentance and change. Tepid spirituality cannot match the challenge of heated secularism. Our vision needs renewing, our passion needs rekindling. What will that take?

It was interesting to note as I gave my message that people began to clap when I mentioned a new point, "a dynamic outpouring of the Holy Spirit…a fresh reading of God's Word,…a new vision of the harvest, empowered gift-based ministries, and flourishing small groups that hold members accountable to each other." To me it felt like a personal vindication and affirmation of what we had struggled to develop for eight long years in the seventies and early eighties in Calgary. The very issues that were major sources of conflict in our ministry were now affirmed with clapping, and even some shouting, as things desperately needed in our churches today and in the coming years. Things have changed over the past 30 years.

It was an electrifying experience for many who attended. Many mentioned that they actually felt proud to be members of the CRC, a church devoted and committed to changing the nation so that Christ would have "dominion from sea to sea!" For me it was a humbling -but wonderful-experience. I was tearfully filled with gratitude that we had stayed in the CRC even though we came painfully close to leaving after the meeting of Classis Alberta South in December 1981, (Chapter 9) when Classis voted to ask me to seek a call. At this inspiring worship service, I felt *all* the pain dissipate. It was worth it!

A "Heart" Challenge

In August 2006, Tyndale requested me to do the entire 35-hour leadership development course in a one-week retreat that would be held at a nice Muskoka area retreat center. It meant a huge amount of teaching, sessions for group interaction, and individual conversations -all within five days, all done by one 67 year old professor.

It went well. I usually woke up at 6:00 AM, a good time to go for a walk in the peaceful wooded areas. On Thursday morning, near the end of my walk I noticed a bit of tightening in my chest and the same again on Friday morning. It was not serious but I did notice it.

After finishing the course, my family picked me up and we stayed in the Havelock area for our family's annual camping weekend. On Sunday afternoon while gathering some campfire wood, my chest became tight again and I had to sit down. While I was sitting I was fine, but as soon as I moved the pain was there. I talked with Jan and she told the kids. In short order we were on the way to Peterborough to be checked at the hospital. They soon informed us that my heart was under stress and I was having a heart attack. I would need to stay and be seen by a cardiologist the next morning. With some meds, I went to sleep for the night. The next day I had an angiogram which showed no damage and no blockage, much to the surprise of the doctor who did the procedure as well as the cardiologist. I was kept one more night in the hospital, and on Tuesday I went home with all the test results and with specific instructions to take them to my own doctor, Len DeBolster, as soon as possible.

When I saw him a few days later, he firmly told me to cancel all my activities for the months of September and October and take it easy. Since those are the start-up months for the church season, I already had plans for preaching appointments and various congregational or Council activities. I canceled them all and spent September around the house, taking short walks and not much else. I had an appointment with Dr. DeBolster at the end of the month for my next check-up. When I saw him, he asked how I was doing. I answered, "Fine." He then proceeded to examine me and announced, "I think you are fine, you can go back to work." He indicated that though I had had a heart attack, called a "non-stemi-infarction," it was not major. I was very thankful but my response was, "Thanks a lot; I just canceled everything. There is nothing on my October schedule."

A New Challenge, Affirmation and God's Timing

Only three days later, when I answered a phone call, I heard these words: "This is Danell Czarnecki from Chino, California. Do you remember me?"

I did; she had been a small-group developer and trainer in the southwest US (California mostly) when I worked with Home Missions. We had met at several Home Missions staff conferences. She explained that her home church, CrossPoint Christian Reformed Church of Chino, was in turmoil. Their pastor who had been there for 23 years had been released for a leave

228

of absence. After his leave and further reflection Council decided not to have him return to the congregation but with the approval of Classis had him declared "eligible for a call" according to Article 17 of the CRC Church Order as explained earlier. Though Council was united in this decision, the congregation wasn't. It had caused damage in two major areas. One, the congregation had drawn many new people from the community who simply did not understand the sudden departure of their "beloved pastor." Instead of challenging the decision, they simply "voted with their feet" and left. And two, the congregation had recently built a beautiful, large, functional facility. It still carried a six million dollar debt, and with people leaving rapidly, debt payments were already in arrears and climbing rapidly.

Danell continued, "It's weird that I call you, but Don Klop, (the associate pastor) and I were talking and we said we needed someone to help us and you came to our minds. I suppose your fall schedule is all booked up, but we wanted to ask you anyway. Is there is any possibility that you could come and help us as an interim pastor for six months or so? We really need someone like you, Henry."

That felt like a "call" from God. I responded, "You'll find this hard to believe, but there is absolutely nothing on my schedule presently. In fact, it is clear."

She gasped and said, "You're kidding me!" When I informed her that I was not kidding, she shouted, "Isn't God good; He's got it all worked out." I too found it more than coincidental. Is this God showing up? I had in fact visited that church for a Sunday service some 20 years earlier while on a California vacation and had mentioned to Jan, "This seems like a nice church to serve sometime." I sensed a beautiful spirit in the congregation and a mission-focused awareness, two things that were both important and attractive to me. The pastor was doing a good work for God.

The Way Church was meant to Be

The timing was perfect for us. I first went for just a weekend visit to meet with the Council and staff, and I preached at the Sunday AM service. It was a mutual opportunity to check the chemistry for possible working together. After further discussion, both Council and I knew we were meant for each other and we were to go there. While there, it became clear that we were a gift of God to the congregation, but really, they were just as much God's gift to us. I still felt we had not had a good closure to our pastoral ministry in Oshawa. It left us with feelings of disappointment. Chino gave us five months in a wonderful pastoral ministry that in every possible way - preaching, pastoring, mentoring and leading a team- brought healing and closure to our woundedness. For me, it was an affirmation that what I believed, preached, and practiced was newly validated as godly ministry.

Amazingly, it brought a good measure of healing to the CrossPoint congregation as well. Authentic public confessions occurred; open forgiveness was sought, granted and declared. We experienced the church at her best; it was the gospel doing exactly what the Lord intended it to do. It was what I had always dreamed ministry would be when I was still young and naïve. I preached my heart out, and the congregation was eager to respond totally, happily and openly. They actually *did* what I preached and together we discovered that God *means* what He says; He blesses faith and humble obedience.

A Challenge to Trust God

For example, I preached a sermon on commitment on Sunday December 3. I urged the congregation to stop wandering to other churches, make a new commitment to God and each other, and support their own church again. It was a time when income was running $250,000, (a huge amount!) behind the needed budget. I challenged the church to tithe as a "starting guideline for giving by setting aside 10% for God and others." I dared them to try it for a two-month period, for the months of December and January, during which time we were back in the Toronto area to spend Christmas with our children and January with Jan's 93 year old father. Early in February we would return to Chino for three months. If anyone regretted the two months of tithing, all they had to do is tell me or the deacons at the end of the two months, and all their donations would be refunded. I added that I would personally add 5% interest on their donated money. I did that not because I was so-well-off or generous but on the basis of experience. I had made that same offer for some 15-20 years to congregations I served in various capacities when I was asked to teach on this subject. *No one has ever* come to collect! Many *did* later thank me and only wished they had been challenged earlier.

The next morning we left for Toronto. In Chino, a large church of about 1,500 members, so many took up the challenge that by the end of the fiscal year, December 31, I received a call from the church's business manager that in four weeks the entire $250,000 in the red was replaced with $100,000 in the black. "Best of all," he said "everybody is really happy and we are having great year-end celebration services. We are excited about the church again." When we came a few weeks later we could seemingly do no wrong; to protect me from a swelled head it was wise for us to leave three months later. We went home at the end of April 2007 feeling fulfilled, blessed, and our ministry completed. It rekindled my passion for the church and the ministry of coaching and mentoring pastors and other leaders. I believe God could not have provided better therapy for me at the time. He showed up in our lives and we are thankful to Him and to Chino CrossPoint for it.

Jan's Dad

While all this was happening in California, we were struggling with Jan's father's health condition. He was 93 and had been quite well. He was happiest if he could spend the winters in his condo in Pompano Beach, Florida, where we annually visited him. Shortly before we went to Chino, we learned that his health was failing and that he was in the hospital with severe diarrhea. We went to Fort Lauderdale to visit him in January and talked to his doctor who told us that the cancer discovered 20 years earlier was no longer dormant but had now spread throughout his entire body. It was time for a nursing home. When we told dad, he said he did not want to go to a nursing home in Florida but much preferred to return to the Christian Rest Home in Grand Rapids, where his wife, Jan's mom, and also her mom had spent their last months. But they had no openings. Three days later we called the rest home again, and amazingly a spot had opened up that very day that dad could have it if we could get him there. We talked to the doctor who said: "Get some airline reservations for Saturday morning. I'll go in and dope him up so he can travel, and if both of you accompany him, he'll be fine."

231

We made plane reservations for the three of us to leave about 8:00 AM on Saturday. When we went to the hospital to tell Jan's father, he was absolutely ecstatic. He clapped his hands, looked up at the ceiling repeatedly, and said, "Thank you, Lord!" at least six times. "I can go home to Grand Rapids, thank you Lord!" He wanted to die in the city where he had been born, lived, worked, and had his family, and in the Christian Rest Home where his wife also died. It was a tearful time for Jan and me but it stands out as a beautiful moment of life with that humble, godly, thankful man. On Saturday morning, I pretty much carried him into the airplane, carried him out of it and into another in Cincinnati, and then out again into a rental car on a snowy (remember it's January in Michigan!) afternoon in Grand Rapids. When we arrived at the rest home, he was utterly thankful and perfectly happy and ready for whatever God had in store for him. He was prepared to die and spoke about it like it would be just one more trip. By about 4:00 PM, he was happily settled in at the rest home where he immediately met a 93-year-old woman who had graduated with him in his high school class 75 years earlier! Exhausted, Jan and I went to a motel and went to sleep with deep gratitude to God and for His unmistakable caring hand of guidance.

Jan's dad urged us to go back to Chino to do what he truly believed God wanted us to do. For his entire life, he had freely and cheerfully released his only daughter to serve God wherever God wanted to use her. If we were happy, he was happy and thankful. There was nothing selfish about him. We went back to Chino and flew back to Grand Rapids for his birthday on March 4, another good event for him. Early on Monday, March 26, Jan's dad quietly slept his way into the presence of God. His funeral was held on Friday morning (March 30) with all his grandchildren present. It was a good celebration and closure to the life of a man who had lived for God, his family, and especially for his daughter. It was hard to grieve his death; his life was complete. Instead we all celebrated his way of doing things, comments he had made, or his crazy clothing color combinations.

After we finished the Chino interim and returned to Oakville, we went to Grand Rapids to settle up the estate for Jan's dad, including the selling of the family home they had owned since 1942. We prayed again that God would send someone who needed the house and would benefit more than

232

just having-a-place-to live. The economy in Grand Rapids was low and house sales were slow. The house sold quickly (about three weeks) to a missionary family returning from overseas with a daughter who was ready to start as a student at Calvin College. We thanked God again. The furniture was dispersed with our children picking whatever they treasured before the rest was sold. It was amazing to us how smoothly and quickly it all went. Not one ripple of dissension. We have been blessed; we both know it well.

Retirement Again

It is now spring 2013, and ministry opportunities are decreasing. Now 73 years old, I am enjoying the feeling of slowing down; I am becoming more detached from churches, pastors, and challenges. It feels like God is preparing me for my assignment whenever and to wherever He calls. Evening meetings, especially those involving travel in cold or wet weather, hold little attraction. A book, a magazine, the fireplace, one or two TV programs, a hockey game to watch, a few Sudoku games or rummy game with Jan easily win out.

We are blessed with good health, our needs are met, and God provides so we can share with others. We have regular contact with our children and grandchildren, even though they are more spread out than we would like. Judy and Edwin and family of four children live in Brampton, Ontario. Barbara, Andre, and three children live in Sao Paulo Brazil for about five years after which they will probably return to Paris, France. Doug and Sharon live in Bowmanville, Ontario with their three children as do John and Grace with their three children. Rob and Christine are settled in Chicago enjoying their jobs and each other. We thoroughly enjoy Christmas and summer get-togethers with most of the children and grandchildren. Regular visits with the Ontario children provide the needed grandfather fixes.

Life is good, it really could not be much better. We anticipate and are confident that the best is yet to be! Before arriving Home we may still have some valleys to cross and some pain and grief to endure as many other people, including Christians, do. We try to leave that in God's hands. His call is still the same as we have heard it our entire lives, "Trust me, believe me, in my Father's house are many rooms…." I believe more than ever that God looks for servants who are sold-out to Him. He and His bride, the church, are worthy of nothing less. They deserve our very best.

So we share this journey of faith and service to God. He was always there but at certain times He showed up surprisingly. We pray our children and grandchildren will carry on where we leave off and likewise experience His blessings and surprises. We also pray that many of God's people including pastors who read this book will boldly continue the prophetic task of His ministry wherever they serve. If so, God is pleased and I will be thrilled and thankful.

Arnold A. Dallimore describes well one of my hopes for this book in the introduction to his two extensive volumes of the biography titled *George Whitefield*, a great evangelist at the time of the eighteenth century revivals. Though the language is dated and the reference to "men" today should surely today read as, "men and women" the challenge is still relevant:

> *Yea this book is written in the desire—perhaps in a measure of inner certainty—that we shall see the great Head of the church once more bring into being His special instruments of revival, that He will again raise up onto Himself certain young men (and women) whom He may use in this glorious employ. And what manner of people will they be? They will be mighty in the Scriptures, their lives dominated by a sense of the greatness, the majesty and the holiness of God, and their minds and hearts aglow with the great truths of the doctrines of grace. They will be men (and women) who have learned what it is to die to self, to human aims and personal ambitions; people willing to be 'fools for Christ's sake', whose supreme desire will be, not to gain earth's accolades, but to win the Master's approbation when they appear before His awesome judgment seat. They will be those who will preach with broken hearts and tear-filled eyes, and upon whose ministries God will grant an extraordinary effusion of the Holy Spirit, and who will witness signs and wonders following in the transformation of human lives.*

That is the longing of my heart for the church; it is my prayer for you, the reader.

Acknowledgements

Because I am first of all a preacher and not a writer, I find that it is easier for me to preach than to write. I am indebted to many for this book. The starts and stops were many over nearly ten years. The stops came from me, the starts from those who said, "Go for it!"

The encouragers were members in the three churches we served. They were colleagues with whom we swapped ministry experiences and stories. They were those whose paths we crossed especially during some of our tough times who said: "Somebody should write this up."

So I did with the help from many of you. Thanks Brian Stiller for "pushing" me on when I mentally quit and then for being relentless about putting out a "perfect" product without you or me realizing just how huge the gap is between my "product" and perfection!

Thanks Amy Woltersdorff (Grand Rapids) for good edits, not only once - but twice! A special thank you is extended to Margaret Dijkhuis of London Ontario, for her creative work in designing the cover of the book. And thanks to Pierre Camy from Schuler Books (Grand Rapids) for great help towards creating a publishable product.

A special thanks to my wife Jan who spent many hours and days with me recalling order of events, specifics that I had missed and then read and reread for grammar errors and typos.

I am indebted in a strange way for the stories, events and experiences which came out of the hearts and lives of God's people in the three churches that I got to know in the unique way of pastor and congregation. When I reviewed all the experiences, the *really good* and the *really bad* I found a common thread tying it all together like someone was in charge coordinating the entire fifty year trip. It makes sense, it has reason, and it is headed in a consistent specific direction to a life of peace, trust, and surrender, and a repeated reminder that I am not really in charge… at all! So I thank God and His church for granting us this journey, and for allowing us to have lives filled with varied experiences that now leave us with vast collections of memories.